Oak Park Public Library

3 1132 01348 0631

MAR -- 2015

OAK PARK PUBLIC LIBRARY

The Formative Years
of an African-American Spy

A Memoir

Odell Bennett Lee

D1446875

Copyright © 2012 by Odell Bennett Lee

All rights reserved. No part of this book may be reproduced in any form without permission in writing from the publisher, except by a reviewer who may quote brief passages as part of the review.

Nothing in the contents of this book should be construed as asserting or implying U.S. Government authentication of information or CIA endorsement of the author's views. This material has been reviewed by the CIA to prevent the disclosure of classified information.

The Formative Years of an African-American Spy by Odell Bennett Lee

ISBN: 0615640362

ISBN 13: 9780615640365

{Dedication}

To my wife, Nora, my son, Marcus, my late mother and biological father, and my fifteen brothers and sisters whom I love very much!

Table of Contents

Preface

This manuscript has been a long time coming. My son, Marcus, persuaded me that sharing stories about my formative years might encourage others, young and old, that have experienced similar difficulties. Marcus wanted to know how I emerged from a turbulent and confusing family environment without falling prey to the evil dark side. Personally, I attribute my survival to family and compassionate friends. The wise souls that guided me through the storms of childhood and adolescence were: Uncle Johnnie Cain, Henry and Opal Hooks, and my grandmother Jannie Mae Bennett. At an early age they helped me to recognize and accept good advice when offered. I should also thank my U.S. Navy friends that reached out to a lonely and naïve sixteen year old, far away from home. These sailors provide real friendship when I needed it the most. But I will never forget my biological father's embrace when I met him for the first time. I was a terrified eighteen year old. Also, I owe special thanks to my friends Joe Call, Greg Nowak, John Miller, and Jim and Marlyn Crampton who led me through a psychological and spiritual renaissance that sustained me and helped me decouple my self-image from the negative impact of my dysfunctional family. Professionally, I want to thank the unnamed colleagues at CIA, especially A.N., who supported my career development and helped me discover my true professional calling. Finally, special thanks to my wife Nora. She believed in me from our very first meeting at UCLA, and her love and compassion put to rest the dark shadows of the past.

Odell Bennett Lee,
Nipomo, California
December 2012

Acknowledgments

My appreciation and thanks to friends and family that read portions of this manuscript and offered valuable suggestions. You know who you are. Special thanks to my late cousin, Wilbur "Sonny" Brown, who helped ensure the accuracy of my childhood chronology. I am especially thankful for the wonderful "Oldies but Goodies" song writers whose lyrics helped me to remember the good and bad times. Listening to songs of the past was like opening a time capsule of memories. Finally, I apologize for holding back certain sections of the manuscript from friends and editors until the whole manuscript was approved by CIA. In this regard, I want to thank the CIA Publications Review Board for permitting me to talk about some of my unique Agency experiences, although the majority of my accomplishments must remain classified.

Disclaimer

All statements of fact, opinion, or analysis expressed are those of the author and do not reflect the official position or views of the CIA or any other U.S. Government agency. Nothing in the contents should be construed as asserting or implying U.S. Government authentication of information or Agency endorsement of the author's views. This material has been reviewed by the CIA to prevent the disclosure of classified information.

Introduction

The Formative Years

As a man thinks in his heart, so is he. (Proverbs 23:7)

I grew up in California at a time when poverty and racism were lesser evils than my experiences in a dysfunctional family. By the time I was fifteen years old, I was the primary caregiver for six half brothers and sisters, ages one to nine. I felt like a modern-day Cinderella: overworked, unappreciated, laden with adult responsibilities, and starving for parental affection. I endured the volatility of a no-nonsense mother who was quick to use the rod at my slightest infraction, and the open antagonism of two stepfathers who sought to isolate me from the family. Despite these difficulties, I was determined that I would not surrender to a life of self-pity and low self-esteem. Out of adversity and chance, I developed an emotional and spiritual outlook that allowed me to work through my frustrations and overcome the sense of abandonment that had followed me into adulthood. My story is about emotional survival, self-definition, and change. It traces my turbulent upbringing, my escape from home, and an emotional and spiritual renaissance that steeled my character and made me an ideal candidate for the Central Intelligence Agency's elite clandestine services.

My difficulties began when my biological father got my mother pregnant and then disappeared. This was not uncommon in the 1940s in Louisiana, especially among the struggling black community. I was two years old when Mother married my first stepfather, a man appropriately called "Fats." Apparently, Fats did not take to me. I was hospitalized for a week because of his physical abuse. When I was three, Fats left me outside in a thunderstorm. Mother returned home earlier than expected and rescued me. She and Fats separated soon after this incident but reconciled when we moved to California. I was five years old when Mother foiled a kidnapping attempt by my biological father. This was the first time I can recall having contact with my dad. Caught red handed, he promised never to bother me again.

Relations with my stepfathers had a significant influence on my personal outlook well into adulthood. My second stepfather "Shorty" came to live with us when I was in the fifth grade. He seemed to have a visceral dislike for me from the moment we met. Mother tolerated Shorty's hostile attitude toward me, while aware that I was always unsettled emotionally when he was around. Only when Shorty got sick did he show me a measure of tolerance. Despite his antipathy for me, he used me as his "bagman" when he was unable to continue his petty drug sales and loan-sharking activities. Shorty schooled me in techniques for braving back alleys, covering my tracks, and keeping secrets. I learned to keep a cool head when facing antagonistic situations, and to "think out of the box." These concepts helped me understand covert activity and to maneuver in potentially hostile environments. When Shorty recovered from his illnesses, I was again the object of his scorn.

Mother and Shorty had five children together, one almost every year. I served as the housekeeper and babysitter for the family until I dropped out of high school and joined the military. My caregiving responsibilities were a depressing restraint to my social interaction with other teenagers. Any complaints about being overworked were handled by Mother's ironing cord. Only after the children were fed and put to bed could I do my schoolwork, or lose myself in my imaginary world that included a loving father figure.

At sixteen, I rebelled against what I felt was unjust treatment at the hands of my parents. One Saturday morning Shorty and I came to blows. He grabbed a butcher knife and chased me out of the house. I ran next door to my grandmother's, and I held him off with a claw hammer while she telephoned the police. I had taken a stand for my personal dignity. There was no turning back. I knew that one of us was bound to get hurt if we continued to live under the same roof. I begged Mother to let me quit high school and join the military. Reluctantly, she agreed and signed for me to join the US Navy. Again, she lied about my age.

Scared and naive, I had no idea where the twists and turns in life would lead me. From the day I sailed off into the sunset, my life has been a relentless march from chaos to order, ignorance to enlightenment, and strength to strength. I welcomed the US Navy's carefully constructed value system that taught me teamwork and personal responsibility. On my seventeenth birthday, I was sailing across the Pacific Ocean on a destroyer escort to such far-off places as Japan, Hong Kong, Guam, and Australia. I discovered that the world was big, complicated, and very different from the world I had known. Yet I felt safe for the first time in my life.

While on patrol in the Western Pacific, I received a letter that jarred my relatively peaceful existence. My biological father wrote that he wanted me back in his life. Until then, I had no idea where he lived or what he looked liked, and I was puzzled why he wanted to see me after so many years. I learned that he had lived only sixty miles from me during most of my childhood. Our encounter after all these years was magical. I did not know how much I needed him, or how much he needed me, until I felt the warmth of his embrace. He said that I was "the missing strand" in his life.

After the navy, it did not take long for me to realize that dropping out of high school had been a bad idea. Without a high school diploma, it took me one year to find a decent job. Unfortunately, my first full-time job proved a bad fit for me, and I was troubled by a variety of ethical and moral issues exhibited by my co-workers. In addition, I found myself isolated from my old high school friends for similar reasons. Most were either in jail, lost to drugs, or caught up in exploring the new morality of the sixties. I realized that I had to change my work and social environment if I was going to survive the frustration. My only hope was to enroll in night school and get a high school diploma. Depressed, I sought guidance from an unlikely source, my mother. I was twenty-three years old.

With a high school diploma in hand, I got a job at the US Post Office. My co-workers soon realized that a career in the postal service was not for me. They urged me to take college courses that steered me toward a different profession. Their wise counsel ushered in an intellectual renaissance that changed my life. Simultaneously, I experienced a spiritual renaissance that helped me to deal with the recurring notion that I was damaged emotionally and psychologically by my turbulent childhood. It required that I let go of grudges that held me hostage to the past, and to quit splitting hairs to justify my bad decisions. Out of all this, I learned to manage my personal relations with people that prejudged me for who I was or was not.

College was a boon for me, and my personal confidence increased dramatically. I was drawn to the fields of psychology, philosophy, and political science. I found myself enmeshed in debating the merits of American involvement in Vietnam, and as president of the International Relations Club at UCLA, I traveled to Vietnam and Southeast Asia. I met my first love, Nora Herron, at UCLA, and proposed marriage on our third date. Six months later, we tied the knot. After graduate school at Johns Hopkins University, I taught at a local junior college before securing a job as an analyst for an international research company. Finally, I took a job representing an American company in the Republic of Singapore. By then, we had a son, Marcus. He was six months old when we moved overseas. After working several years in the Republic of Singapore, rather than relocating the company's offices to Jakarta, Indonesia, I decided to accept a job with a company back in the States. This was not a good move. Frustrated for a variety of reasons, I applied for a research analyst job with a "think tank" based in Washington, DC. To our surprise, a representative from the Central Intelligence Agency visited at our home. The CIA officer said that I had "come to the agency's attention," and that I was the person they wanted for an unspecified job. The officer cited a variety of reasons that made me attractive to the CIA: my military service, international work experience, foreign-language ability, academic credentials, and personality traits. Finally, he said that I had come "highly recommended."

My interview with the CIA forced me to examine whether or not I was psychologically and emotionally cut out for this kind of work. While my desire for self-discovery had always been deep, I had never asked myself, "Who am I?" I had always known. This does not mean that I fully understood why I was the way I was, nor why so many good and bad things happened to me. Nonetheless, I never had trouble being me. Following the crowd was never easy, and I had trouble embracing a lifestyle that did not feel right. Most importantly, I refused to allow others to define my worth. In this regard, I was well suited to work alone, "out in the cold," so to speak.

The interview also brought to mind the practical lessons I learned from my stepfather, Shorty. The things he taught me about clandestine activities proved helpful in discussing covert strategies. In addition, Mother's insistence that I take responsibility for my actions helped me to develop a high level of self-reliance. Any difficulties with the children had to be managed intelligently, and often without Mother looking over my shoulder. As a result, I learned to work independently, without fretting. Finally, my experiences in the US Navy taught me the value of teamwork, loyalty, and comradery. I learned what it means to be a friend. A discussion of ethical behavior was also an important part of my interview. I admitted that my Christian faith was an important factor in defining my character, and that my values kept me grounded in difficult and ambiguous situations.

In sum, my life can be measured by how I have managed to turn my bad experiences into positive factors. Throughout this book, the reader can look over my shoulder and observe how I worked through some of my personal struggles and escaped a series of potential dead ends. Finally, a discussion of a few of my operational experiences will shed some light on how I utilized lessons from my formative years to manage spy operations. My hope is that anyone lamenting negative life experiences, or feeling psychologically and emotionally damaged by their childhood, will find something useful in this book.

Chapter One

How It All Began: The Perennial Stepchild

I was three months old when my dad saw me for the first time. He picked me up, kissed me, and carried me outside into the sunshine. My mother observed while he examined my face, fingers, and toes. He returned to the house with a huge grin on his face, announcing: "Yep. He's mine." Mother and Dad met in Delhi, Louisiana. Dad was a migrant construction worker, and Mother was a waitress in a small café frequented by the local black townsfolk. Dad pursued Mother with a passion. They fell in love, and I was conceived a few months later. Times were difficult for my mother's family, and my grandfather, Papa, had been out of work for almost a year. Dad talked his boss into taking Papa on as a part-time carpenter. This was a godsend for the family.

Unfortunately, Dad's job ended before I was born, and he moved to Texas to find new work. Mother did not see him again until he showed up one day wanting to see his baby. A few weeks later, Dad disappeared again. Mother did not know that he had another family in Texas. Therefore, the impact of this single event on my life should have been small. Unfortunately, this event set forth a series of actions that affected my life well into adulthood.

My Grandmother, Grandy; My Grandfather, Papa; Mother, Mary;
And Aunt Queen Ester

Two years later Mother married Adam Lee, a longtime friend. Adam was a large man, and everyone called him "Fats." Fats was a part-time police officer, and he moved us closer to his job in Alexandria, Louisiana. We lived in a small house just outside the city limits. I had to sleep on a mattress in the kitchen. At night, I watched the rats scurrying about looking for food. One night I woke up and saw a rat staring at me. It was smiling, and I thought I was going to be his next meal. When I cried out, Mother rushed in and the rat ran away.

By all accounts, Fats seemed to resent me as his stepchild. One day he was dressing me and suddenly, I cried out hysterically. Aunt Hattie was visiting at the time and accused Fats of doing something to my genitals. Fats denied any wrongdoing. Whatever the case, the problem was serious enough to put me in the hospital for several days with swollen testicles. On another occasion, I was playing outside and it started to rain. I dashed for the house, but Fats would not let me inside. He told me that I had "mud" on my shoes and that I would mess up the house. The house did not have a porch, so I stood under a tree for shelter. I do not know how long I would have stayed out in the rain had Mother not come home earlier than expected. I was crying, wet, and cold. I told Mother what Fats had said to me. She was furious. Fats had picked on me once too often. They argued, and they separated shortly afterward. Fats was distraught over the separation. It came at difficult time for him. He had been laid off by the police department and was having trouble finding another job.

Around this time, several relatives decided to move to California to look for work. Rumor had it that blacks were finding good jobs on the West Coast supporting the war effort. Uncle Johnnie and his family were the first to leave Louisiana. He found a job right away and convinced my grandparents, Papa and Grandy, to join him in San Bernardino, California. Uncle Johnnie even rented a house for my grandparents to move into, and had a job lined up for Papa with a company that built barracks and other facilities for the air force. After a few short months, Papa's boss recognized his carpenter skills and made him an assistant foreman. Back in Louisiana, it would have been unheard of for a black man to supervise whites on a job. Fats heard about the opportunities and followed Uncle Johnnie and Papa to California. He landed a job in Alameda, California, with the police department. Fats wrote to Mother and asked if she would join him. With most of our relatives heading west, Mother was feeling isolated in Louisiana and agreed to reconcile with him. Fats sent money for our train tickets, and off we went to California.

The Train To California

I remember the train ride to California as an exciting experience. We sat in the "colored only" coach because public transportation in the South was racially segregated. Mother and I celebrated my fourth birthday on the train. According to Mother, I was quite active. I walked around the coach and talked to anyone that paid attention to me. The train stopped in Lake Charles, Louisiana, and a white couple boarded. They were French nationals on vacation in the States. They stopped to talk to me as they made their way through our coach. I told them that it was my birthday. Later, the French couple returned and asked Mother to let me sit with them for a while. Since I was very young, the train conductor allowed me to sit with the couple in the "whites-only" coach. I can remember sitting on the man's lap while his wife stuffed me with goodies that they bought from the snack bar. Mother became concerned after a couple of hours had passed. She asked the train conductor to find me. I was still with the French couple. They were preparing to get off the train at the next stop. The conductor asked them to return me to my mother. They refused to give me up and said that Mother had given me to them. They were adamant that I was now theirs. I might have been had the conductor not threatened to have them arrested when the train pulled into the next town.

San Bernardino, California

We spent two months in San Bernardino with my grandparents before joining Fats in Alameda. Papa and Grandy's house was a huge gray brick house. I had never seen an all-brick house before. There was a large black walnut tree in the front yard that looked dead but had lots of dark walnuts on it. Along the street was a row of straggly green hedges that separated the yard from the street. On one side of the house was a huge row of large leaf cactus plants. They were twice my height. On the opposite side of the house was a large plot of land with several rows of almond trees. They were loaded with almonds. Next to the almond grove was a high fence. Behind the fence was an ironworks factory. Hanford Foundry fabricated iron rods and metal plates. Dark gray smoke covered the area around the foundry yard.

The neighborhood was racially mixed and vibrant. There were lots of children my age. Saturdays were the most fun. We all got together and went to the early-morning cartoon shows at the Studio Movie Theater downtown. After the movies, we went to Meadow Park to play. There was a small grocery store nearby where we could buy ice cream and candy. Across the street was an active bar and café. The bar was popular with local adults, and Mother was a regular visitor. On our trips to the park, our parents would not let us walk on the same side of the street as the bar.

I had never been to a public park before. It had two banks of swings, a sliding board, a teeter-totter, and public toilets for boys and girls. There were lots of trees in the park. A small creek filled with crawdads and polliwogs flowed near the edge of the park. Periodically, Uncle Johnnie took us there to catch crawdads. He deep-fried them for us, and I can still remember the good taste of the salt-and-peppered crawdad tails. We also caught polliwogs and put them in fish bowls, hoping to see them develop into frogs. They all died, but we kept trying, anyway.

Finally, Mother and I took a train to Alameda, California, to join Fats. Shortly after our arrival, I met Joyce, a girl who lived next door. She taught me to play jacks and other games that I had never played before. One day Joyce suggested that we play doctor. She asked to examine my genitalia, and she allowed me to examine hers. At one point, she asked me to look inside her vagina and tell her what I saw. Unfortunately, her mother caught me in the act, and we were not allowed to play together after that.

To satisfy Mother, Fats formally adopted me. Unfortunately, the reconciliation with Fats did not work out, but Mother got pregnant during our brief stay. We moved back to San Bernardino, and my brother Roy was born a few months later. Although pregnant, Mother got a job making beds at a hotel downtown, and on weekends she waited tables at the neighborhood bar and café. She enrolled me in elementary school so that she could work full-time. The idea of going to school had never crossed my mind, and I had difficulty with just about everything, including recess. Learning to write in cursive was my biggest challenge. The teacher was patient and convinced that I could do the work. She kept me after school a few minutes every day to practice cursive writing. Watching the other children leave on time and knowing I had to walk home from school alone was frightening to me. I was determined to work hard so I could walk home with my friends. I learned later that Mother had lied about my age and I entered the first grade earlier than most children did.

I have fond memories of living with my grandparents in the brick house, and going to the movies and to the park on Saturdays. Years later, during a visit back to San Bernardino, my friend Denny Shorett took me on a tour of my old neighborhood. The area had changed completely. We found the corner where my grandparents' brick house used to sit. The old black walnut tree, cactus plants, almond trees, and the Hanford Foundry were all gone. Denny said the city had razed the whole neighborhood to make way for a promised Urban Renewal project that never took place. Although Meadowbrook Park was still there, the creek that once teemed with crawfish and polliwogs had all but dried up.

Papa was making good money working as a carpenter. He decided to buy a bigger house on the west side of town. This time, the house was all wood with a long front porch. All rooms were warmed with beautifully flowered wallpaper. A large pepper tree graced the front yard and gave off a piquant aroma in the springtime. A small peach tree stood in its shadow, with plants and flowers growing all around them. In the backyard, a wash-house and storage room stood between apricot trees and a large fig tree that produced fruit every year. Several relatives moved in with us: Aunt Queen, Uncle Doc, and their son Arthur, Jr., took one bedroom. It had an outside door to the front yard so they could enter without going through the house. My cousin Frank and my half brother, Willie, whom I thought for a long time was my cousin, bunked in the second bedroom. Mother, Roy, and I took the back bedroom. It had a door to the backyard, but it was locked. Papa and Grandy had the master bedroom. Our only bathroom in the house was located off the master bedroom.

Mother enrolled me in second grade at Harding Elementary School in the downtown part of the city. The walk to school was much longer than to Burbank. I remember my first visit to the school library and being amazed to see so many books in one place. Our teacher showed us a *Webster's Unabridged Dictionary*. It was the biggest book we had ever seen. The librarian helped us with our first class assignment, which was to look up our first and last names in the dictionary. I learned that "Odell" had a Greek root and meant a "joyful melody" or "short poem." My last name, "Lee," was defined as the "sheltered side," away from the wind. The teacher suggested I translate my name as a "joyful shelter." This would turn out to be prophetic.

Papa worked a lot of overtime. Often, we did not see him for days. I do not know where he found the time, but soon after we moved into the new house, Papa started converting the washhouse and storage room into a small house for Mother, Roy, and me. We moved into the house six months later. The small house had two bedrooms, a kitchen, and a bathroom. By the time I left for the US Navy many years later, Papa had added two more bedrooms to the house to accommodate our expanded family.

I entered the third grade at Mount Vernon Elementary School. This was my third school in three years. Mount Vernon was four blocks from our new house. I never knew why I had ended up at Harding the year before since Mount Vernon was so much closer. The first day at school was confusing for me. The classroom had more students than seats, and several adults were standing in the back of the room. It was an orientation meeting for all third graders. After a selection process, students were directed to different rooms. Miss Brigitte was my third-grade teacher. She was young and beautiful. I liked her, and I was convinced that she liked me. My cousin Frank was also in our third-grade class, although he was three years older than me. Word had it that Frank had failed third grade several times. Mother said that Frank was "a little slow." I did not believe it. I thought Frank was very smart.

My First Friend, Rudy

The walk to school took me by Weber's Bakery and a house that was almost too nice for the neighborhood. One morning, a boy was leaving the house for school. I cannot remember which one of us spoke first, but we connected right away. Rudy Valdez was his name. I liked Rudy a lot, and I made sure that I was outside his house early enough each morning to walk to school him. Rudy and I were best of friends throughout elementary school. We walked to school together for four years.

Fourth grade at Mount Vernon was a challenge for me. We had to do a lot of reading aloud and long-division arithmetic. Our teacher, Mrs. Smith, was strict and never in a good mood. We could speak only when she spoke to us. When we misbehaved or did not perform to her satisfaction, she would often grab us by our shoulders and shake us violently. She would not hesitate to send a tearful student off to the principal's office for more scolding or a paddling.

Mrs. Smith did not allow eating of any kind in class. One day on the way to school, I bought a roll of Necco Rainbow candy from Johnny's Grocery store. I told Rudy that I was going to sneak the candy into Mrs. Smith's class. I tried to share some candy with him, but he wanted nothing to do with my plan. When Mrs. Smith left the room, I took out the candy, ate a piece, and gave a piece to another student. I did not notice that Gwen, a girl who walked to school with us occasionally, saw me eating the candy. When Mrs. Smith returned to the classroom, Gwen raised her hand and blurted out that I had candy in my desk. My punishment was not physical this time; I had to give each student a piece of my candy until it was all gone. I was furious at Gwen. I decided to beat her up during recess. It was easier said than done. Gwen fought back. I claimed victory when Gwen started crying. Unfortunately, Gwen had another card to play. She told Mrs.

Smith that I had hit her during recess. Mrs. Smith sent me to the principal's office, and I was summarily paddled. I was afraid that the principal would call my mother to come in for a talk. Thankfully, the principal let me off with just a paddling because it was the first time he had seen me in his office.

Chapter Two

Shorty, Mother, And Me: Radical Rupture—My Stepfather, Shorty

In the fifth grade, profound changes at home overshadowed my school activities. One day, Mother introduced me to a man that she said would be living with us. She told me that she was pregnant with his baby. My relationship with Shorty was a negative experience from that day on. Mother introduced him as "Mr. Cooper," but she called him "Shorty." He was just over five feet tall. Shorty's reaction to me was strange. I sensed immediately that he did not like me, and the idea of him living with us seemed to unsettle me. My anxiety began to affect my behavior in school. Miss. Harrison, my fifth-grade teacher, noticed that I had become unfocused and more introverted. She asked if there was something wrong at home. I was afraid to tell her about my new stepfather, so I told her that I did not feel well. I buried myself in schoolwork after Shorty arrived. My sister, Barbara Jean, was born the following December. She was a beautiful baby, and I like taking care of her when I had the chance.

Things began going wrong in the sixth grade. I remember that on a cold November morning, soon after Shorty came to live with us, I stood too close to the open-face gas heater, and my clothes caught fire. I started screaming. Mother heard my screams and ran from the kitchen. She tore my clothes off and put out the fire. Shorty was lying in bed just a few feet from me. He was propped up on his elbow and just looking at me. I don't know if he was startled or confused by the noise, but he did not come to my rescue when he heard me screaming. I thought about this incident as I walked to school later that morning. I was upset at myself for allowing my clothes to catch on fire, and I was angry with Shorty for not helping to put out the fire. I recalled that Shorty never involved himself in my problems. This incident was no different. Several times, when I fell and hurt myself while running or bumped my head on something in the house, he would just look at me as if he were loath to touch me or even ask if I were OK.

At the end of the year, our teacher called each of us to her desk to discuss our report cards. She congratulated me on a job well done and said that I had passed to the seventh grade. Nevertheless, her remarks under "Teacher's Comments" bothered me. She wrote that I showed signs of being "emotionally upset" for reasons she could not fathom. She recommended that I talk to my parents about the problem. I read the teacher's comment over and over again. I wasn't sure what the words meant, but I knew it wasn't good.

As I walked home that day, I found it hard to be excited that school was out for the summer. I showed my report card to Rudy. He didn't know what the teacher meant either, but he reminded me that I had passed the sixth grade and that this was the important thing. After leaving Rudy, I walked home thinking about my home situation. Shorty rarely spoke to me, and it was clear that he wanted nothing to do with me. I was so down about it all that I did not bother showing my report card to Mother. I knew that she was not interested in my grades, anyway, only that I did not get into trouble at school. At first, I was curious about Shorty because he seemed so intelligent and clever. I wanted to know personal things about him: who his parents were, where they lived, his personal likes and dislikes, and his favorite things to do. I was curious about where he grew up and went to school. It took some time for me to get the message that he wanted nothing to do with me. Whenever I asked him about his life, he responded, "Don't you have something else to do?" We lived in the same house for eight years, and he remained a stranger to me. For a long time, I thought that if I had been smarter and had done more to please him our relationship would have been different. I wondered if I was responsible for our bad relationship, but I did not know how to fix it. I will never know why he did not like me, but I suspected that it was because I was not his biological child. I did not belong to him.

Caregiving For My New Family

Before Barbara could walk, Roosevelt, the second baby, came along. Mother had four more children, the next four years in a row: Rosemary, Jannie Mae, and Gary. A fourth between Roosevelt and Rosemary was stillborn. Mother worked part-time during all but one of her pregnancies, and I was the primary caregiver for the little ones. I did the washing, ironing, and housecleaning after school. Mother had dinner ready each day when I got home from school so at least I did not have to cook, but I had to help feed the children and wash the dishes. It was only after the children were fed, bathed, and put to bed that I could do my homework.

With each addition to the family, my personal needs became less important to the family. By the time I entered high school, I was fully engaged as the primary care giver to my brothers and sisters. My weekends were completely occupied with caring for the children. Mother's attitude toward me had also changed. She seemed agitated most of the time, and if one of the children got hurt playing around, or broke her glass bottle, it gave her an excuse to whip me for being irresponsible. Keeping up my schoolwork was a challenge. I got very little sleep because I had to get up and help care for the babies during the night. I was always tired and did not get the grades I hoped for. Shorty rarely helped with the chores or got up at night to see after the kids. He said he needed his sleep because he had to go to work the next morning. I resented him because I got up earlier than he did to go to school.

In the eighth grade, my mother kept me out of school the maximum days allowed. If it were not for the aggressive San Bernardino school policy requiring students to maintain a certain attendance level, my parents would have kept me home a lot more.

Barbara Jean   Rosemary, Roosevelt, Jannie Mae

There were times when I thought I would not survive the task of child rearing. My brother Roy was a godsend. He was too young to help me with the household chores, but he was always willing to help me take care of the smaller children. He learned how to warm the babies' bottles and to help feed the smaller ones. Unfortunately, Roy was also my responsibility. I had to dress him in the mornings and make sure he did not get into trouble. Roy had a gift for mischievousness and had to be watched closely. He bullied the neighborhood children, and was a natural manipulator. Roy would come home with toys that he said were gifts from his friends. In fact, he had taken the toys from other boys and bullied them into saying that they gave the toys to him voluntarily.

Odell And Brother Gary

One spring, three of the children had the whooping cough at the same time. Barbara Jean was the sickest, and the doctors considered putting her in the hospital. I had to help her get her breath during coughing episodes. I can remember feeling so sorry for her. At the smallest cough, she would run to me for help. I tried to convince Mother to take her to a hospital, but the doctors said that she could be treated at home. The children were sick for months, it seemed, and I was exhausted from having to care for them at night and get up for school the next morning.

A Message Etched In Bronze

I was thirteen years old when Shorty revealed his true feelings to me. He had been out of work for a while and finally got a new job. When he got his first paycheck, he went to the supermarket and bought lots of groceries. He also bought some toys for the smaller children and a box of my favorite breakfast cereal. He handed the box of cereal directly to me. It was the first act of kindness that I had experienced from him. Everyone was excited. The small children were showing each other the presents he bought, and yelling, "Look what Daddy brought me!" In a moment of reckless abandon, I shouted, "Look what Daddy brought me!" What did I say that for? In a rage, Shorty turned to me and said, "I am not your father. Don't you ever forget that!" Then he stormed out of the room. We were all stunned. There was a deafening hush in the room. I felt like a fool. Honestly, I cannot remember what happened next.

Mother heard his comments but did not react at all. I felt completely isolated. A black cloud hung over our house for several days; even the little children seemed in a funk. Shorty's outburst changed my perception of him and poisoned our relationship for years to come. He never showed any remorse or guilt for having slam-dunked me that day. His words stayed with me as if they were etched in my mind. Shorty had drawn a line between us that day, and I was old enough to understand its significance. The more I thought about his words, the more depressed I became. Mother's reaction to the outburst also troubled me. To my knowledge, she never discussed the event with Shorty, and she made no effort to console me. I thought about my schoolmates, and their stepfathers that often attended school events and church picnics with them. Some of them called their stepfathers "Dad." Roy was four years old when Shorty came to live with us. Shorty seemed to accept him as his own, and Roy called him "Daddy." I recalled that I had never called anyone dad or father until that day, and the results were devastating.

My responsibilities prevented me from participating in school events and playing with kids in the neighborhood. Some of my classmates would make remarks about my absences at school events and other activities that led to a number of scuffles. After one fist fight in junior high, I was sent to the dean of boys' office. Dean Thorsall accused me of starting the fight. I tried to explain that I was not at fault, but he would not listen. He said, "Don't make excuses; just make good!" It was the same message I got at home: do not complain about anything. If I did complain, the consequences were swift and grave. I often felt attacked from all sides, so I folded into myself. I wanted so much to run away from home, but I had no place to go.

Nonetheless, there were some pleasant times with my brothers and sisters. On Saturday afternoons if the weather was good, I took them to the

Ninth Street Park to play and relax. The park was five blocks from home. During summer vacation, we went to the park almost every day, except Sunday. Our trips to the park were well planned. We packed a picnic lunch and filled several baby bottles with milk, water, or orange juice. I took extra diapers and clothes for the children. We had a good strategy for getting the children to the park. We used an old red wagon to transport the toddlers. My brother Roy pulled the wagon and I pushed the stroller. I held Barbara Jean's hand as she walked along beside me.

The park was fantastic! There were two three-wall handball courts, a swimming pool, a teeter-totter, a merry-go-round, two sliding boards, and two banks of swings. There were also tennis courts and public toilets. While we were at the park, Mother used the time to shop, clean house, and do the wash. I preferred taking the children to the park rather than helping with the wash and cleaning house. Occasionally, some of my schoolmates would show up at the park to swim or play three-wall handball. One friend, Arthur Paul, was always willing to come over and sit with me while I babysat. Sometimes if Arthur agreed to watch the children, I was able to join in on a handball game.

By my junior year in high school, I had learned to make the best of a difficult situation. I tried not to focus on my restrictions and lost opportunities. I buried myself in caregiving. I read nursery rhymes to the children, played games with them, put together their toys, and comforted them when they were hurt. I chose most of their birthday and Christmas presents, also. The unexpected benefit of this strategy was the opportunity to reflect on my responsibilities at home and the impact on the family if I ran away. Who would take care of them? As they developed and grew, I saw things that I taught them take shape in their lives. Their innocence and dependence on me for guidance and security when Mother and Shorty were not home helped me endure the burden of my caregiving responsibilities. Although the children developed different personalities and anger flash points, they showed respect for one another at an early age. I was content in knowing that I was a major factor in their healthy development.

My chores became easier when I allowed myself to think about positive things while washing dishes, ironing, and cleaning the house. I also realized that increasing my knowledge of the world by listening to the radio and doing my homework for school brought mental satisfaction. I was generally ignored by Mother and Shorty when I mentioned news items that I had heard on the radio or things I had learned in school. They were unimpressed when I told them that I had won the eighth grade world geography contest. I was able to name the most capitols of foreign countries. I was also fascinated with rockets, airplanes, and electricity and I tried to recreate experiments that I had learned about in science classes. Mother and Shorty were convinced that I was learning nothing worthwhile in school and would probably burn the house down.

Bagman, Soldier, And Spy

Shorty kept the family in food and clothes by working part-time at the American Legion Hall in "Little Harlem," a small nightclub area a block from our house. He was also the house card dealer at the Legion's clandestine gambling room. Among other things, Shorty ran a small money-collection operation for a friend who lent money out at high interest rates. He made it known that he was licensed to carry a gun so that there would be no problem when he went to collect money. I don't believe Shorty ever threatened anyone with his gun, and I am positive that he could never have shot anyone. His gun stayed at home in a special hiding place, and it was never loaded.

Not long after Shorty dismissed me as his stepson, he had a heart attack. His illness increased my responsibilities at home. In addition, Shorty depended on me to run errands, act as messenger, and be the eyes and ears for his moneymaking schemes. He took me into his confidence and introduced me to some of his nefarious activities. I learned that Shorty sold marijuana cigarettes for a small-time drug pusher. When clients came by the house to buy cigarettes, Shorty would send me out the back door, and I would crawl under the house to get the cigarettes. I had clear instructions not to tell anyone about the hiding place and never to bring the jar out into the sunlight. After each sale, I counted the cigarettes and wrote down the number sold on a piece of paper that he kept inside the jar. Periodically, I was sent to the store to buy cigarette paper and had to help roll the marijuana stokes.

Shorty trusted me to help him count the money he collected from different sources, and to meet clients outside bars and restaurants, and in alleyways. I passed notes and verbal messages, received packages, and made small deliveries. Shorty taught me how to be discreet and how to make sure I was not followed back home after meetings. I found these activities exciting, and I had no problem going along with his schemes. Observing him and following his orders taught me a lot about the subculture operating in our neighborhood. During one of my deliveries, I learned that Shorty's opinion of me was not all bad. I passed a message to a man who told me that Shorty was proud of me. Shorty had told him that I was mature for my age. He also bragged that for a thirteen-year-old boy, I could be trusted to do what I was told. I suspected that my stepfather's comments were designed to build confidence in the people who had to deal with me. Mother repeated similar things to me. I did not believe her either. I took her comments as attempting to trump my complaints against Shorty. I was convinced that she just wanted me to tolerate his behavior and not get upset with him so often. Whether or not Shorty was dedicated to our family was never a question for me. He was a good provider for the family, and he was willing to steal and cheat to keep the family afloat. Despite my difficulties with him, I admired him for his intelligence, resourcefulness, and cleverness. We rarely suffered from wanting, and he was a loving father to his five children, as well as Roy. Until his outburst, I had convinced myself that I could live with Shorty, despite his disdain for me.

Mother And Me: The Good And The Bad

My relationship with my mother was all-important to me. Before Shorty moved in with us, we shared a special relationship. Often she took me shopping downtown with her. I was with her when she bought new furniture for the house, Christmas gifts, and clothes for Roy and me. I can remember when Mother took me to my first real restaurant downtown. She gave me instructions on how to hold a knife and fork properly, and to remember to place the napkin in my lap. She taught me to observe people closely in restaurants and public places and to imitate them. She said that if I were confused, I should try to blend into my environment. The time I spent with Mother diminished with the arrival of each new baby. Nonetheless, we spent some special moments together. One of my best memories was when she took me along to shop for Christmas toys for the children. I helped her pick out the appropriate gifts for everyone, including myself. That evening after the children were asleep, she and I wrapped the gifts and put the children's names on them. Christmas became a special night for me. It was just she and I, like in old times.

Mother was barely five feet tall and very pretty. She was also sheer dynamite, and just as volatile. She could beat both of my stepfathers in a fight. One night my mother and Shorty had one of their violent fights. The furniture was crashing, and we could hear glass breaking. Barbara Jean, the baby, was crying. Roy and I were frightened and stayed in our room. During the fight, Mother stabbed Shorty in the leg with a knife. The wound was deep enough to cut an artery. Mother made me get up, run over to Grandy's house, and call an ambulance. They took Shorty to the hospital, and he stayed there for over a week. The police interrogated us, but we feigned ignorance of what had happened. When Shorty got out of the hospital, he returned home as if nothing had happened.

All of us were victims of Mother's volatility at one time or another. She did not believe in sparing the rod. Electric ironing cords were her favorite whipping tools. If they were not available, she would use whatever objects she could find. Often, she would exhaust herself while whipping us. One afternoon when I came home from school, Mother asked me to bottle-feed one of my baby sisters. I cannot remember what went wrong, but Mother got so angry with me that she tried to hit me with the handle of a broomstick. I lifted my hands to protect myself and the broom handle struck the glass bottle in my hand. The broken glass cut a nerve in my right index finger. I could not understand why I made Mother angry so often since I took my home chores and responsibilities for children seriously, which made it possible for her to work and to entertain her friends.

One day Mother caught Roy smoking a cigar in the washhouse. She made me chase him down and bring him to her for a whipping. Since Roy was known to run away from a whipping, Mother made me tie him to a tree until she found her ironing cord. Having compassion for him, I tied him to the fig tree outside, but loosely enough for him to escape. Mother was evidently in a whipping mood. She whipped me because Roy had untied himself and gotten away. After dinner that night, Mother decided to whip Roy for what he had done earlier in the day. Despite our frequent beatings, we were all certain that Mother cared for all of us deeply. She just had little tolerance for our stupidity and disobedience.

When I was in the eighth grade, I asked Mother to buy me a wristwatch for my birthday. She was noncommittal. One Saturday I finished the ironing and began putting the clothes away. I discovered a box hidden in a drawer under some clothes. It was a brand-new wristwatch. I told Mother that I had seen the watch, and I asked her if she would let me wear it right away. She said that I had to wait for my birthday. A couple of days later, she agreed to let me wear the watch. I was so excited. It felt so good knowing that Mother had bought me a watch because I asked her to buy me one. As she put the watch on my arm, I saw my friend Arthur Paul walking by the house. I wanted him to be the first one to see my watch. I charged out the house, and my watch hit the door facing as I rushed out. It did not hurt, so I continued to run toward my friend. When I stopped to show Arthur the watch, I saw only the watch casing. I could see my wrist through the watch crystal. The watch had no face and no back. I was devastated and knew instantly what had happened; I had destroyed my watch. Arthur and I traced my steps back toward the house, and we found the inner work-ings of the watch on the porch. They were intact and were still running. We put the watch back together, and it seemed to work OK. There was a small dent in the back casing, which made it difficult to keep the back cover attached. I used Scotch tape to keep it on. If I told Mother that I had broken my watch, I was surely headed for a beating. The watch stopped frequently, and soon it stopped completely. When I complained to Mother that the watch did not keep good time and that it stopped frequently, she said that she was not surprised because it was an inexpensive watch. What a relief! Mother refused to buy me another watch, so I never owned another one until I bought one after I joined the US Navy.

My grandmother was the only one who could influence my mother. We could appeal to her and sometimes it would help. However, that depended on how bad the infraction. Grandy used to tell us stories about Mother. She said that Mother got her personality and tough attitude from our grand-father, Papa. Consequently, she received more whippings than her siblings did. Grandy told me that Mother was kicked out of school in the eighth grade. The school was small, and all the elementary school students met in the same room. Mother overheard the teacher talking to the older students about fire and things that are hot. The teacher was telling the students that experiencing some things directly was not necessary for a good observer. As an example, she asked the class if it was necessary to touch a hot stove to prove that it was hot. She asked my Aunt Queen to put her hand near the stove. Mother misheard and thought the teacher was asking my aunt to touch the hot stove. She jumped up, grabbed the teacher's hand, and put it on the hot stove. She told the teacher, "Now you know what it feels like to touch a hot stove, you bitch!" That was Mother's last day at school. She was condemned to working in the fields helping the family pick cotton. Mother hated picking cotton. She soon got a job working as a domestic for several well-to-do white folks in town. Because she could cook, read, and write and had "light skin," it was easy to find a job as a domestic.

According to Grandy, Mother was run out of Monroe, Louisiana, by the sheriff when she was only nineteen years old. The sheriff told her that the town was not "big enough" for both of them. Mother had previously been arrested twice for causing a disturbance in a nightclub. Once, someone told her that a woman was beating up my Aunt Queenie in a bar next door. Mother rushed to the bar and could not get in because of the people blocking the entrance. She pulled out a knife and started cutting her way through the crowd, injuring several people. When she got to my aunt, she put her knife away and beat up the other woman.

Mother was a wonderful storyteller. When she was in the mood, she entertained us with stories about growing up in Louisiana. I can remember a story she told us about an outing with my biological father. She said that she was pregnant with me and had a craving for watermelon. She asked my dad to buy one for her. He told her that it was not a good idea because they were a long way from home, and that he did not want to carry it. Mother insisted that she wanted a watermelon and that she would carry it herself. My dad bought one for her. A short time later, Mother asked him to carry the watermelon, but he refused. Not to be outdone, she rolled the watermelon all the way home.

Our favorite story was about the "whipping snakes." Mother told us that the schoolchildren had to run to school and back because of an area infested with whipping snakes. She said that she had witnessed a child being attacked by a whipping snake. The snake coiled itself into a circle, then put its tail in its mouth and lifted itself up like a bicycle tire. It rolled after the students. When it caught the student, it wrapped itself around the child's legs, tripped him, and then whipped him to death. The snakes would not stop whipping a person until the sun went down. Mother would mesmerize us with stories about growing up in the country.

Mother worked as a waitress during each of her pregnancies, and she was always rehired after having her babies. Once, Shorty sent me to a café where Mother worked to pass along a message. I could tell that Mother enjoyed her job, and she seemed popular with the customers. They called her "Mae." Mother introduced me to several customers, and they seemed happy to meet me. While Mother wasn't looking, one of her friends let me taste a beer for the first time. It was so bitter I spit it out. They all laughed.

By the time I entered high school, Mother seemed to have little time for me. We hardly ever talked. She was working part-time and always seemed busy. Twice a month, her job took her away on Fridays, and we would not see her until Sunday night or Monday morning. I was always afraid that something had happened to her and that I would be forced to live the rest of my life with my stepfather. When she returned, I would sing my favorite song to celebrate her return. I was fourteen years old when the singing group called The Counts released the rhythm and blues ballad, "My Dear, My Darling." The ballad has been named as one of the best one-hundred doo wop songs ever. The words reveal the depth of my feelings for my mother, and the maturity I was feeling at fourteen regarding the meaning of a love relationship. The lyrics have stayed with me all these years:

My dear, my darling,
I'm so glad that you've come home to me,
All my life, my love, my all to be.
My dear, my darling I've missed you.
My dear, my darling,
I'm so happy that you're here at last,
And I'm glad to know what's past is past,
Oh, how I long to kiss you.
My nights will no longer be lonely,
My days will be filled with joy,
My mornings I will share with you only,
Like a baby with a brand-new toy.
My dear, my darling,
I will never, never let you go,
Cause' my darling, dear, I love you so,
My dear, my darling, I need you.

The Counts

If Mother did not come home by Sunday night, my grandmother had to come over and stay with the children so I could go to school. Shorty was working full-time and could not stay home with the children. Grandy was not happy about having to babysit, but she always agreed to stand in for me. I had a terrible day at school when Mother did not show. I felt so alone. Fortunately, she was always home when I got out of school.

I was frequently disillusioned by Mother's attitude toward things important to me. When she had to go to school on parents' day, or she had to take me to the doctor, I sensed that it was out of duty, not out of concern for me. I never knew for sure what she was feeling about me. When she looked at me, I saw compassion and sometimes puzzlement in her eyes, but never hatred. I imagined that she was sorry that I had to carry the major burden of caring for my brothers and sisters. By the time I entered high school, Mother's lack of interest in my life had become more obvious. I began to think that she saw me as a necessary burden to bear, an unwanted product of her regrettable early lifestyle. She got pregnant with me when she was twenty-three. I loved Mother as much as I feared her, and I believed she loved me in her unique way.

I Was No Angel

As a youngster, I did some things that were patently irresponsible. These things undoubtedly contributed to Shorty's negative opinion of me. In junior high school, I was interested in electricity, airplanes, and rockets. I remember building a small rocket. I looked around the house for chemicals, found none, and decided to check out our medicine cabinet in the bathroom. I used several bottles of medicine that contained alcohol and mixed them into a paste using gunpowder. I had taken the gunpowder out of the cartridges of Shorty's .38-caliber pistol. I used two pairs of pliers and carefully removed the bullets from the casings, poured out the powder, and replaced the bullets back into the cartridges. Shorty noticed that his bullets had been tampered with, and he confronted me. Initially I denied my involvement, but I confessed when he showed me the gunpowder residue that he had found in my room. Instead of yelling at me or even telling Mother, he just shook his head and walked away. The rocket lifted off then exploded. Unfortunately, it sprayed yellowish liquid on some clothes that happened to be hanging on the clothesline near my launch site. Mother whipped me good, and I had to wash the clothes again.

After the rocket disaster, I turned to electronics. I decided to turn our new television set into a radar console by shifting the tubes to different locations. I had to force some tubes into different sockets because they would not fit. In one case, I attached a thin wire to the tube ends and stuck the wires into the holes to make the connection. I noted the original location of the tubes so that I could put them back in their proper place. After reconfiguring the television and plugging it into a wall socket, I went outside to look for airplanes. I was sure that our television antenna would act as a radar screen and monitor airplanes taking off and landing at Norton Air Force Base, which was just outside town. Upon returning to the house, I discovered that the television was spewing smoke. I push it out on the porch before it caused any damage to the house. Surprisingly, I was able to convince the repairman, a close family friend, not to tell Mother or Shorty what had happened, but only after I confessed to what I had done. Shorty easily figured out what had happened to the television. My indiscretions supported his conclusion that I was capable of anything.

My Secret Counselor, Uncle Johnnie

Uncle Johnnie was a true outdoorsman, and I respected him a lot. When I was in elementary school, he took us to animal auctions and other agricultural events. He had a small farm that he spent time cultivating. It was more of a hobby than a major source of income. He had chickens, pigs, and other animals. In his garden, he grew tomatoes, squash, collard greens, corn, and cabbage. He let us watch when it was time to slaughter his pig and other animals. Once, Uncle Johnnie gave me a rabbit to raise. I was eleven years old. He would visit us periodically to make sure I had cleaned out the rabbit's cage. If I didn't have time to clean the pen, he would do it for me. One day I came home from school and the rabbit was missing. I later discovered that Mother had cooked the rabbit for dinner. I did not know that we were eating my pet rabbit. I was sick to my stomach for several days when I found out.

By my junior year in high school, my caregiving and household chores became more burdensome and prevented me from participating in school projects and extracurricular activities. My cousins were involved in all sorts of activities, and I envied them. I mentioned my frustrations to Uncle Johnnie. He was aware of the pressure I was under at home and gave me pep talks to cheer me up. He told me that he thought it was wonderful that I was able to take care of my brothers and sisters and still get good grades at school. He praised my good manners and intelligence, and told me to be patient and persevere for as long as I could. He said that I would grow up to be a better man if I kept a cool head.

Uncle Johnny, My Counselor

I could talk to Uncle Johnnie about most things. There was one problem that I wanted desperately to tell him about, but I was afraid of the consequences if he revealed it to anyone. An older member of my family had forced me to engage in some immoral activities with him. I was convinced that if I told someone and it got out, my relative would beat me up. Worse, what if no one believed me? On the other hand, if the news got back to Papa, I feared that he would kill the relative. For some strange reason, Papa was protective of me, but his wrath was worse than Mother's. Once, Papa brutalized my cousin for picking on me. Papa knocked him down with his fists, grabbed a bucket, put it over his head, and then kicked the bucket. If Grandy had not intervened, Papa might have injured him severely. So far as my older relative's actions were concerned, I solved the problem myself, but not without Uncle Johnnie's indirect counsel. I decided to call his bluff. I became wildly uncooperative and threatened to tell everyone about what he was doing to me, whether anyone believed me or not. It worked; he left me alone after that. I always felt better after my talks with Uncle Johnnie, and I believed him when he told me that if I were patient and persevered, things would surely get better. His faith was unwavering. He also told me that my experiences would work to my advantage someday. Unfortunately, he offered no canned solution for escaping from my difficult home life. He felt that I was smart enough to use my imagination and sense of right and wrong to find my way.

Chapter Three

Dreams Of My Father: Mother's Memories Of My Biological Dad

While doing the weekly ironing one evening, I saw how gentle and caring Shorty was for his children. He placed two of them on his lap and read to them. I also noticed that he hugged them a lot. I wondered if my biological father had ever cared for me in the same way. One day, when we were alone, I asked Mother to tell me about my biological father. She burst with enthusiasm to my question. She said that the last time she saw my dad; I was just five years old. She claimed that he had tried to kidnap me when we first arrived in San Bernardino. As Mother talked about my father, I remembered bits and pieces of the event.

My dad drove up to my grandparents' house in a brand new automobile and parked in our driveway. I was playing in the front yard with several neighborhood friends. He picked me out of the group, called me over to the car, and asked my name. I told him that my name was "Beebe," which was my nickname. He smiled broadly and asked if I wanted to go for a ride. I refused to get in the car. I did not know that my father's name was Beebe. This confirmed to him that I was his child. There was a two-year-old boy in the car with him. Mother saw me talking to the man in the car and came out to see the stranger. She was surprised to see that it was my biological father. Mother had not seen my dad since I was a baby in Louisiana. She asked him why he was there and how he knew where we lived. He did not respond directly but asked her if she would like to go for a ride. Mother got in the front seat of the car, and the little boy and I got in the backseat. Dad told the small boy to say hello to his "big brother." As we drove off, Mother asked my dad why was he in San Bernardino. He told her that he lived in Los Angeles and was working in the navy shipyards in Long Beach, California. As he talked to Mother, I remember that he kept looking back at me and smiling. Finally, Mother told me that the man was my father. I wasn't sure what to make of the situation, and I was reluctant to talk to him. I thought Fats was my father.

When we returned home after driving around for an hour or so, Dad gave Mother some money and told her that he would like to come back and see us. Mother told him that she was now married and that he should not bother us because it would only make trouble for her and Fats. She did not tell my dad that she and Fats were no longer together. She also told my dad that Fats had adopted me. Dad was visibly disappointed and agreed that he would not bother us again. Nonetheless, he looked directly at me and asked, "Son, would you like to come live with me?" Mother answered for me by saying that I was to stay with her. As Dad was leaving, he smiled and waved goodbye to me. I heard him tell the little boy with him, "Say goodbye to your brother." Mother said that it was the last time she saw my dad.

All I Had To Do Was Dream

Mother's fondness for my father was obvious, and my desire to know more about him became a reverie. I wondered what life would be like for me if he had taken me away that day. My dreams about him started after hearing Mother's story. He appeared to me in all races, colors, and professions. Sometimes he appeared to me as a famous movie star, a firefighter, or a schoolteacher. The dreams always had a similar theme: we rode horses, sailed on ships, climbed mountains, and strolled through beautiful green meadows holding hands. My father figure was always explaining something to me and encouraging me to be patient and strong. I had a secret world that seemed to balance things for me. All I had to do was daydream. Thinking about him took the edge off my problems.

My fantasies helped me persevere against social isolation. During my first year in high school, I was sick often. My complaints of stomachaches and of pains in my back and groin fell on deaf ears. Shorty accused me of faking. Once he said to me, "I notice you are never too sick to go to school." He was correct; I loved school. It was a wonderful escape from the burdens I felt at home. Mother was sympathetic enough to keep Pepto-Bismol on hand for me. Finally, I complained to my grandmother about the stomachaches. Grandy agreed to take me to our family doctor. After examining me, Doctor Ingram told her to take me to the hospital for a more thorough examination. He suspected that I might have an ulcer.

Unfortunately, I had to go to the hospital alone. Mother stayed home to take care of the children, and Grandy could not go with me. I had never been to a hospital before, and I waited at least an hour in the reception room before the nurse called my name. When my name was called, the nurse asked if my parents were there. I told her that they had to work. She seemed annoyed that I was there by myself. She took me into a room where several men dressed in white uniforms were working. The nurse told me to undress and put on a white robe. I was very nervous. My fear was so apparent that one of the men in white held my hand and told me to relax. Someone brought him a chair so that he could sit next to the bed. He continued to hold my hand until the examination was over. I heard him tell the examining doctor that I should be given something to help me relax. I can't remember the diagnosis, but they gave me some orange-looking medicine to take and wrote a note excusing me from school for two days. The medicine worked, but I never found out if I had an ulcer or not.

By the time I was fifteen, Shorty's antipathy toward me was apparent to everyone. The older I got, the more agitated he became when I was around him. He often complained to my mother about my attitude no matter how hard I tried to please him. I was crushed when one of my sisters told me that Shorty asked her if I mistreated them when he was not around. Whatever he was saying to them, they soon learned that they could get away with just about anything if they told him that I had done it. My denials were met with a haunting response, "Children don't lie." On the other hand, as the children grew older, they would defend me, but only when it suited their purpose.

My First Father Figure: Henry Hooks

After Mother's divorce from Fats, and long before Shorty moved in with us, I used to visit our neighbors Henry and Opal Hooks. I was drawn to them because they seemed so different from the other friends that came by to see my folks. Mrs. Opal was more educated, poised, and sociable than any adult I knew. Her husband, Mr. Henry, was very tall, intelligent, and handsome. Mrs. Opal invited me into her home often, and she never failed to ask me how I was getting along. She was the only adult beside Uncle Johnnie that seemed to like talking to me. She asked lots of questions, and she would just let me talk on. Mrs. Opal seemed to have confidence in me, and she even let me borrow some of her music records to take home and play on our record player. This made me feel special because I was sure she did not lend her records out to other children my age.

One day I asked Mrs. Opal if I could watch Mr. Henry work on their new house that was only a few doors away. She said that her husband would be happy to have me watch him work on the house. I liked Mr. Henry, but he seemed aloof to me. Although he was kind and responsive to my many

Henry And Opal Hooks

questions, he was always focused on what he was doing. I was concerned about being an annoying distraction to him while he worked. On occasion, he would ask me to bring him a piece of material or a tool that he needed. I think he would send me off to get something for him when he got tired of answering my many questions. Sometimes Papa and my Uncle Doc would be there to give Mr. Henry a hand to lift something heavy. Mother used to tell me not to bother Mr. Henry while he was working, but I would slip off to see him work anyway. Periodically, I dropped by the house when Mr. Henry was not there so that I could see his progress.

By the time I entered junior high, my thoughts and dreams about a father figure included Mr. Henry. It was not long before it occurred to me that the Hooks had no children. I asked Mrs. Opal if she and Mr. Henry would adopt me. She laughed off my suggestion. However, to my surprise, she mentioned my comments to my mother. Both thought that I was kidding. Eventually, I became embarrassed that I had dreamed about Mr. Henry being my father. I feared that he might have perceived my thoughts.

After returning from the navy almost ten years later, I encountered Mr. Henry at a bookstore. He seemed happy to see me. We chatted for a few minutes and then went on our separate ways. I could not help but wonder what my life would have been like if he and Mrs. Opal had adopted me. I reestablished contact with the Hooks and started visiting with them periodically. While writing this manuscript, I shared my childhood fantasies with them. They confessed that they knew how I felt all along and were aware of my difficulties with Shorty. I was happy to see that they had lost none of their kindness toward me. My special regard for them is still strong.

Chapter Four

Relationships And Background Noise: The Trouble Being Me

Independent but seen as needy
Strong but perceived as weak
Intelligent but thought limited
Wise but seen a fool
Qualified but seen as unqualified
Honest but thought duplicitous.
Kind when he should be bitter
Compassionate when he should be
unforgiving
Patient when he should be rebellious
Daring when he should be discouraged
Comfortable when he is himself.

Odell Lee

I was never at the center of any social activities as a teenager or as a young adult. My caregiving responsibilities severely limited my social contacts outside my family. Most of the information I got on managing interpersonal relationships came from friends, books, movies, and music—mainly music. The lyrics of songs often expressed my changing moods and my feelings of loneliness and disappointment. With my active imagination, I loved and lost through the lyrics of songs. I was around thirteen years old when I first heard the ballad sung by Johnnie Ace called "The Clock" while visiting the Hooks' house. I asked Mrs. Opal to lend me the record for a few days. The lyrics of the song resonated with me even at age thirteen:

I look at the face
Of the clock on the wall,
But it doesn't tell me
Nothing at all.
The clock on the wall
Just stares at me,
It knows that I am lonely,
And always will be.

It was a profoundly sad song, and it seemed to personify what I was feeling in my youth. On the other hand, another song made me hopeful that someday things would change. One of my favorite songs was "Gonna Find Me a Blue Bird," by Marvin Rainwater. The lyrics:

"Gonna find me a bluebird,
Let him sing me a song,
Cause my hearts been broken
much too long.
Gonna chase me a rainbow
up in heaven a blue,
'Cause my hearts been longing
just for you."

For me, the bluebird symbolized freedom and my longing to escape from home.

My childhood interest in girls was partly peer-driven, except for the first girl that I had a crush on. I was in the sixth grade, and Geraldine sat at a desk just behind me. I made it a point to talk to her as often as possible. She had long black hair and bright blue eyes. A few days before

Valentine's Day, the teacher asked us to send Valentine cards to other students in the class. I was thrilled to get a card from Geraldine. I had sent her one. Although nothing developed between us, she was truly my first love interest.

In junior high, I did not have the opportunity to date. On the other hand, it seemed to me that most of the guys fell into dating relationships without even trying. Rumors were always flying about who liked whom. The rumors I heard about me were disappointing. I was seen as a standoffish and as a guy that didn't go to parties or play sports. Only a handful of my schoolmates knew what was really going on in my life. My freedom to go on dates, parties, movies, and even after-school activities had virtually ended by the eighth grade. I was confident that I could handle relationships with girls if I ever got lucky enough to go on dates. After all, I had memorized the lyrics of hundreds of love songs that talked about all manners of love relationships.

Once I telephoned a radio station and asked the disc jockey to dedicate a song to a girl I liked. Irene was the sister of a friend. I knew that she did not have a boyfriend, so I thought she might become interested in me if I showed some interest in her. I was hoping the song dedication would start a rumor that we were dating and that it would become fact. It seemed that everyone at school heard the radio dedication of "Earth Angel," by the Penguins, except Irene. When she learned about it, she was annoyed. She told me that she did not appreciate what I had done, and she asked me not to do that again. Irene was mature about it all and said that she did not want to give me the wrong impression. I got the impression that she was not interested in boys at all. On the other hand, the girls that showed interest in me had bad reputations. They were on the wild side and were considered "easy" by the guys in the know. Once two girls followed me partway home after school and made seductive gestures. They joked with me and speculated about my private parts, and asked if they could touch them. I was more frightened than flattered and ran home.

In high school, most of my classmates were involved in extracurricular activities. My first cousins were on the school's varsity teams, and other classmates were involved in local clubs and church activities. The only time I participated in these activities was when Mother was well along in one of her pregnancies and needed to stay at home. Curiously, I do not remember reflecting much on my future. Most of my schoolmates had dreams of doing something useful with their lives. My dreams were different. I dreamed about running away from home and finding my biological father. I do not remember ever dreaming about going to college, deciding on a profession, or becoming rich or famous.

By the eleventh grade, things began to turn around for me. Uncle Johnnie convinced Mother to give me more freedom to socialize with my peers. Occasionally I was allowed to go to dances at the community recreation center, called the REC. The REC was started to help keep the neighborhood high school students off the street. Although there were no chaperones that I could see, the disc jockeys were all adults. The music was loud and the ambiance was just right. The disc jockeys turned the lights down low for the slow songs and raised them during the fast ones. I was one of the better swing dancers, and I did my best to impress the girls when they danced with me. Some guys only danced during the slow songs while others did not dance at all. Unfortunately for me, most girls came to the REC looking for someone special, and they would only dance with their boyfriends or someone they already knew. I always went to the REC dances alone and left the same way. This was just another example of being on the fringes of social activities.

My Nemesis: Willie

One afternoon I was at my grandparents' house listening to music and dancing by myself. Willie's girlfriend dropped by to see him. Since she planned to wait for him, she offered to dance with me. We were having a lot of fun. However, as if out of television soap opera, Willie came home while we were dancing. When he saw me dancing with his girlfriend, he went berserk. He attacked me viciously. I fought back as best I could, but I was no match for him. He was six years older than I. Grandy and Olean were screaming for him to stop. Not until we broke Grandy's expensive three-foot-high floor vase and the living room window did Willie stop hitting me and run out of the house. I was beaten up badly, and I could not go to school the next day. No one saw him for two days. When he returned, Papa dealt with him in his usual brutal way. Willie seemed prepared for his medicine.

Me, Age 5, And My Brother Willie, My Nemesis

This incident revealed just how much Willie disliked me. He abused me in all sorts of ways when the grownups were not around. He was wild, devious, and unprincipled. In my view, he rebelled against everything good and decent. I did my best to avoid him if no adults were around. Unfortunately, Willie had a difficult childhood, too, but his response to misfortune was one of open hostility. He was my half-brother, but he never lived with us. I did not learn that he was my brother until I was in the third grade. I thought he was my cousin. Willie lived with my grandparents, and I was sure that Papa hated him. I do not know what happened, but he did not get along with Mother either. They rarely spoke. It was as if Mother had disowned him. His father got Mother pregnant when she was seventeen. They never married.

One day, Willie disappeared. Mother told me that he had gotten into trouble so they had sent him to live with his biological father in Illinois. I was relieved that he was not coming back. As fate would have it, Willie returned to San Bernardino for a short visit a year after I got out of the navy. He told my mother that he had returned to seek our forgiveness for the problems he had caused the family. He also wanted to see me. Mother telephoned me and asked me to come to her house to talk to him. I was stunned by the call but decided to see him. When I arrived at my mother's house, Willie was asleep on the sofa. I stood over him and studied the man that had caused me so many problems. I wondered what I had done to him to cause him to hate me so much. Willie was slightly heavier than I remembered, and his face was puffy. I sensed that he was ill. Finally, he woke up and saw me. He smiled and said "hello." We were now about the same height although he was six years older.

Willie said that he was proud to hear that I had been in the navy. I was not thrilled by his small talk. Finally, he asked if I would forgive him for all the bad things he did to me when I was younger. He talked as if he were reading from a script. He said that he had come back to make peace with the family. Despite my skepticism, I told him that I had forgiven him already and that I harbored no ill will toward him. This was the truth, but I can remember saying to myself, "I can forgive you, but I will never forget." Willie died several months later in Illinois from cirrhosis of the liver. When I heard of his death, I understood why he came back home. I asked Mother if she wanted to go to his funeral in Illinois. She responded, "No, his family will bury him."

Shorty And Our Final Conflict

Turning sixteen brought a sea change in my attitude toward Shorty and my mother. A few months before school was out for the summer, Shorty and I came to blows. We might have hurt each other if Grandy had not called the police. It all started on a beautiful Saturday morning in April. I was upset that my mother had not come home the night before. Shorty, for his part, seemed unperturbed by her absence. In fact, that morning he decided to fix a big breakfast for the family. He cooked bacon, eggs, grits, and pancakes and called everyone to the table.

After helping the smaller kids get seated, I noticed that there was no chair at the table for me. Shorty said, "You can fix your own breakfast after we're done. Then, you can clean up the kitchen." He had a smile on his face. There were pots, pans, and dirty dishes everywhere, and no food for me. I remember being so mad that I yelled at him, and this is what started the fight. I cannot remember what I said to him, but whatever it was, it sent him into a rage. He bolted from the table and began yelling at me. I stood my ground and yelled back. I was furious, and so was he. Suddenly, he grabbed a butcher knife from the counter and rushed toward me. I could see the fury in his eyes. I threw a plate at him and ran out of the house. He ran after me. He was cursing and waving the knife. Grandy heard all the screaming and came to the door to see what was happening. I almost knocked her down as I ran past her into the house. Shorty was in hot pursuit. He pushed Grandy aside and ran into the house after me. Grandy got to the telephone and called the police. I made it to the back porch of her house where she kept a small workbench. I grabbed a claw hammer and started swinging at him. We heard the police sirens, but that did not stop his effort to get to me. We were at a standoff when the police arrived and separated us. By this time, I was hysterical, he was yelling, and Grandy was screaming. I had never seen Shorty so angry. And I had never been so angry with him.

I was depressed for weeks after the fight, and I realized, painfully, that I would never win over Shorty no matter how hard I tried. I reflected on our relationship over the years and I could not recall one instance when he was a father to me or offered me counsel. I finally came to believe that he resented my presence as part of the family. I could see that there was something visceral about his dislike for me. Mother's reaction to the fight added to my uncertainty. In my mind, her subdued reaction to this incident meant that she would choose Shorty in a crunch. I could not believe she did not jump all over him for treating me the way he did at breakfast and then threatening me with a knife. I saw this as a defining moment for me. I had to escape from home.

Except for his previous outburst when he brutally reminded me that he was not my father and that I meant nothing to him, Shorty and I never had a shouting match. Instead, he was a master at playing psychological games with me. Shorty's comments at the breakfast table that morning were just another example of the tactics he used to show his antipathy for me. Sometimes he would make hostile faces at me when I entered a room where he was sitting, or he would give me the silent treatment when I asked him a question. I could handle his silent treatment, but not his hostile looks. I felt that he was using me as a negative example to the children. This hurt the most. One day we were all watching television together; everyone was quiet and enjoying the TV puppet show. Unexpectedly, Shorty gestured at me and asked my little brother, "Doesn't Odell look a little like Fi-Fi?" Fi-Fi was an ugly black dog in the puppet show.

Shorty tried to keep me off balance all the time and, more and more, Mother would ignore his comments to me. I finally concluded that Mother was no longer concerned about protecting me from the men in her life. This realization put me down in the dumps and fostered a radical change in my behavior. I would now have to fend for myself. Somehow, I got up the nerve to tell Mother that I could not live in the same house with Shorty much longer. She was surprisingly sympathetic. She told me that she was aware that I had "endured a lot of abuse" from the men in her life. Nevertheless, she offered no suggestions on how to solve my problem with Shorty. It was up to me to figure a way out of the situation. A few weeks later, Mother and Shorty had another one of their famous fights, and Mother kicked him out of the house. Shorty got a room with some friends about a block away. My brothers and sisters took this very hard. They were very young. I knew that Shorty would be back in a few weeks or so, but the children were afraid he would never return. They loved him and he loved them.

Donnybrook In The Park

After the altercation with Shorty, my attitude toward my relatives and schoolmates changed dramatically. I felt nervous and agitated most of the time. I got into several fights at school, some with a couple of my friends. Although my grades remained good, I was tense and short-tempered. Several friends accused me of having a chip on my shoulder, and my cousins just avoided me. One morning a couple of my schoolmates, Virgil and Brigham, were joking about my change of attitude. We joked with each other all the time, but I got angry and slugged Virgil. The moment I hit him, I knew it was a mistake, but I could not bring myself to apologize.

Later that day, he told Donnie what I had done. During the lunch hour, before several students, Donnie promised to take care of me after school. I took this threat seriously since Donnie was about six feet tall and weighed about 170 pounds. He had long arms and big hands. He had a wild streak about him and we did not see him as altogether stable. This made Donnie doubly dangerous.

The news spread fast that Donnie was going to deal with me after school. I liked Donnie, although we had never been close friends. I decided that I did not want to fight him, so I had to do something to deter him. During my wood shop class, I went into the storeroom and stole a piece of wood about three feet long and a couple of inches thick. It was just long enough to be intimidating. I hid the plank in the bathroom until school was over. Then I carried it with me onto the school bus. Donnie sat across the aisle from me during the bus ride home. He looked at me and asked what I was going to do with the piece of wood. I said that it was for my protection. By then, everyone on the bus knew what was about to take place. Donnie was silent during the thirty-minute bus ride. Finally, the bus stopped at Ninth Street and Mt. Vernon Avenue near the park. Half the students on the bus got off to watch the fight. I tried to appear unafraid, and I walked straight into the park. We went to the center of the park and squared off. Donnie did not believe I would use the stick, but he was wrong. When I refused to put down the stick, he charged me. I stepped aside and hit him in the nose with my left fist, and I drew first blood. When he charged me again, I threatened him with the stick and he backed off. Each time he tried to charge me, I would threaten him with the stick. Finally, he retreated and said he was going to find something to even the odds.

When Donnie disappeared into the crowd, I decided it was time to go home. Suddenly, one of my cousins yelled, "Odell, look out! Donnie is coming!" Donnie was rushing toward me with a large board that he had broken off a nearby fence. His board was much bigger and longer than mine. In a flash, I headed for the baseball diamond backstop, which was about fifty yards away. I made it there safely. With the backstop between us, Donnie could not get to me. When he tried to come around one end, I would take to the other end. He was so frustrated that he asked someone in the crowd to help him catch me. Nobody moved because my cousins, Cleopas and Hayward, were in the crowd. They made it clear that if anyone intervened, they would enter the fray.

The standoff lasted about ten minutes. Finally, Cleopas talked me into facing Donnie without the stick. He was convinced that I could take Donnie. He reminded me that I had already given him a bloody nose. Actually, I had no choice. Donnie showed no indication of letting me escape. Moreover, I was concerned about getting home late and having to face Mother's wrath. I did not want to be beaten up by Donnie either. When we finally squared off, Donnie asked if I was ready. Instead of answering, I hit him in the nose again. Donnie went wild. One of his blows glanced off the side of my head and took at least two inches of hair with it. Blood was everywhere. Donnie was trying to stop his nose from bleeding, and he began swinging blindly. I outmaneuvered him easily and kept aiming for his face. Finally, Donnie astounded the crowd by saying in a loud voice, "I quit. I don't want to fight any more." He was afraid that I had broken his nose. I did not know if this was a ruse or not, but I wanted to stop, too. I had a terrific headache from the blow I received to the head.

The next day at school, I was on red alert. I saw Donnie several times that day, but he refused to look at me. I did not trust him. I was convinced that he would slip up to me from behind and crown me with a board or something. When nothing happened between us and he did not take the same bus home after school, I was relieved. The following Saturday I dropped by my cousin's house and Donnie was there. He acted as if nothing had happened between us. I apologized for fighting with him. Donnie was still upset about the whole affair. He admitted that he should not have called me out for a fight. His parents saw the blood on his shirt and wanted to know why he had been fighting. They could not believe that Donnie had been fighting with me. We felt bad about the whole thing. None of us doubted that Donnie could take me in a fair fight.

Chapter Five

Off To The Us Navy

I CALL IT AN *"ESCAPE FROM HOME"*

DREAMS
If while pursuing distant dreams
Your bright hopes turn to gray,
Don't wait for reassuring words
Or hands to lead the way.
For seldom will you find a soul
With dreams the same as yours.
Not often will another help you
Pass through untried doors.
If inner forces urge you
To take a course unknown,
Be ready to go all the way,
Yes, all the way alone.
That's not to say you shouldn't
Draw lessons from the best;

Just don't depend on lauding words
To spur you on your quest.
Find confidence within your heart
And let it be your guide,
Strive ever harder toward your dreams
And they won't be denied.

Bruce B. Wilmer

I talked to some friends at school about leaving home. A schoolmate mentioned that he was thinking about joining the US Navy. He said that he saw a newspaper advertisement about the Navy recruiters forming an "All–San Bernardino County Company" of young men that would go through basic training together. After school, he talked me into going with him to check out the possibilities. The recruiter was excited to see us, and he gave us a nice talk about the benefits of a career in the navy. Unfortunately for me, the minimum age for entering the navy was seventeen and required a parent's signature as proof. I had just turned sixteen. I talked to Mother about signing up and tried to convince her that it would be a good thing for all of us. I do not know how it happened, but not only did Mother agree to let me join the navy, but also she agreed to affirm that I was seventeen years old and to sign a statement to this effect. As fate would have it, no one could find my birth certificate to verify my age. The State of Louisiana searched for my birth certificate under my adopted name, Odell Lee, but I was born Odell Bennett. Finally, the navy agreed to accept the San Bernardino City School records that put my current age at seventeen years old. Apparently, Mother had lied about my age when she enrolled me in the first grade. I was so relieved; I do not know what I would have done if I had to live in the same house with my stepfather, Shorty, another year.

US Naval Training Center, San Diego, California (USNTC)

When school was out, I went to the Navy Recruiting Office and signed up for the All–San Bernardino County Company. The navy also offered the Kiddie Cruise Program, which was an experimental recruitment option that reduced the length of navy service to three years instead of the usual four. The "all county" idea worked. About thirty of us signed up for the program. A couple of weeks later, we reported to the recruitment office and were bused to Los Angeles for processing. A complete medical exam was an unusual experience for most of us. After the blood tests, X-rays, and eye exams, they herded us into a room and told us to strip down to our underwear. The doctor checked our knees, feet, and the curvature of our spine. Next, we had to undergo a hernia and rectal examination. None of us had had such a thorough physical examination like this one. Everyone passed.

After the medical exam, we assembled in a large classroom for a general-knowledge and career-placement test. The recruiters scored the tests on the spot. Those of us scoring above average on the general-knowledge exam were asked to take additional tests to qualify as candidates for the pre-Officer Candidate School (OCS) training. I knew that I had done well on the knowledge test, but I was concerned that if selected I might not be ready for such an honor. As expected, I was asked to undergo further tests. The recruiter said that the navy was looking for qualified Negroes to attend pre-OCS training. He confirmed that I had done well on the initial test but that he needed to know the year I had graduated from high school. I told him that I did not graduate. He was visibly disappointed and said, "How far did you get?" I told him that I finished the eleventh grade but that I did not attend the twelfth grade at all. Finally, he apologized and said that he could not continue the process since a high school diploma was a minimum requirement for entering the pre-OCS program. He sent me back to join the others in the waiting room. In truth, the possibility of becoming an officer in the navy was more than I had bargained for. This was my first indication that dropping out of high school was not a good idea.

Mother agreed to attend the swearing-in ceremony with me. I was nervous and she noticed it. She gave me a pep talk and said that she was confident that I would be fine. She reminded me that my Uncle Emeal had served in the army and had fought in Korea. A recruit wandered over and introduced himself to me. After some small talk, he said, "Do you think we are doing the right thing?" Earl had a crop of blond hair that made him look like a young Val Kilmer, the movie actor. He said that he decided to join the navy because he had "nothing better to do." I noticed that Earl arrived with several friends; his parents were not there. Earl's friends joked with him, saying that he wanted to have "a girl in every port." After the ceremony, Mother gave me a strong hug and left in a hurry. I saw her wiping her eyes as she walked away. The new recruits were given time to get to know each other before boarding the bus to the Naval Training Center in San Diego.

USNTC Company 322

The Naval Training Center was animated. Several busloads of new recruits arrived around the same time. After looking over the other recruits, I was happy with my group. Our group had already begun to meld. On the bus trip to San Diego, we discussed our backgrounds and got to know one another. Several had college experience, and others had been working full-time. Still others, like me, had not finished high school and had lived most of their lives in the same place.

The first thing we did after our arrival was to turn in our civilian clothes and pick up our military uniforms. We received shoes, socks, dungarees (trousers and shirts), belts, underwear, t-shirts, traditional white navy uniforms, and toiletries. We were then escorted to our barracks and given bunk assignments. The next stop was the barbershop. The military haircuts changed our looks. Dressed in our dungarees, it seemed that our identities merged. During our first drill practice, a recruit that was marching directly behind me said, "You don't have an ass!" Then he said, "You don't recognize me, do you?" It was Earl. His hair was gone, and he looked physically different to me in his dungarees. When we reversed directions, I told him that he didn't have an ass either. He responded, "I know."

At first, the basic training program was difficult. Getting up at 5:30 a.m. for "muster" (early morning roll call) was a struggle, and learning to stay together and move in a synchronized fashion during marching drills was a challenge for us. In addition, we had inspections of our physical cleanliness at muster and weekly inspections of our lockers. It was imperative that our uniforms were clean and neat, our bunks made up the "navy way," and items in our lockers folded properly and arranged correctly. If too many failed inspection, the whole company was sent out to the field for additional drills. Soon, we learned to check each other's lockers to prevent problems. Often we had to herd the slowpokes out of the shower and out of the mess hall to make muster on time. Most of us made it through the first few weeks without problems. A couple of recruits dropped out of training after three weeks, but none of us knew why. One day, we returned to our barracks and discovered that the beds had been stripped and the mattresses folded in half. A new duty roster was published that omitted their names. No explanation was given to us regarding their departure.

Nothing in my previous experience had prepared me for what I was doing. The lectures and training courses were like learning a foreign language. We learned to read a compass, use firefighting equipment, tie naval knots, use proper navy terminology, identify profiles of warships, fire a rifle, do different kinds of exercises, and drill in unison. The physical exercises were easy for me since I was in good shape. In high school, I played three-wall handball every day during the lunch hour and enjoyed gymnastics, softball, football, archery, and tennis during our physical education classes. One day our company was punished for laughing and making light of an exercise session. We were forced to squat and "duck walk" back to our barracks in a squatting position. Our company commander was not happy when he found out that several of his men were responsible for the problem. Lucky for us, he thought the duck walk back to the barracks was punishment enough. Unfortunately, a few days later I developed a severe pain in my groin and my company commander sent me to the infirmary. I had developed a hernia and needed surgery. I remained in the Balboa Naval Hospital for five weeks. I was not discharged until I was fully able to continue my training, marching drills and all. There is no such thing as "light duty" in basic training.

Balboa Naval Hospital

While in the hospital, I was depressed most of the time. I missed my family and my new friends. I wrote to Mother, told her that I was in the hospital, and asked her to come visit me. The hospital was only two hours from San Bernardino by automobile. She never answered my letters, and no one from home came to see me during my stay. The only telephone call I received while in the hospital was from Earl. He wanted to know how I was doing and to bring me up to date on happenings in the company. He also informed me that I would not be coming back to Company 322 because I had missed too many weeks of training. I was disappointed but not surprised. Our training program followed a tight schedule. I never saw any of my San Bernardino navy friends again.

The only bright spot in the hospital was the special attention I got from Boyson, a medical corpsman. He was the petty officer in charge of my medical ward. Boyson was a tall redheaded sailor with lots of freckles. From the start, he did not hide his interest in me, and before long several sailors recovering from the same type surgery began calling me "Boyson's pet." Boyson seemed amused by their comments and did nothing to change their opinion. One day while Boyson was taking my temperature (we normally took our own temperature), he told me that I was a "special patient." He reminded me that I was the youngest sailor on the ward, the only Negro, and the only sailor still in basic training. On occasion, some patients made negative comments about Boyson's reddish complexion and freckles. It occurred to me that Boyson and I were both minorities.

Occasionally, Boyson would sit in a chair next to my bed and talk to me about his family and his experiences in the navy. He mentioned his desire to go back to college when he got out of the military. He asked me about my family, where I was born and grew up, and what kind of assignment I was looking for when I finished basic training. Boyson could not believe that I had dropped out of high school so close to finishing. At times he reminded me of my Uncle Johnnie because he was always giving me pep talks. Also, every few days he would bring me a paperback book to read so I would not get bored.

I will always remember one humorous incident during my stay in the hospital. A week or so after the surgery several of us complained about being constipated. This was a common problem after a hernia surgery. Boyson told us that using a laxative just after surgery was not good for us. The men got together and decided that I should use my influence with Boyson to convince him to change his mind because I was his "pet patient." Boyson listened to me patiently, and just when I thought he was going to give in, he replied, "You'll shit or blow up, and I don't think you will blow up." We laughed so hard that we almost popped our stitches. The problem solved itself a couple of days later.

All ambulatory patients in the navy hospital were required to do small tasks while recovering from surgery. We dusted furniture on the wards, distributed towels, made beds for the disabled, and ran errands for staff. One day I was feeling out of sorts, and I told Boyson that I had a headache. I asked him if I could stay in bed. Boyson stared at me for a few seconds and then asked, "Why haven't your parents come to see you?" He knew my parents lived only a couple of hours away. I did not respond. Finally, he said that I could stay in bed. He told the ward doctor that I had a slight temperature.

When the doctors cleared me to return to basic training, Boyson accompanied me through the checkout process and walked me to the bus that would take me back to the training center. I appreciated this gesture.

Saying goodbye to Boyson was difficult. I had seen him almost every day for over four weeks, and I had enjoyed his company. I wanted to embrace him but was not sure how he would react. After he walked away, we both turned around and waved goodbye again. I will never forget his kindness to me.

My relationship with Boyson caused me to reflect on the friends I had back home. I seemed to have at least one good friend at every stage in my life. Rudy Valdez was my friend in elementary school. We walked to school together for four years, and I felt that he understood me better than anyone. Rudy was the first person that I confided in about my problems with my stepfather. In junior high, Casper Willis was my best friend. We just seemed to hit it off well. We walked to school and ate lunch together. When Mother allowed me to go to the movies, Casper was the first person I thought to call. In high school, my best friend was Corneal Crayton. He was so easy to talk to and nonjudgmental. Most of our conversations took place at school because I was unable to see him on weekends. One day Roy, a football player, pulled a button off Corneal's new shirt, just to be mean. I tried to get Corneal to do something about it, but he was afraid of Roy. I confronted Roy and told him that he should be ashamed of himself for mistreating Corneal because he never bothered anyone. Roy threatened to do the same to me. Fortunately, my cousin Hayward got between us and said, "If you touch him, you'll have to deal with me." Hayward acted as if he was ready for action. Roy backed off and apologized to Corneal. Corneal and I agreed that I must have been crazy to challenge Roy. I don't know how I got the courage to stand up to Roy that day.

The only other close friend I had in school was Arthur Paul. He lived a few doors away from our house. He was the only friend that came to visit me at home without being invited. Arthur stuttered when he spoke, and I was one of a few kids that did not make fun of him. He was also a little overweight, but none of this deterred him from hanging around the "cool" guys at school. Arthur kept me informed of what other kids were doing after school and on weekends. He and his family moved away when I was in high school, and we never saw much of each after that. I realized that saying goodbye to Boyson was different. I was slightly emotional about not seeing him again, and I thought about him a lot after I left the hospital. He brought friendship to a new level for me.

USNTC Company 363

I was assigned to Company 363 after my discharge from Balboa Naval Hospital. The company had reached the training point where I had left off with Company 322. The dynamic of Company 363 was very different from company 322. Individualism was very strong in the company, and a few recruits were openly hostile to each other. Some complained about others talking too loud in the evenings or playing music that they did not like. There were a few scuffles and shouting matches. Even so, Company 363 did well in the training program. We worked hard to measure up to navy expectations, and we had a lot of fun.

Seaman Recruit Mike

I had only one close friend in Company 363. Mike was from Mississippi. He rarely talked to anyone, and he stayed mostly to himself. One day he approached me and asked me to go on liberty (weekend leave) with him. He said that he had heard that the San Diego Zoo was interesting but did not want to go there alone. I accepted his invitation. We visited the zoo and the harbor area, and Mike took pictures of our outing. He asked some passersby to take pictures of us together so that he could send them home to his parents. Mike reminded me of a young, unpretentious boy that I had met during my visit to Louisiana when I was ten years old. One summer, my grandmother wanted to visit our relatives but did not want to travel by herself. She thought it would be a good idea to take me along so that I could learn something about my roots.

Our relatives lived on a large farm just outside the town. My great-uncle Ned grew tomatoes, black-eyed peas, okra, squash, carrots, green beans, collards, turnip greens, and watermelons. I had never seen so many vegetables growing in one place. We had to pump water from a well and carry it to the house in a bucket because there was no indoor plumbing. There was also an outhouse. I had never seen one before, and I held on tight when using it from fear that I would fall into the cesspool underneath. I had never seen so many large green flies.

One morning a boy named Peter dropped by the house and introduced himself to me. He said that he lived on the farm just down the road. He asked me to go bike riding with him. I was excited to see someone my age. We rode around for a couple of hours and ended up at his house. His mother made sandwiches for us and said that she was happy Peter had found someone to play with during the day. We saw each other every day for two weeks and enjoyed riding his family's horse together and trekking in the woods.

One day Peter invited me to a movie at the local theater. He said that he would pay for the tickets. After he bought the tickets, the movie usher directed me upstairs to the balcony. Peter froze. Finally, he said, "I forgot." Neither of us had focused on the realities involving skin color in Louisiana. I was the only person in the balcony. After the movie, we talked about the situation. Peter told me that he had some black friends but had never gone to a movie with them. He asked me about the racial situation in California. I told him there were no "whites only" drinking fountains and that we could sit wherever we wanted to in the movie theaters. Peter found my description of California fascinating. Finally, he confessed that sometimes he drank from colored fountains when he was thirsty.

Mike, on the other hand, was self-conscious about his southern accent. He told me he knew that some of the sailors laughed at him because he was from Mississippi, and that he felt isolated from the group. I thought to myself that Mike brought some of this on himself. He rarely talked to anyone except me, and he rarely participated in evening activities with the other sailors. He usually went to his bunk to write letters and afterward buried his face in a book. One day Mike said that I was his best friend and that he had told his parents about me. He said that his folks were coming to our graduation ceremony and that they wanted to meet me. He showed me a letter from his mother. She wrote that she and his father were eager to meet his new friend, and that they were so glad that he was "making friends with sailors of different backgrounds."

Mike sent pictures home along with his narratives of everything he had done in basic training. Sometimes he let me read his letters before mailing them. His letters described our training and social activities. He was a wonderful writer. A couple of times a week, we walked to the post office so that he could mail the letters. In turn, his folks wrote to him often. I was moved by Mike's close relationship with his family. I had no contact with my family while I was in boot camp, even though I wrote to them several times.

Company Commander Barr

Mr. Barr, our company commander, was a no-nonsense type. He wore his cap low over his beady eyes, and he never smiled. We all thought he was really a tough Marine Corps officer disguised as a navy warrant officer. Mr. Barr was very strict and impressed on us the importance of obeying boot camp regulations, on and off the naval base. He told us that he was determined that all of his men would graduate and that he would not tolerate our embarrassing him or our company. I liked Mr. Barr, but I was uncertain if he even noticed me. He never showed any favoritism that I could see.

Ralph, a recruit from New York, was the only one in the company that defied the commander. He was streetwise and stretched the regulations to the limit. Ralph would often regale us with his stories about life in New York City. One day he went downtown and got a small tattoo on his left shoulder. Mr. Barr had given strict instructions that if anyone in his company got a tattoo, he would send them to the brig. Ralph told us that he wanted a tattoo and that he was going to get one. No one believed him. We were shocked when he displayed the tattoo to us one evening. Not surprisingly, Ralph got a slight infection in the area around the tattoo. Since we figured that we would all get into trouble if the commander found out, we stuck together and helped him treat the problem with various ointments that we could find.

On graduation morning, I went to the head (navy term for toilet) and saw Mr. Barr standing in front of the mirrors. He was wiping tears from his eyes. I thought that maybe someone had died. He looked at me and said, "It's always the same; I love you guys. But, I will survive." Finally, he asked me if I was happy with my duty assignment after leaving boot camp. I was unhappy with my assignment, but I was not going to tell him that. I told him that it was not what I had expected but that at least I was going to sea. He replied, "Life on a destroyer escort is the real navy. You will love the duty."

My ship, the USS Foss DE-59, was based at Pearl Harbor, Hawaii. I wanted duty on a cruiser or aircraft carrier, but most of all I was hoping to stay in California. In addition, I wanted to go to Radioman School, but this was denied too. It seemed that those of us that had not graduated from high school did not get a specialized school, no matter how well we did in basic training. I talked to the training assignments officer to see if I could get an exception. He recommended that I apply to become a radioman "striker" when I reported aboard ship. He thought I had a good chance because my general knowledge scores were high.

USNTC Boot Camp Graduation Day

We assembled in front of our barracks and marched to the parade grounds for the final review and the graduation ceremony. Although I accepted the fact that my folks would not be at the ceremony, I scanned the visitors and onlookers for a familiar face, desperately hoping that someone from home would be there to see me graduate. Many graduates did not bother inviting their relatives to the ceremony because they lived too far away. They got together and planned a graduation picnic at the beach before departing on home leave.

Mike introduced me to his parents. They were kind and considerate, and entertained me as if I were their own. I suspect that Mike asked them not to mention my parents because it was a sore spot with me. Nonetheless, we had a wonderful meal at a restaurant in town. Mike and I took his parents to the zoo and other places that we normally visited while on liberty. Mike was going off to a navy school, and I was going to sea. We knew that it was unlikely that we would see each other again. We exchanged addresses, hugged, and promised to say in touch.

After boot camp, I returned home for two weeks' leave. During my absence, mother and Shorty had gotten back together. I did not know this since I had not heard from home in three months. Shorty was not happy to see me and did not speak to me during my visit. Of course, this was his normal response to me. On the other hand, my brothers and sisters had missed me, and I had missed them too. I tried to connect with several of my high school friends, but they did not have time for me. It seemed that I was a forgotten entity. I felt that everything had changed in just a few months; even the house looked smaller. Before long, Roy told me that Mother asked him if he knew how long I was staying. I had already decided that I should not have returned home after basic training. I had brought home lots of photos, but only Roy and the small children were interested in looking at them. I could feel the tension in the house building every day. After six days, I said goodbye to everyone and took a taxi to the Greyhound bus station. No one came to see me off.

The bus ride from San Bernardino to San Francisco was long and tiring. I took a navy shuttle bus to the naval station at Treasure Island. I was not expected to arrive for another week, so I had to go through a special check-in before I was assigned a bunk in the temporary duty (TDY) barracks. Three weeks later, I boarded a military plane to Hickam Air Force Base in Hawaii. I had never been on an airplane before. The C-124 was a four-engine prop military transport plane. It was uncomfortable, noisy, and cold. There was no wall padding or lining in the passenger cabin, and the seats had metal frames with sagging canvas suspended over them. We landed in Oahu eight hours later.

Seaman Eugene

When my shuttle bus from Hickam Air Force Base arrived at the Pearl Harbor Naval Base, Hawaii, the USS Foss was not in port. She had left a few days before for sea operations. I was concerned. However, the shuttle driver told me not to worry, that the TDY barracks would put me up until my ship returned. The wait turned out to be a good thing. I met one of the most interesting sailors of my navy tour. I was checking into the barracks when a sailor introduced himself and suggested that we go to dinner. Gene said that he was waiting for his ship to return from Japan and that he had been in the TDY barracks for two months. I took a bunk across from his, and we walked over to the mess hall together. Gene was tall, handsome, and physically fit. He wore a tailored bell-bottom white navy uniform. I learned that Gene was twenty-one years old, on his second tour in the navy, and that his wife was in the process of divorcing him. Although he was much older than me, I was surprised that he seemed to want my company.

One evening, Gene volunteered that he had been in the brig because he had gotten into several fights while on liberty and on board ship. Unfortunately, his ship, a navy supertanker, had left for a three-month cruise just before he was released from the brig. Every evening Gene wanted me to go to the base non-commissioned officers' (NCO) Club to drink beer and listen to music. He prided himself in being able to suck beer out of a can in ten seconds. I was charged with timing his feat when he felt like showing off. On occasion, I had to help him back to the barracks after our nightly visits to the club. When he was drunk, he talked about his wife and cried because she was divorcing him.

I surmised that Gene had been reduced in rank at least once for fighting. Nevertheless, he was a wealth of information. He made my transition to "real" navy life easier. Some of his advice dealt with practical issues and others with philosophical ones. Gene suggested that I should buy additional dungarees, underwear, T-shirts, and toilet articles while I had the chance. In addition, he encouraged me to buy a camera to take pictures of the sunsets while out at sea. I had never owned a camera, so he showed me how to work it. He treated me like a younger brother, and I appreciated his looking after me. Every evening, we took long walks after dinner and he told me about his navy experiences. Gene said that he had joined the navy before he got married. When his ship's homeport moved from Stateside to Hawaii, his wife refused to accompany him. A couple of years later, she wrote him and asked for a divorce. I could see that Gene loved the navy, but in his mind it had cost him his marriage. When the USS Foss returned to port, we did not see much of each other. Our ships were rarely in port at the same time. One day Gene showed up at the USS Foss to tell me he was leaving the navy, and he gave me his address in the States. I never saw him again. I wrote him, but he never answered my letters.

Anchors Away! The USS Foss DE-59

The USS Foss was larger than I thought it would be. She was 306 feet long, about the length of a football field, and carried a complement of 185 sailors in peacetime. She was a Buckley-class destroyer escort and had a unique appearance. Her superstructure was higher than the other destroyer escorts classes, and this made her look top-heavy. For armaments, she had three open-mount 3-inch caliber canons, two forward and one aft, 40-millimeter canons, a pod of hedgehogs, and depth charge racks. The USS Foss was also equipped with ship-to-shore electric power generators. The power reels were located on the second deck, amidships, just behind the smoke stack. The Foss could provide emergency electric power to a small town using its turboelectric generators and engines.

Everything was arranged for my arrival. I had an assigned bunk in the deck force berthing space, and my name was on the ship's "watch" roster. In addition, I was assigned to a "general quarters" (battle station) duty position.

The enlisted crew's bunks were made of a sturdy canvass. Each had a thin mattress, a pillow, sheets, and blankets. The bunks were in pairs and three high, each separated from its neighbor by two five-inch pipes that supported

USS Foss DE-59

the bunks. Two chains with clips were attached to the outer edge of the bunks for support and were used to raise the bunks out of the way when we needed to get into our footlockers. Although the bunks were comfortable and wide enough for an average-size sailor, they were not far enough apart to prevent encroachment into the neighbor's bunk. We had to make up our bunks every day, and the covers had to be neat and tight.

The first thing I did was to unpack my sea bag and change into my dungarees. The footlockers under the bottom bunks were small but sufficient for our basic needs. Our dress and heavier clothes were put in storage in another part of the ship.

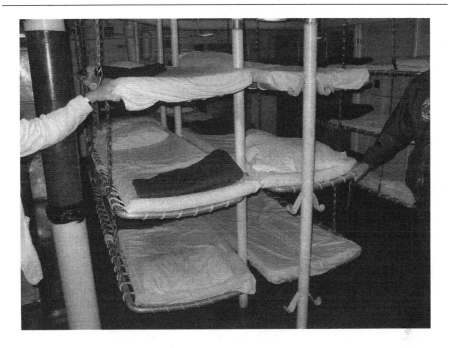

Typical DE Bunk Arrangement

A petty officer was tasked to familiarize me with different compartments. The Head (toilet) and shower areas were my biggest surprise. There was practically no privacy. The toilet stools had no partitions between them and had barely enough elbowroom between commodes. Things got complicated when sailors rushed in to the toilets to throw up. My tour guide reminded me that the USS Foss was a warship and not a luxury liner, and that toilet conveniences were secondary to the main purpose of the ship. The showers on the Foss were similar to our high school showers. They were in a single space with several individual showerheads. The washbasins were across the passageway and closely spaced. There was always a line for the showers and washbasins during the morning rush. Some sailors would get up very early to take their showers or the night before to avoid the morning rush.

My tour guide showed me the location of other berthing spaces, the mess hall, radar, and radio shack, and the Combat Information Center (CIC). On my second day, I toured the sonar and engine rooms, and several storage areas. The mess hall had a refrigerated storage area that was packed with foodstuffs. The most fascinating space that I visited was the machine shop. Sailors were cutting, welding, and shaping different pieces of metal and pipes. The USS Foss carried its own complement of sailors trained in a variety of trades. The ship was like a small self-contained city.

I worked in the deck force for about two months. We were responsible for handling mooring lines while docking and undocking, lifting and lowering the anchors, polishing brass, chipping rust, and painting the outer areas of the ship. We also had to wash down the bulkheads and the outside decks to get rid of salt and other contaminants. The work was mostly busywork and was not difficult at all. However, several shipmates warned me to look busy when the chief boatswain mate was around because he might give me extra work to do. One morning the chief boatswain informed me that my request to become a radioman striker was approved, and he ordered me to move my belongings to the berthing space where the radiomen, radarmen, and quartermasters slept. I counted six blacks including myself on board ship. I was the only one in my new compartment. A couple of blacks were stewards, and the rest worked on the deck force or in the boiler room.

The USS Foss was designed to escort convoys and to search out and destroy enemy submarines. We had the latest sonar and antisubmarine-detection equipment. However, during my tour on the ship, our activities were limited to antisubmarine exercises in and around the Hawaiian Islands using depth charges and hedgehogs in concert with other destroyer escorts and destroyers. We also practiced antiaircraft combat using our forty-millimeter and three-inch canons to fire at targets pulled along by aircraft. On one occasion, in an exercise to rescue wounded marines, we used rubber rafts to land sailors on a beach to rescue the marines. Several of our sailors became violently ill when they came upon marines with horrific wounds on their bodies. They were moaning, crying, and bleeding profusely. Several had deep stomach wounds and legs blown off. Some of us were shocked to discover that the wounds on the men were faked. They looked so realistic.

In general, the training we received emphasized ship readiness, knowledge of our jobs, and getting to our assigned battle stations in a timely fashion. My primary battle station was to a starboard side depth charge position. More than once, we got underway in full battle readiness when alerted that suspected Russian submarines were lurking around the entrance to Pearl Harbor. Our mission was to find them and follow them around.

Sometimes the chase lasted for days. We tried to wait them out and force them to surface, but there was no attempt to engage the subs in a military confrontation, although we were prepared for a potentially hostile response.

During non-working hours at sea, the captain encouraged us to organize evening activities on the ship's fantail. It was the best place for watching movies in calm weather, and the fantail was our main physical-exercise and sunbathing area. Sometimes we fished, listened to music, and danced to rock 'n' roll songs. In addition, Sunday-morning religious services were on the fantail for sailors who wanted to practice their faith, whether in port or at sea. Our meals were always hearty and high quality. I could not believe the wonderful breakfasts, lunches, and dinners served at sea. Wednesdays and Sundays were my favorite days. We usually had large T-bone steaks at lunch on Wednesdays and wonderful desserts after the Sunday brunch. The mess hall was the center of our indoor recreation activities and late night chats. Pinochle, whist, and cribbage were the most popular card games. Dominoes and checkers were also popular. Sometimes the cooks baked cakes or cookies for late-hour snacks. A task of the "messenger of the watch" was to keep the coffee pot perking at all times. There was no night curfew like in basic training, although we were encouraged to get sufficient sleep if we wanted to stay healthy.

"Male" Problems

After about six months on board, several sailors developed rashes under their foreskins. After several unsuccessful treatments, the ship's medic sent me to Tripler Army Hospital in Honolulu for evaluation. The doctors at Tripler decided that circumcision was the best option to deal with the persistent problem. I was not happy about the proposed surgery, but I did not have a choice.

After surgery, I joined at least twenty other patients in recovery. A medic gave me a small silver canister filled with a freezing solution to kill spontaneous erections, which was a common problem after this kind of surgery. He said that the canisters had to last a week and that there were no refills. With more than twenty of us on the ward, the canisters were in use almost constantly, day and night. Some used their canisters more than others did, and a few sailors ran out of the freezing solution early. When this happened, we all cooperated to deal with the situation. A full erection was very painful and could tear the stitches, requiring additional surgery. Most of our problems occurred late at night or early in the morning. Although we all got refills (contrary to what the medic had told us), we did not trust anyone to handle our personal canisters from fear that he would use too much spray. Instead, we would use the spray on each other to solve a comrade's problem. The experience was an important lesson for all of us. We lost any shyness regarding what was happening to our bodies and were even able to joke about our difficulties. When I returned to the USS Foss, I was the focus of immense curiosity. My shipmates wanted to know "how it felt" to be newly circumcised and jokingly asked for a show-and-tell.

Bad News From Home

The Christmas holidays brought some sad news from home. Mother wrote that our house had burned down on Christmas Eve and that the family had lost everything, including the Christmas presents I had sent home from Hawaii. Although it seemed the whole town had responded with gifts and clothes, Mother asked if I could send money to help. I asked the chief responsible for personnel matters what I should do. I asked him if I should take a "hardship discharge" so that I could return home and help my family. The chief was sympathetic but said that a discharge from the navy was not a good idea. He told me about cases where sailors had left the military to help their families and ended up becoming an additional burden because they could not find a job. The chief suggested that I sign up for a monthly allotment to my family. In hardship cases, the navy would provide matching funds to augment the amount a family would receive. He warned me that I would have to make some sacrifices because they would reduce my monthly salary by half. I opted for the allotment and continued it until I got out of the navy.

I learned a lot about the navy in boot camp, but the experience did not fully prepare me for my duties aboard ship. Serving on a warship taught me what it meant to be a "shipmate" and "in the same boat." We recognized our responsibility to our jobs and knew where we should be when danger threatened the ship. Thanks to this experience, I developed a responsible work ethic that has stayed with me through my other assignments. I will always remember my life experiences aboard the USS Foss and the men that taught me how to be a sailor. After serving one year on the USS Foss, she was ordered to return Stateside for decommissioning. I was transferred to the USS Walton DE-361, another destroyer escort in the same squadron.

Chapter Six

My Navy Western Pacific Cruise (Westpac): The USS Walton DE-361

y transfer to the USS Walton went smoothly. While on the USS Foss, we had conducted antisubmarine and war-fighting exercises with the USS Walton, and I had met several members of her crew while in port. The USS Walton was a Butler-class destroyer escort. She had a lower superstructure that gave her a lower profile at sea. She was roughly the same size as the USS Foss and carried similar armaments, except the USS Walton had two five-inch gun turrets, one forward and one aft, instead of three open mount three-inch guns. The living spaces, mess hall, and upper decks had the same configurations as on the Foss. Finding my way around the ship was easy. The Heads were a welcome change; they were configured differently and upgraded. Shortly after I arrived on board, the USS Walton and the USS McGinty DE 365 set sail for a Western Pacific cruise (WESTPAC) with planned visits to Midway, Japan, Hong Kong, Guam, Philippines, Australia, and American Somoa. I was very excited.

The WESTPAC cruise was everything the other sailors said it would be. The experience opened my eyes to a new reality about peoples and places. Our first stop after leaving Pearl Harbor was Midway Island. I was awestruck by the idea of traveling to such a historical place. I learned that

USS Walton DE-361

the "Battle of Midway" had turned the tide of the war against Japan during World War II. Topographically, the island was flat and narrow with a winding coastline. It was so small that as our ship approached it, we could see the ocean on the other side of the island's coastline. We spent several hours on the island and checked out the historical points as well as the notorious Goonie birds. Our next stop was Yokosuka, Japan.

Our Visit To Japan

Several days out of Japan, the chief medic ordered all hands to the mess hall to watch movies about venereal disease (VD). We attended in shifts. The films were the most disturbing movies I have ever watched. They focused on the potential consequences of unprotected sex and the dangers of not reporting symptoms of venereal disease to a doctor immediately. The men featured in the movies had rotted penises, some of which were full of open sores and fissures. Some men showed signs of brain damage and diseases akin to leprosy. These were conditions caused by untreated syphilis and gonorrhea. The message to us was that we were going to a place where VD was rampant.

The "old salts" (sailors with lots of experience) mocked the film and claimed that very few people caught VD in Japan. For me, the movie was scary, and I had trouble getting some images out of my mind. I was struck by the wisdom displayed by a particular sailor. Bill said that the film's purpose was to encourage sailors to use protection when having sex. He said that we should see it for what it was. Bill was a tall, handsome, and athletic black sailor. His two front teeth were slightly gapped and he had a wicked smile. He was from Little Rock, Arkansas, and had been on the ship almost a year. Bill and I struck up a wonderful friendship during our WESTPAC cruise. He became my best friend in the navy.

Before leaving Hawaii, I had made friends with Jim, a white sailor who was also from Little Rock. Jim was always helpful and took me under his wing when I first came on board the USS Walton. We seemed to hit it off right away. He looked like a real country boy and spoke with a pronounced southern accent. It was hard for me to believe that he and Bill grew up in the same town. Bill seemed better educated and from a higher economic class. Bill and Jim rarely interacted with each other. If one saw me talking with the other, he would pass us by without speaking. I was determined to find out why.

We spent two months in Japan. Since the ship was in dry dock most of the time, we had a chance to explore the country. I could not wait to take pictures and send copies home to my family. While entering the port at Yokosuka, we sailed past several US warships. The aircraft carriers USS Hancock and USS Hornet were moored at a pier, and several cruisers and destroyers were anchored offshore. As I walked along the pier next to the USS Hancock, I was amazed at its height and length, and I wondered how that much steel and iron could float.

The first night on liberty, three of us took a taxi to downtown Yokosuka. We saw dozens of nightclubs and bars filled with sailors from different ships. At one club, we stopped to take a closer look inside when an arm reached out and grabbed one of my friends, pulling him into the club. The woman that grabbed him was naked. She insisted that we come in and watch the show. Three women were onstage, dancing erotically. They were all naked as well. The sailors in the place were cheering wildly. We stayed in the club only a short time before moving on to check out other clubs.

The next club seemed a lot tamer. A woman was doing a striptease dance and was removing her clothes in a seductive manner. She had a lot more class than the first three women we saw. The nightclub was packed with sailors, many from our ship. We decided to join them. I saw sailors being led by women to a back room located behind a curtain. They were gone for about twenty minutes or so and returned alone. The women returned a few minutes later and tried to woo other sailors to join them behind the curtain. A couple of sailors had women sitting on their laps. The women were laughing, wiggling, and whispering in their ears. I almost choked on my beer when I realized that they had been doing more than laughing and talking. They had been having sex. Ironically, they were sitting near a sign that read, in English, "No Lewd and Improper Behavior Allowed."

Sex was on our minds all the time. It did not take long for the impact of the movie on VD to fade from our memories. With the encouragement of some older sailors, we decided to throw caution to the wind and go to a house of prostitution. A couple of older sailors that had visited Japan previously took us to their favorite house. They said that they had lost their virginity there. They told us that the women in Mama-San's House were "certified" VD free, so that using a condom was not necessary. We arrived at the house en mass (about six or us).

We entered a large reception room where the Mama-San and a dozen or so women were waiting. To our horror, the Mama-San insisted that she inspect our genitals to see if we were disease free. The women standing along the side of the room were smiling, whispering, and pointing to us as if they were deciding among themselves which sailors they wanted. Our mentors told us to relax and let the women lead the way. They told us to take our time, and that everything had been paid for in advance.

Tom, a tall, big-boned sailor from the Midwest, was upset because the women said that his penis was too large. They feared that he would ruin them for other men, and they wanted nothing to do with him. Tom's penis was the size of a healthy young ear of corn, and he was sometimes the object of jokes on board ship. This time, Tom was embarrassed, and he turned beet red and bolted for the door. The Mama-San stopped him and told him not to worry, that they would take care of him. The old salts talked Tom into staying. They pointed out that he could not leave Japan still a virgin.

We were taken to separate rooms by the women, but it did not matter since we could hear everything going on through the thin walls. The woman I picked seemed eager to please, and that made everything easier for me. She was very good in making me think I was taking the lead and that I was the best lover she'd ever had. I was not fooled by her comments and erotic behavior. Afterward, I felt a lot more grown-up. I could hardly wait for my next experience. On the other hand, some of us could not wait to get back to the ship to take a shower. Others went bar hopping until curfew. Surprisingly, we never discussed our experiences with each other. The exception was Tom. The next morning we saw Tom in the showers, and he confirmed that he was no longer a virgin. He stunned us all when he said, "Having a big dick is no fun."

For the next two months while in Japan, we had to report to the infirmary every two weeks for a checkup, whether or not we had participated in any sexual activities. The medical corpsmen working in the infirmary used flashlights and swabs to check over our groins for indications of "crabs" and other sexually related culprits. After the flashlight inspection, they performed another process: they captured any suspicious results for analysis. Finally, they sprayed our groin area with a disinfectant. The experience was debasing, but we knew it was for our own good. For me, it was reminiscent of the recovery room in the circumcision ward at Tripler Army Hospital. There were no secrets.

When rumors had it that a couple of sailors had come down with VD-type symptoms, the news dampened our sex drives. There were also false alarms among the sailors. By the time we left Japan, all of us wondered if we had been exposed to something that would show up years later. My friend Bill rarely left the ship. He said that he did not want to engage in any of the risky sexual activities. One day I asked him to go to a bar with me. He refused. He said that he was not interested in getting drunk and making a fool of himself. Bill was also furious that he had to go to the infirmary for VD tests even though he had not engaged in any sexual activity. After pleading with him for days, he finally gave in and agreed to have a beer with me and to visit a few shops to look for postcards and trinkets to send home. Bill enjoyed the outing, and a couple of weeks later, he asked me to go with him to Tokyo.

One evening I went out with some sailors from the deck force. I got sick after drinking several beers, and I felt that I was going to pass out. The last thing that I remembered before fading was Jim, my other friend from Little Rock, rushing toward me. He made everyone move back, and he picked me up and said, "We've got to get you back to the ship." Jim rallied a couple of other sailors to help. They hailed a taxi so that we could avoid running into the shore patrol. I had already vomited in my hat, so Jim put his hat in my lap just in case I vomited again. When we got back to the ship, Jim helped me to get undressed and into my bunk. He brought me something to drink and he stayed around until he was satisfied that I was going to recover. I was touched by his concern, and I was reminded of the compassion shown by Petty Officer Boyson at Balboa Hospital.

Recreation At Sea

Our Visit To Hong Kong

Our trip through the Taiwan Straits to Hong Kong was a frightening experience. We ran into a typhoon. The ship was bobbing up and down and tilting left and right from the wind and waves. An alarm bell started ringing indicating the danger of capsizing. Several sailors that did not have time to buckle themselves in their bunks rolled out and hit the deck. A couple of sailors were slightly injured. The mess hall and kitchen were the hardest hit. The captain returned to the bridge and told the officer of the deck that he had talked with the captain of the USS McGinty. They had decided to move into closer visual range of each other just in case one lost power or got into difficulty. The captain ordered all hands below decks, except those of us on the bridge. We had belts that tied us in place. Unlike in the Hollywood movies, no sailor came out on deck and was swept overboard because he did not get the message.

Our visit to Hong Kong was a disappointment for me. First, we anchored at some distance from the shore and had to take the whaleboat to the pier. It was no fun when we had to cross the wake of another ship, and we could get only a few sailors on the boat at one time. It was first come, first served, and often we had to wait for two or three trips to connect with our buddies. The city was dirty, and abject poverty was in bold relief. In addition, I was overcome by the unusual smells and felt nauseated most of the time. Bill and other sailors loved Hong Kong. Several sailors had clothes made and bought different kinds of jewelry to send home to family and friends. After I returned to the ship, I canceled any plans to return to Hong Kong and resisted efforts by Bill and others to change my mind.

Unbeknownst to most of us, the captain had arranged to have the exterior of our ship painted by a Chinese company. It was a lot of work for us too. We had to stay ahead of the painters by chipping and sanding rust spots. We also had to paint the more sensitive areas of the ship and watch the painters do their work. The Chinese painters were fast and efficient. A couple of Chinese representatives appeared in the mess hall during lunch and dinner every day to collect the food scraps. They brought two large trashcans, and they separated the food they wanted to keep from what they could not use. Some of us were convinced that we were providing food scraps for the "starving children in China," and I was horrified by this idea. I thought, "Why not share our food with them beforehand?" I talked several sailors into eating everything on their trays so that we would not participate in this tragic situation. One day I asked the officer of the deck about the "food for paint" agreement. He told me that the food was to feed hogs and chickens, not humans. I felt like an idiot. Twenty years later, I visited Hong Kong on business and was thoroughly impressed by the city's modern skyscrapers, upscale hotels, fancy restaurants, and comprehensive transportation system. The city was teeming with excitement; it was nothing like I remembered at seventeen years old.

Shipmates Bill And Jim

Sometimes out at sea we would entertain ourselves by having boxing matches, dancing, singing, and joke contests. My friend Bill organized a doo-wop singing group, and we serenaded the crew during these down periods at sea. My buddy Jim was one of the best joke tellers. Unfortunately, Bill wanted nothing to do with Jim. As far as I could tell, the feeling was mutual. I told Bill about Jim coming to my rescue in Japan, but he was unimpressed. He commented that any of the other sailors would have done the same thing. I protested and accused Bill of not wanting to give Jim any credit at all. Finally, Bill agreed to talk me about the issue, but not aboard the ship. We took a walk around the base that evening, and I learned that Bill and I had very different reactions to white people.

Bill said that he had never interacted with whites until he joined the navy. He admitted that it was a big adjustment for him. When whites had befriended him, he was forced to change his opinion somewhat. In fact, Bill had several close white friends on board ship. He was especially fond of a white sailor from Beaumont, Texas. We dubbed him the "lady killer." Bill liked the Texan because he knew all the rock 'n' roll songs, and when he was on the dance floor with a girl, everyone stopped to watch them. Beryl said that he learned to dance by watching blacks dance at mixed nightclubs in Beaumont, Texas. Growing up in different parts of the country was the primary reason for our divergent views. I grew up with the view that there were good and bad people of all races. Although my adult relatives were born and raised in the South, they never taught us to distrust other races. While growing up I was only vaguely aware of the depth of racial prejudice confronting blacks in other states, except for my experience with Peter during my visit to Louisiana when I was ten years old. For example, I cannot remember ever discussing the US Supreme Court 1954 Brown v. The Board of Education ruling neither at home nor in school. The Court ruled that "separate but equal" laws justifying segregation of schools by race was "inherently" unequal. According to Bill, this was a major topic of discussion in homes, churches, and schools in the South. My high school was integrated, and the ruling did not seem important to us.

My mother was born and raised in Louisiana near the Mississippi border. She rarely spoke about her experiences with racism. Papa seemed to have no problem with the issue either. My grandmother, on the other hand, was born in Mississippi and was half-Cherokee. She was less trusting of whites, but she had white friends her age that came by the house on occasion to visit. The black community in San Bernardino was diverse and was not concentrated in one area of the city. There was no recognized black leadership in town, and most of us did not automatically "relate to each other" because we were black. The blacks that lived on the west side of town had little to do with the blacks that lived in the suburbs or the valley. I think that the general division among blacks was based on economic standing and church affiliation. On this point, it seemed that the black churches in the city did nothing to foster political unity in the black community. Religious segregation and doctrinal differences seemed more important than politics and prevented any real notion of "black unity." On the other hand, the blacks and whites that had moved in from the South found themselves going to school with races that they had never encountered before. They took their cue from the rest of us and adjusted to their new environment.

Our family had the first television set in our neighborhood. I can recall Mother ushering us into the house to watch black performers on television. We would rarely see black faces on TV except on shows like *Amos 'n' Andy*, *The Little Rascals*, boxing, and wrestling. These were very popular shows in the black community. The civil rights movement in the early sixties and the birth of the Nation of Islam organization sought to convince blacks that programs like *Amos 'n' Andy* were denigrating to black people. My parents loved the *Amos 'n' Andy* show and *The Little Rascals*, and were offended that some blacks criticized these programs.

I cannot recall any of us being denied service in a place of business in San Bernardino, California. However, there were areas of town that were almost exclusively white. The Perris Hill Park area on upper Highland Avenue comes to mind. Nonetheless, blacks went to the park often to watch people play tennis after school and on Saturday mornings. Our junior high school boy's swim classes were at the YMCA and fully integrated. For health reasons, students and coaches had to swim naked. We were required to take a shower, monitored by the coaches, before entering the pool area.

On my nefarious missions for my stepfather, Shorty, I noticed some racial separation in bars and nightclubs. For example, although there were whites that lived in our neighborhood, I rarely saw a white face in "Little Harlem," which was a block away. In the so-called "red-light district," on East Third Street downtown, there were several bars—some all black, some all white, and some thoroughly mixed. It was the favorite area for airmen from March and Norton Air Force Bases and for soldiers from Fort Irwin.

During one of my discussions with Bill about institutionalized racism, I recalled an incident in junior high school when a counselor told me that I would be wasting my time by taking language courses because, according to him, most Negroes did not go to college. This was the only case of racism that had a personal impact on me while growing up in California. Bill, on the other hand, said that he grew up in an openly hostile racial environment. He said that black and white kids threw rocks at each other and called each other names when they passed on the street, and that black and white adults did not mingle unless they worked together—and even then, they ate in different areas and drank from different water fountains. I mentioned my positive experiences with Peter during my visit to Louisiana while in elementary school and my friendship with Mike during basic training. Bill said that he knew of isolated incidents of blacks and whites in the South becoming close friends, but said that it was not the general order of things.

Ironically, the 1957 federal-court-ordered integration of Central High School in Little Rock, Arkansas, started heating up during our WESTPAC cruise. Arkansas Governor Faubus threatened to call out the Arkansas National Guard to prevent desegregation of Central High School. President Eisenhower dispatched federal troops to Little Rock when Governor Faubus, standing behind a mob of white protestors, refused to let black students enter the high school building. In an unprecedented move, the captain of the ship made it clear that he would not tolerate any racially motivated incidents on his ship. His pronouncement effectively eliminated any open discussion about the Little Rock situation.

The Little Rock situation deeply affected Bill and Jim. They were the same age and keenly aware of the inbred hostilities that were fanning the flames in Little Rock. It was unusually hard for them because we all knew that both of them were from Little Rock. If they were home, they might have been involved in the struggle. Bill told me that he had nothing against Jim personally, but that Jim had the "look" of some militant whites he had encountered in Arkansas. One day I asked Jim about the Little Rock situation. Jim put his arm around my shoulders and said, "Lee, let's not talk about Little Rock. Let's just be friends."

Despite Bill's opinion, I considered Jim one of my best friends. Jim was also a natural-born comedian. Standing watch with him on the bridge was always fun. He entertained us with his off-colored stories about living on a farm in Arkansas. One evening, I was getting some training on the ship's helm while Jim was learning about the duties of a quartermaster. He told a story that was so funny, I was laughing so hard that I allowed the ship to drift several degrees off course. The officer of the deck, who was also laughing, reminded me that I had to keep my eyes on the helm. Jim swore that his story was true. It involved two young boys trying to have sex with a cow. He said that the cow kept backing up against the boys until she pressed them against the barn wall. The boys started screaming, then the wall collapsed and the boys were caught in the open with their trousers down. Jim was fond of referring to animals, birds, and southern food by names that he had made up to confuse us sailors from the city. One night he asked if we knew what a "bittie" was. He was surprised that I knew it was a "baby chick."

Guam And The Western Pacific Islands

We sailed from Hong Kong via the Bonins, the Carolines, and the Northern Mariana Islands to Guam. The weather was beautiful all the way. We operated out of Guam for two months and conducted surveillance cruises around the Marianas. On one trip, we seized a Chinese boat that was "allegedly" fishing illegally off the islands. We stopped the boat, and several of our sailors boarded it. After checking their cargo, we instructed them to follow us to Saipan, where they would be fined for trespassing. On the trip to Saipan, we got a message from another ship, some miles away, that they had a sick sailor on board and needed to get him to a hospital. We rushed off to rescue him. We gave the captain of the Chinese boat explicit instructions to stay on course for Saipan. Two days later, we caught up with the Chinese vessel, and it had followed our orders exactly.

We stayed in Saipan only a few hours before we were off to an island called Tinian. The captain granted shore leave, and we visited a village there. This was the first time I had been to a place where the women did not wear coverings over their breasts. We were instructed to refrain from staring and making improper comments. Although some islanders wore Western clothing, most wore different-colored cloths around their waist. Some Tinian women posed for our cameras—for a fee. We left Tinian and visited several small islands nearby. We anchored off one island and conducted "man overboard" and "abandon ship" drills. Rope ladders were placed over the side of the ship for the abandon-ship exercises. The coordinators timed all of our drills. After the drills, we went swimming in the ocean. We put a couple of sailors with rifles in the whaleboat to act as lookouts for sharks. All was fine until a shark was spotted. We had no problem getting the men out of the water. Luckily, the rope ladders were still in place.

Guam was a desolate place, and the weather was hot. Most of us slept on the open decks at night to take advantage of the cool ocean breezes. While in port, we were restricted to the base area. I never got a chance to see how the people of Guam lived. There seemed to have been some kind of conflict between the local government and the US military authorities, and we were restricted to the military base during our entire stay in Guam.

Aboard the ship, we had to make our own fun. We had portable record players and all kinds of music. On weekends, we had dance contests, singing contests, boxing matches, pushup contests, and other crazy activities. Periodically, the captain and the officers attended these events. A couple of officers had beautiful voices and played musical instruments. I was a member of Bill's doo-wop singing group. During one performance, Bill pantomimed the words of the song "Rockin' Robin," and I did a solo dance to the music. I flapped my arms like wings and mimicked how I thought a robin would dance to the music. The dance got a lot of laughs. We tolerated and accepted each other's foibles during these fun times.

Recreation At Sea

One evening I went to the NCO club for happy hour. The club was packed with military men from different services. I did not know that there were so many military men stationed on Guam. The music was wonderful. The DJ was playing all the latest rock 'n' roll songs from the States; most we had not heard before. I remember the DJ playing Ivory Joe Hunter's new song, "Since I Met You Baby," and he was asked to play it over and over again. A sailor asked me if I had ever tasted a "whiskey sour." I had not, so he bought me one. I loved it, and I had four of them and a Zombie drink before the evening was over. Just as we were leaving the bar, a fight broke out. Before the action got to us, we headed out the door. It was the first time I had ever seen a movie-style free-for-all fight.

By the time we got back to the ship, I was not feeling well. My head was swimming and my stomach was burning. I did not sleep at all that night, and I went to the infirmary the next morning. I told the chief medic that I had insomnia and felt nervous. He gave me some aspirins and told me that I had a hangover and that I should be fine in a few hours. The APCs did nothing to solve the problem. I felt tired all day, and I had trouble concentrating and did not sleep at all the next night either. Finally, the chief medic asked me if I ever had any problem with sugar. Mother told me that once I passed out from eating a large quantity of candy. I was in the hospital for a few days. The chief was relieved to see that my health records showed that my sugar levels were normal during the last test. He suspected that I had a sugar "overload." He thought I would be better in a few days. I swore off whiskey sours and mixed drinks after that.

The Letter

Mother had started writing me every few months to bring me up to date on the news at home. In every letter, she mentioned how grateful she was to receive the allotment check each month. I was amused when she mentioned that Shorty was having a difficult time understanding that I cared enough about the family to send money each month. This was proof that Shorty knew so little about me, and that he could not see my loyalty to the family.

Mother was the only person that ever wrote to me, until one day when I received a letter from an unexpected source. While underway off Guam, we pulled alongside a much larger ship to receive supplies and a couple of mailbags. I received a letter from a person named "Louise." The letter was one page long and was posted in Los Angeles, California. Louise wrote that she was writing the letter for my father and that he wanted me to come visit him. She said that she was happy to know that she had a big brother. I was speechless, and frightened. Was this a joke? I had not seen nor heard from my dad since I was five years old, and I barely remembered meeting him. The first thing I did was to share my letter with Bill. I told him about my family situation and about some very personal details about my childhood. Bill seemed intrigued by my story. He said, "Now that is really interesting." I was puzzled by his remark, and I felt that I had revealed more about myself than might have been wise.

After thinking it over, I decided not to answer Louise's letter. Instead, I wrote to Mother and asked her what I should do. I enclosed the letter and the envelope. Not long afterward, Mother wrote that the letter was, indeed, from my father. She suspected that a relative in the family had given him my address. Mother said she had no idea that someone in the family was in touch with my dad. Nevertheless, she urged me to write him back. For days, I tried not to think about the letter, but it was always in the back of my mind. I feared that my dad might not like me. In addition, what if I did not like him? My heart told me not to take a chance. I concluded that my need to know my father was not a priority for me, and I decided not to respond at all.

Crossing The Equator

After leaving Guam, we headed for Subic Bay in the Philippine Islands. We refueled in Subic Bay, sailed a couple of days along the Philippine coast, and then headed southward toward Australia. We crossed the equator just north of Papua New Guinea. The navy initiation ceremony for crossing the equator was an ironclad tradition and an experience I will never forget. It was at once fun and brutal. Although some have dubbed the experience the "highlight of their naval career," I am glad that I will never have to go through that experience again. The navy officially recognizes the crossing of the equator and provides sailors with certificates authenticating the crossing. The date, time, and longitude are logged in our service records. Tradition said that it was the sworn duty of "shellbacks," who had crossed the equator and gone through the navy initiation before, must ensure that "polliwogs," who had not crossed the equator, were properly initiated. This was by order of the fictional "King Neptune Rex" and his royal entourage. All polliwogs, even a commanding officer of a navy ship, had to go through the initiation.

Our first indication that something was amiss was when we noticed that there was very little garbage being thrown overboard. Unbeknownst to us, the garbage had been stored in a secret hiding place to be used to fill a garbage chute that polliwogs had to crawl through as part of the initiation. The exact timing of the crossing was secret, but there were some very clever polliwogs on board, and they did a good job eliciting information from unwitting shellbacks. A couple of days before the crossing, the shellbacks were busily mapping out a gauntlet path with bright tape along the decks and hiding objects covered by canvasses. The shellbacks guarded their projects. The polliwogs were not allowed near them. The day before the crossing—some said it was tradition—the polliwogs attempted to take over the ship and turn it northward. A couple of polliwog officers barricaded the bridge and threatened to stop the ship and delay our crossing. The siege did not last long. We were overcome by shellbacks that were prepared for this eventuality. There was also an attempt the night before to lock all the shellback officers in their quarters. That did not work either. A group of shellbacks intercepted the ship's chaplain, who was trying to take the canvass off one of their secret props. They tried to tie him to the barrel of the forward gun mount. A message sent from the captain of the USS McGinty foiled the plan when one of her lookouts reported a lot of activity on our forecastle. The shellbacks were warned that this was a time of fun and not intended to injure anyone.

On the morning of the crossing, the polliwogs were not allowed to conduct any activities that would delay the initiation ceremony. We were gathered on the forecastle and fed some unsalted, bright-green-colored spaghetti for breakfast. Shellbacks had steak and eggs. Finally, we were led to the port side of the ship to face the first of several gauntlets. There were at least twenty sailors standing on each side of the gauntlet. Each sailor was holding a piece of fire hose about eighteen inches long. As we walked through the gauntlet, we were smacked on the rear with the hoses. It was not a pleasant experience. I admit that I got a bit angry when a shellback made me go through a gauntlet twice. He said that two of the forty-odd men that tried to smack me had missed. I kept my anger to myself. Most shellbacks let me pass without hitting me again. On the other hand, some shellbacks claimed that they had waited years to be on the giving side of the gauntlet and that they wanted to give out what they got. One overweight polliwog was afraid that a particular shellback had planned to work him over. The shellbacks had commented that the pollywog looked "too well-fed." Instead of brutalizing the polliwog, the shellbacks merely touched him on the rear with a fire hose and laughed.

After the first gauntlet, we were brought before the hairdressers to prepare us for our audience with King Neptunus Rex, his queen, and the royal court. Axle grease was combed into our hair, and some of us got designer haircuts. Throughout the process, we were told to bend down from the waist and pick up things or to kiss icons or pieces of cloth consecrated for the ceremony. Of course, each time we bent over, someone was there to smack us on the rear with a hose. Those who got angry at being hit were sent to the "stockade" where they were held until most of the polliwogs went through the ceremony. Then the new shellbacks were asked to join the gauntlet to punish the uncooperative prisoners who had jeopardized their fate. Most of the new shellbacks were too weary to inflict a lot of pain on the others.

Finally, the polliwogs were presented to King Neptune Rex and his queen. The sailor playing the queen was dressed in women's clothing with exaggerated breasts and buttocks. We were obliged to confess our wrongdoings and then kiss the king's foot, which was covered with hot sauce, mustard, and an unknown gooey substance. Our faces were pushed into the gooey substance. The court passed judgment on each polliwog. Those that were stupid enough to deny the charges were sent to the stockade to await further punishment. After the judgment, they sent us to the dentist to have our teeth checked. During the dental examination, a large quantity of hot sauce was squirted into our open mouths. Some of us were blindfolded and forced to turn around and around until we were dizzy, then they smacked us for looking drunk. By this time, we were so confused that we had no idea what was going on. Finally, they forced us to get into a ten-foot long garbage chute filled with garbage that smelled as if it had been decaying for weeks, not days. The garbage chute had to be entered headfirst. This meant that our rear ends and legs were the last to go through. They smacked us until we got completely inside the chute. A few of sailors were too large to get through the opening and were allowed to bypass the chute. When we exited the chute, we were washed down with a fire hose. According to the royal decree, this was to clean us up before Neptunus Rex and his royal court could formally induct us into the "mysteries of the deep."

After the initiation, they gave us a big lunch. Many of us had to eat standing. Our rear ends were black and blue, and raw. A couple of sailors had to go to the infirmary to be checked over. All of us had recovered within a few days. I was glad that I took the punishment without reacting to the pressure. It was an unforgettable experience. At times, the ceremony had some humorous overtones. The costumes, cages for the stockade, posters, and props were imaginative. Initially, some polliwogs were concerned that certain shellbacks had it in for them and would use the initiation as a cover to get them. If that occurred, it was not apparent. The shellbacks posted monitors along the path to observe the process and to prevent anyone from being overly brutalized. My impression of the initiation was that it was brutal, egalitarian, and lacking in evil intent.

Townsville, Australia

After crossing the equator, we headed for Townsville, Australia, which is on the northeast corner of the continent. Our trip took us through the waters of Indonesia and Papua New Guinea. I was amazed at the lava formations and the volcanic cones spewing smoke and bubbling lava into the air. Some volcanic cones were no more than ten feet out of the water, and some less. We were sailing through a fantasy world reminiscent of the geological scenes in the science fiction thriller *Lost World*. The ocean was bluer and clearer than usual, and the islands dotting the area were nothing but smoldering lava beds. We took lots of pictures. In the radio shack, we picked up a Townsville news station that mentioned our planned visit. The radio station urged citizens to come out to welcome the "two big" American destroyers that were on a courtesy call to Australia arrival. The announcer noted that we were the first American warships to visit Townsville since the World War II. Our arrival was on a local countdown clock.

Our reception in Townsville was overwhelming. There were hundreds of people on the dock waiting to greet us. There was a band playing the American National Anthem, street singers, dancers, and all sorts of activities. We were invited to a party at the town hall, and the single girls in town were more than willing to show their hospitality. Beer was free to American sailors in the bars across town. Some black sailors were concerned that they would not get the same courtesy as white sailors, but these fears were put to rest immediately. As the sailors left the ship, each were handed an invitation to dinner or an outing with an Australian family.

Docking Two Abreast At Townsville, Australia

Townsville seemed like an American frontier town of the late thirties. The buildings in town were mostly made of wood, and there were few multistory high-rise buildings. We saw very few new cars, trucks, or modern machines and equipment. The people had the friendliness and hospitality normally found in rural America. They were also heavy beer drinkers. We were amazed at how many beers the Australian men could consume in bars and at home in one day. Our arrival seemed to augment the festive atmosphere that increased the alcohol consumption. The Australians seemed to hold their alcohol well and were reasonably tolerant of those that could not. Although I never visited Townsville again, years later I had the opportunity to visit Sidney, Canberra, and Melbourne. I noted that the openness and generosity of the people had not changed, nor had the average consumption of beer and wine.

Just before our departure from Townsville, we were supposed to take on board stores of beef products and other food for the trip back to Pearl Harbor. Unfortunately, the beef cargo never arrived. Amid great apologies, the town officials rounded up crates of frozen kangaroo meat for us. We ate kangaroo meat for the next three weeks. The cooks prepared it in every way possible: baked, boiled, roasted, minced, and chipped pieces in cream sauce over biscuits that the sailors described as another version of "shit on a shingle." They could not figure out how to cook it to our satisfaction.

After Townsville, we set sail for Pago Pago in American Samoa, the first stop on our voyage back to Pearl Harbor. We ran into rough weather, and for some strange reason, a cap on one of our fuel tanks ruptured. Fuel oil, about a foot deep, backed up into one of our berthing compartments. Clothes and other valuables in the footlockers were ruined. We had to pump most of the fuel overboard; consequently, our fuel level dropped dangerously low. Matters got worse when the storm got intense and we faced a strong head wind.

The last few days before entering American Samoa were scary. Although the weather had improved, we shut down some systems to save fuel and limped into the harbor on one propeller. As we entered the harbor at Pago Pago, the winds picked up, and we had to drop the anchor to stop the ship from drifting toward the wrong side of the port. Our anchor got stuck on submerged wreckage, and we could not raise it. We stayed an extra day while divers worked to free the anchor. Finally, the decision was made to cut the anchor chain and leave the anchor at the bottom of the harbor. The McGinty decided to continue to our next port of call. We expected to catch up with her after we refueled and retrieved our anchor. But things did not go as planned. While we were tying up to the pier, some local women were performing lewd acts for us. One woman sat on the bollard, preventing us from attaching one of our mooring lines. She pulled up her dress and screamed, "F–k me! F–k me!" It was truly an unbelievable sight. The port authorities had a tough time controlling the women trying to greet the sailors.

The next night there was a fight in a bar downtown between some sailors and locals. A group of locals chased the sailors back to the ship. A sailor was screaming, "Pull up the gang plank!" After the sailor jumped aboard, the officer of the deck pulled in the gangplank. The locals threw bottles and rocks at the ship. The local authorities tried to intervene but were ineffective. The next day several locals were massing on the pier with sticks and rocks to attack the ship. The authorities asked the captain to move the ship away from the pier because more angry citizens had entered the port area. Luckily, we had already refueled and taken on supplies and were planning to leave port that morning. The captain called "general quarters" and we pulled away from the pier. Some local merchants were furious at the rioters and protested our early departure. They got into small boats and tried to sell the trinkets to us while dodging the rocks and bottles.

Pago Pago Merchant

The rest of our voyage was less eventful. We sailed around several small islands and took soundings before catching up with the McGinty. We arrived in Pearl Harbor a few weeks later. Our cruise to WESTPAC lasted almost six months and was as interesting as it was exhausting, but we were all ready to return home. Shortly after our return to Pearl Harbor, the USS Walton went into dry dock, and our sailors were housed in barracks on the base. Since we had to eat all our meals on base, our crew was obliged to send men to help on mess duty at the base dining hall. Several other ships were in dry dock, and we took turns working lunches and dinners. After dry dock, we were back to sea exercises and war fighting drills. We operated in the Hawaiian Islands for another five months.

Dreams Do Come True: Meeting My Biological Father

I did not hear from my sister again until we returned to Pearl Harbor. Her second letter was a plea to respond. I ignored that letter also. Then an unexpected thing happened: the USS Walton got orders to return to the States for possible decommissioning or conversion. Bill and I were selected to return with the ship to Long Beach, California. The plan was for us to remain on the ship until we were reassigned. The idea of returning to California made me edgy. Long Beach was only a few miles from Los Angeles. I knew that I would have to revisit the question of whether or not to see my biological father. While in Long Beach, the USS Walton underwent a top-to-bottom inspection. Nonessential sailors were assigned to temporary quarters on base, or allowed to take home leave, if desired. My family lived in San Bernardino, which was only seventy miles away, so I took some home leave.

Everything seemed different at home. I felt welcomed, and Grandy had reserved a bedroom for me at her house. The family prepared a big dinner for my homecoming. Shorty shook my hand and thanked me for sending the allotment each month. He said that they could not have made it without my help. His change of attitude stunned me, but I was still suspicious of him. News that my biological father had made contact with me was the main discussion at the dinner. Mother was adamant that I see him. I felt that everyone, including Uncle Johnnie, supported the idea. I think most just wanted to see who had fathered me. The only person cool to the idea was Grandy. She said that she could never forgive my father for running off after getting my mother pregnant. I can remember Mother and Grandy arguing about my father. Mother defended him and claimed that she drove him off. She forced Grandy to concede that Dad helped the family out by finding a job for Papa. Despite Grandy's reservations about my dad, she thought I might as well see him if he wanted to see me. For my part, I was concerned about having another painful experience like the one I had when Shorty blew up at me for calling him "Daddy." His firm rejection of me had effectively eliminated the word from my vocabulary.

Although I was happy to be home, time was passing slowly for me, and I was getting bored. One day I ran into Jeremy Brown at Sally's Groceries on Eighth and J Streets, a couple of blocks from my Grandy's house. We had been friends since junior high school. Jeremy looked unkempt. He was driving an old truck that looked like it had been in several accidents. We chatted for a few minutes, and he asked why I had come back to San Bernardino. I told him that I was still in the navy and was on leave for a few weeks. He replied, "Good. We said that you were one of the lucky ones; you got away from here." Jeremy confirmed that a lot had changed in San Bernardino since I had been gone.

A Day And Night To Remember

With just a week or so left on home leave, I yielded to family pressure and agreed to travel to Los Angeles to see my father. The sixty-mile train trip from San Bernardino to Los Angeles seemed like the longest ride of my life. I arrived at four o'clock in the afternoon and made my way to my father's neighborhood. His house was easy to find. It was a modest little house with a well-kept yard. I went up to the house but did not knock because it seemed that no one was home. I felt relieved and walked back to the corner bus stop, sat on a bench, and waited. From my vantage point, I could see anyone approaching the homes on the block. After a couple of hours, I was getting hungry, so I took a walk around the neighborhood and found a restaurant. I stayed in the restaurant for a couple of hours drinking coffee and reading a book before returning to my bench. It occurred to me that I did not have a place to stay that night so I had to go through with the visit.

Around nine o'clock that evening, I decided to approach the house again. My heart was beating so loudly that I thought I might pass out from the tension. Finally, I knocked on the door. A boy around thirteen years old greeted me at the door. I told him that I wanted to see his sister, Louise. He called out to Louise and ran off, leaving me standing in the doorway. Louise came to the door and asked me what I wanted. She was wearing a robe and I could see that she had been in bed. When I told her who I was, she shouted, "Are you Odell, our big brother?" She was embarrassed that she was in her nightclothes and said, "You should have told us you were coming!" Her excitement awakened the whole house. Kids came from everywhere. That night I discovered I had seven additional brothers and sisters. Their response overwhelmed me. One child said, "I didn't know we had a big brother." They asked me all sorts of questions about where I grew up, the navy, and how long would I stay with them. I felt comfortable with them and, for some reason, I felt that I belonged.

Me With Sister Louise

After an hour or so, I asked Louise if she had a picture of my father. I confessed that I did not know what he looked like. She went into the master bedroom and returned with a picture of him and her mother, Bertha. Both appeared to be in their thirties. Dad was handsome but had a stern appearance. Bertha had a kind face and she was smiling. I asked Louise to tell me what I should call him? She seemed puzzled by my question. She said, softly, "Call him, 'Daddy,' like the rest of us." Suddenly I felt very tired. I thought to myself, "I have tried that before, and I'm not about to make that mistake again." At the same time, I knew that with all the children around, I could not call him Mister, as I referred to Shorty. I decided to play it by ear.

We were enjoying ourselves when we heard a car pull in the driveway. The kids ran back to bed. They seemed terrified. Louise said that Daddy had strict rules about their bedtime. The door swung open and my dad entered. I would not have recognized him on the street. He was athletic, ruggedly handsome, and well groomed. We were about the same height, skin color, and build. In a hostile tone, he demanded to know what was going on. I was not prepared for his angry demeanor, and my heart sank. Before anyone could answer, he saw me. At first, I thought he might think that I was one of Louise's boyfriends. I was nervous and tried to smile. Suddenly, without prompting, he screamed, "My son! My son! Hey, boy!" and he rushed over and grabbed me. He embraced me for a long time. He told the kids to go back to bed, and the room cleared without a murmur. Suffice to say, it was love at first sight. We stayed up the whole night talking. Dad put his arm around me and kept me close to him. He said that he thought we would never be together again. He told me why he and my mother parted.

My Biological Dad Beebe Charles Mason

It was the same story Mother told me when I had asked about my dad. He confirmed the watermelon fiasco and said that my mother was just too difficult to live with for him. Dad said that he lost track of us when Mother moved us to California. He met a friend of our family in Los Angeles who told him that we were living in San Bernardino. Dad confessed that when he saw me as a five-year-old, he wanted to take me from my mother, but she foiled his plan. Mother made him promise not to bother us again. I told him that I remembered meeting him but that I was afraid of him.

Me (Back Center) And Nora (Front Center)With Grown-Up Dad's Side
Of My Family.

Before long he asked me the big question, "Are you angry that your daddy was not there to raise you?" I was surprised by his comments for two reasons: first, the idea of being mad at him had never occurred to me, and second, he referred to himself as my "daddy." When he said it, the word lost all of its negative connotations. Mother told me my dad was the most wonderful man she had ever met and that she was a fool to "drive him away." I told him that I had nothing against him but that I had wondered if I would ever meet him. Taking a big risk, I called him "Daddy" for the first time. I could see him get teary eyed. The whole encounter was a new experience for me, and I was not sure if I was dreaming. For the first time, I felt emotional about not having had my dad around. Literally, I wanted to fall in his arms and never go free.

Dad told me several stories about his childhood. Our experiences had a similar theme. His mother and father divorced when he was very young, and he ended up living with an aunt and uncle. He said that he had thought he was an unwanted burden on them, so he had been looking for an opportunity to leave. When he was thirteen years old, his uncle told him where he could find his father. Dad said that he slipped away from his uncle's house and set out to find his father. He said he lived with hobos for a while and stole rides on freight trains until he got to his father's place.

Dad showed up at his father's house, unannounced, and told him that he wanted to live with him. His father was overjoyed to see him, but his stepmother was cool toward him. All was fine for the first few months. Dad said that he helped his father around the farm and tried to earn his own keep. He was happier than he had ever been in his life, but it was too good to be true. One night he heard his father and stepmother arguing about him. His father was pleading with his wife to let him stay a little longer.

Dad said that he packed his things that night and that early the next morning he hopped on a freight train. He did not say goodbye, and never saw his father again. Dad said that this was the beginning of his adventurous life. He met an older guy by the name of Manny who took him under his wing. Dad said that he never went back to his uncle's house. I think Dad told me this story because he wanted me to believe he understood my emotional longing. We stayed up all night talking. Finally, he said that he had to go to work. He went to his bedroom, showered, got dressed, and kissed me goodbye. There was real chemistry between us.

Over the next few days, we stayed up late and talked every night. My feelings for him grew stronger and stronger. I had never felt such a strong emotional attachment to another person before that night. Dad told me that I was the "missing strand" in his life, and he wanted me to live with him when I got out of the navy. I knew then that I loved this man.

My Stepmother, Bertha

After Dad went to work that morning, and the children went off to school, I was sitting in the living room reflecting on how lucky I was to have found my father. All my fears about a potentially negative experience had dissipated. Suddenly, the door to the bedroom opened, and my dad's wife, Bertha, the mother of my newly found brothers and sisters, emerged. She asked me if I wanted some breakfast. I was too shocked to respond. She had been in the bedroom when I arrived the night before, and had wept silently through all the commotion. In all the confusion, I did not recall anyone mentioning that she was in the house.

Over the next few days, she and I had several long conversations. She was kind and considerate, and she wanted to know all about me. At first, I felt a little awkward being at home alone with her most of the day. Because of her basic kindness, we became good friends. One day she told me that she never knew I existed until I came to the house that night. She said she was deeply hurt when I showed up, but she knew that it was not my fault and that she did not have anything against me. I did not try to respond. I realized that Dad had done a similar thing to his wife that his father had done to his stepmother.

My Stepmother Bertha

I never saw my dad and stepmother speaking during that week. She was always in the bedroom when he returned from work. I was fortunate that she was kind enough to see to my needs, talk with me, and engage me in conversation when we were alone. I often wondered why Dad had never told her about my existence but did not dare ask. Years later, Louise confided to me that Dad had forbid any mention of me to anyone else, including her mother. She was frightened of my father and kept the secret. It was unfair of Dad to force Louise to keep such an important secret from her mother.

That weekend Dad took me to visit family relatives and friends. He bragged that I was in the navy and forced me to wear my uniform a couple of times to prove it. One day he took me to work with him and introduced me to his supervisor. He also introduced me to his cousin Myrtle and her husband, and my stepmother's brother, Uncle Theodore, and his wife, Elizabeth. Uncle Theodore's nickname was "Uncle Piggy." Most of the people that Dad introduced me to were shocked that I existed, except Uncle Theodore, my stepmother's brother. Apparently, Dad had confided in him years before. They were very close, and Uncle Theodore had not broken confidence about my existence to anyone, including his sister.

In reality, I felt like the Prodigal Son. I was home at last. Our relatives indulged my father so as not to take away his joy. I felt closest to Uncle Theodore. He was almost seven feet tall and weighed at least two hundred and eighty pounds. I noticed that he had a strong influence over my father. Just prior to returning to the USS Walton, Uncle Piggy telephoned me and asked me to come to his house, alone. We had a long talk, and he confirmed that my stepmother was hurt when she learned about me. He had consoled her about the situation. Finally, he said to me, "Your Dad needs you, and I think you are a good example to your brothers and sisters."

I learned that my father was an austere and serious-minded man. He was not amorous with his children at all. He and my mother had similar views on discipline and demanded strict obedience. The consequence for disobeying was a thorough beating. Ironically, my joining my dad's family made life a little easier for my siblings. As time passed, Dad's affection for me seemed to spill over to his other children. He started embracing them as he did me. In addition, Dad would calm down when I spoke up for the other children. All agreed that I seemed to have a calming effect on him. The USS Walton remained in Long Beach for a couple of months. I invited my shipmate Bill home with me a couple of weekends, and we double dated with my sister Louise and her friend Rita. Occasionally, on weekends Bill and I took the Red Car trolley together between Long Beach and Los Angeles. I got off in East Los Angeles to see my dad, and Bill would take the trolley all the way to downtown Los Angeles to see his distant relatives.

We finally received reassignment orders. Bill was assigned to a ship based in Long Beach, and I was reassigned to the USS Vance DER-387, a radar picket ship that had just changed its homeport to Pearl Harbor, Hawaii. I was not happy about returning to Pearl Harbor. Saying good-bye to my dad was difficult, but I thought we needed to put some space between us. I was tired of following him around town and visiting his friends on weekends, and neither of us was getting the rest we needed because of our long talks at night. Nonetheless, the more I talked to my dad, the more I realized that having grown up in broken homes gave us something in common, at least from my point of view. One day I arranged for my dad and several of my new siblings to travel to San Bernardino to meet my mother's side of the family. Mother and Dad had not seen each other since I was five years old. I would make sure we all got together, periodically. Shorty was always conspicuously absent during these visits.

Before my return to Hawaii, Dad surprised me with a question that echoed in my mind for the next year. He asked, "What do you plan to do when you get out of the navy?" He was the first person to remind me that I had to think about my future beyond the navy. Unfortunately, when I got out of the navy, I still had no answer. Without a high school diploma my choices were limited.

Me Onshore At Pearl Harbor Navy Base

Chapter Seven

The Final Countdown: USS Vance DER-387

The USS Vance was about the same size as the USS Foss. She had the newest 3.5-inch rapid-firing deck guns, and she was built with the most sophisticated radar and sonar detection equipment in the navy's inventory. I reported aboard the USS Vance a week after she returned from her tour on station as part the Distant Early Warning (DEW) line. The DEW line provided radar coverage from Alaska to the Midway Atoll in the Pacific Ocean. It was established to warn against potential air and sea attacks on the United States from across the northern Pacific Ocean. The ships that worked the DEW line spent a cycle of twenty-eight days on station and fifteen days in port. The US Air Force had a contingent of aircraft equipped with the latest radar and sonar that also worked the DEW line with the radar picket ships.

USS Vance DER-387

My tour of duty on the USS Vance was problematic. I was assigned to the deck force while the chiefs decided what to do with me. I had been a radioman on the USS Foss and the USS Walton, but the USS Vance had a full complement of radiomen, and there was no room for another one. I was disappointed to lose my job as a radioman. I had worked so hard to get it. In addition, this affected my eligibility for a promotion to petty officer. Moreover, I had to work for a chief boatswain mate that everyone on the USS Vance loved to hate. I soon learned why. On my first voyage out of Pearl Harbor, the chief told me that he had no love for "radiomen types." He said we were all "softies" and did not like to work. The older sailors on the deck force told me to ignore his comments because he had something negative to say about everyone. Nevertheless, I felt that the chief singled me out for special ill treatment. One day I went to sickbay to get some APCs. The chief medical corpsman was there. He asked how I was adjusting to my new ship. I told him that my only problem was the chief boatswain mate. The medical chief laughed and said, "The boatswain actually likes you. He thinks you are smart, and he talks about you often in the chiefs' quarters." As far as I was concerned, the chief boatswain's attitude towards me told me all that I needed to know about him.

Emergency Leave

It seemed that my family at home went from one problem to another. On returning from one of our four-week DEW line missions, I received a message from the personnel officer that my stepmother, Bertha, had died and that my family requested my return home for the funeral. I remembered my stepmother's kindness even though she was having a difficult time dealing with my arrival. I returned to Los Angeles and attended her funeral. Dad had a difficult time dealing with the situation. He kept me close everywhere he went. While at home, I learned that my family in San Bernardino had fallen on hard times again. Mother asked me to send more money to help. When I got back to the USS Vance, I asked to increase my allotment, but the personnel officer refused to allow it. He said that I barely had enough money to live on and that he had to protect my interest. His counseling was a good thing. It helped me understand that I could be concerned about my family but that I also had to think about my own welfare. In short, I was still a prisoner of my family.

Tripler Army Hospital

On my third DEW line voyage, I injured my right wrist. Despite my badly swollen wrist, the chief boatswain accused me of faking my injury to get out of work. The chief corpsman confirmed that there was definitely something wrong with my wrist, and he put me on light duty until I could get it checked out back in Pearl Harbor. The chief was angry, or at least he pretended to be when he was around me. After X-rays at the clinic on base, I was sent to Tripler Army Hospital for wrist surgery. The doctors had to operate on the upper and lower sides of my right wrist to free a trapped nerve. In addition, calcium had restricted movement in my wrist, and I was losing sensitivity in my right little finger and along the outer edge of my right palm. I spent two full months in the hospital recovering from surgery and undergoing physical therapy.

Seaman Stewart

I was so disappointed over being in the hospital yet again, and I was lonely. I decided to start visiting the recreation room in order to talk to other patients. Occasionally I would join a card game or find someone to play checkers with.

While I was watching television one evening in the recreation room at Tripler Hospital, a sailor sitting next to me on the couch fell asleep with his head on my shoulder. I decided not to wake him. Soon he stirred and apologized for falling asleep on me. I am not sure why he was in the hospital since he showed no outward sign of being disabled. Surprisingly, after this incident, we encountered each other frequently in the cafeteria or recreation room. We started meeting for coffee and often took long walks together around the massive hospital complex. Stewart was from Memphis, Tennessee. We spent a lot of time discussing our very different childhood experiences. His family had none of the tensions that had plagued my dysfunctional family, and he had trouble believing some of my stories. However, unlike Bill, Stewart was a good listener and never argumentative; and unlike Jim, he did not enjoy bar hopping with other sailors.

When I returned to the ship, the chief boatswain mate made it a point to ignore me and did not show that he regretted calling me a faker. I ignored him too. While in port, I had weekly appointments at the base clinic for physical therapy. Despite the chief's apparent disdain for me, I learned that he was concerned about my condition. He told all of the petty officers on the deck force to make sure that I did not re-injure my wrist. Their orders were to give me only light tasks until he decided differently. Eventually my wrist got better, but the chief made sure that I did not have to do any heavy lifting or pulling on the ropes when we docked. In a sense, he became protective of me, but he still had on his angry face whenever he saw me.

Several weeks after I was discharged from the hospital, I met Stewart as I was walking across his ship to the dock. (Our ships happened to be tied up at the dock, three abreast.) The USS Vance was the third ship out. I had not seen Stewart since my discharge from the hospital, and I had forgotten the name of his ship, although it was in our squadron. We rekindled our friendship and started going into Honolulu and to Waikiki Beach together. Often, we would watch movies together on board our ships. He helped convince me that no matter where I lived and worked, I would have the opportunity to have one good friend.

Seaman X

My long absences from the USS Vance limited my opportunity to develop and maintain the kind of friendships that I had established on the USS Foss and USS Walton. I got into my first and only fight in the navy while aboard the USS Vance. Seaman X bullied several sailors and threatened to beat them up if they told anyone. On occasion, I noticed Seaman X glaring at me, but he never did anything to provoke a confrontation. He and his friends generally met in the mess hall after hours to play pinochle. His friends were equally obnoxious but generally friendly toward me when Seaman X was not around.

One day while the ship was on station off Alaska, Seaman X made his move against me. The weather was bad, and the ship was pitching and rolling. Some deck equipment came loose, and the boatswain mate sent me to look for Seaman X. I found him in the aft compartment talking to one of his friends. I delivered the chief's message. As I was walking away, Seaman X came up behind me and said, "I am going to kick your ass." Fearing an attack, I turned around and slugged him in the stomach, and followed up with a barrage of blows to his body. Before he could throw a punch, he was on the floor and I was on top of him. His friends were astonished. The ship was rolling back and forth, and each of us was trying to take advantage of the ship's motion to gain the upper hand. Finally, I pinned him so he could not move. Suddenly, he tried to bite me. His friends were horrified and intervened. They pulled me off him and criticized him for trying to bite me. They knew that any evidence of a scuffle, and particularly bite marks, would have landed us both in the brig.

Seaman X was upset that he got the worst of the fight, and he promised to take care of me later. I responded that I was not through with him either, and told him that if I ever saw him in the aft compartment (where my bunk was), I would finish the job. Finally, he remembered that the chief had asked for him, so he ran out of the compartment. That afternoon, Seaman X showed up in the infirmary for medical treatment. He told the chief corpsman that he fell down during the storm. Word spread rapidly around the ship that I had bested Seaman X. His reputation fell further when others learned he tried to bite me during the fight. I never had another problem with Seaman X, and his behavior toward other sailors changed remarkably. Soon we were playing cards together, but we were never close friends.

General Quarters—Battle Stations

On occasion, the USS Vance kept Russian trawlers under surveillance in the Western Pacific. We got a real scare when we slipped up on a Russian submarine that was refueling from what looked like a Russian cargo ship. We picked up a very large image by our surface radar that appeared dead in the water. The Russian ships had turned off their radar to avoid detection by American radar picket ships equipped with listening-type ECM (electronic counter measures) gear. We were in visual range before we realized that the image was of two ships, a submarine refueling from a cargo ship. We went to general quarters. Our ship's photographer took several photos of what we saw using a high-powered photo lens before the Russian ships noticed us.

When they spotted us, the submarine submerged quickly and headed away from us. However, the cargo ship started acting erratically, speeding up, slowing down, and then turning toward us. It was gigantic in comparison to our ship. We had visions of a World War II "Q-ship." The Q-ships were ships deployed by some navies to lure U-boats and other enemy combat vessels closer by giving the appearance of being poorly armed. They sat high in the water and were virtually unsinkable by torpedo. Under attack, they would hoist a white flag. Usually, the submarine would surface in order to sink the ship using deck canons, to save their torpedoes; the Q ship would lower its side panels and fire deck guns or torpedoes at the enemy vessel. The USS Vance could handle the submarine in a fight but was not prepared to deal with a submarine and a suspected armed surface ship at the same time. We radioed our situation and location, and soon a couple of US fighter aircraft from somewhere in the Aleutian Islands circled our position as a show of force and returned to base. We were amused to learn that another ship, the USS Savage DER-386, had left her DEW station and was racing to assist us. She was about two hundred miles away and sailing at flank speed (twenty-five knots) to assist us. Obviously, by the time she arrived, we would have been long gone. The USS Vance provided solid information on how Russian diesel submarines could operate off the Western coast of the United States. The submarines were refueling from Russian cargo ships doubling as tankers for submarines.

I served on the USS Vance for eight months before my honorable discharge from the navy. The end-of-tour physical exam brought some unexpected news. The doctors instructed me to have my right wrist reevaluated by the Veterans Administration Hospital after my discharge. As I departed the USS Vance, I said goodbye to several of my shipmates. I was at the gangplank when the chief boatswain came up to me and said, "Leaving without saying goodbye?" He apologized for being so hard on me and extended his hand. I shook his hand and said goodbye. Those observing the event were visibly shocked. The chief seemed reflective, and said that he was sure I would be a success at whatever I tried. I am not sure what provoked his civility, but when he came to attention and saluted me, I felt his remarks were sincere. I wondered if the chief Medic was telling the truth when he said that the Chief Boatswain spoke highly of me in the chiefs' quarters.

Shortly after my discharge, I received a letter from the VA Hospital in Long Beach, California, requesting that I make an appointment to have my right wrist evaluated. After the examination, the doctors determined that I qualified for a "service connected disability."

Bon Voyage!

My navy experience changed my perception of the world around me. My visit to Asia, Micronesia, and Polynesia introduced me to peoples and places that I had only seen in the movies. Their cultural patterns defined the word "foreign" for me; even more so, the lifestyle and living standards of Japan and Hong Kong were remarkably different from anything I could have imagined. It was hard for me to comprehend the abject poverty that I saw in some of these places. I felt truly blessed to have grown up in America. On the other hand, the sailors I lived, worked, and played with taught me that there were levels of friendship and loyalty that I did not think were possible among men. It seemed that every sailor was fundamentally lonely from being so far from home. Friends were our only solace. Most of my friends I will never see again, but I will never forget them; they will continue to live in my heart and thoughts. Not a day passes that I don't think about some of them. Starting with basic training, I was strengthened, humbled, and encouraged by the comradeship exhibited by fellow sailors.

I will always remember one special friend most vividly. Bill and I spent many hours discussing our views on everything from racism to wine and cheese. Bill had fixed views on subjects I had never thought about before. He was smart, confident, and clearly the master of his own destiny. He took note of the world around him and was determined to live life as he chose to live it. At the same time, he was scrupulous in his observance of navy regulations and protocol. After my discharge from the navy, I lived with my dad in Los Angeles. Bill was still stationed at the Long Beach, California, Naval Station. Sometimes we drove down to San Diego together to visit our friend Beryl, a sailor we met in Pearl Harbor. Bill and Beryl were very close.

When Bill got out of the navy, he went back to Arkansas and I did not see him for several years. I never knew how to contact him. It seemed that each telephone number he gave me had been disconnected or the wrong number. However, he never had trouble finding me. One day Bill telephoned and said that he had moved back to California and was living in Hollywood. I remember asking him how he found me. He responded, "How many Odell Lees can there be in the San Bernardino, California, telephone book?" Bill invited me to a bar in downtown Los Angeles for a drink. I drove to Los Angeles periodically to see him. Bill always had a couple of parties to attend, and I was eager go along with him. Some parties brought together people of all kinds of backgrounds. Once, he left me alone with his friends. It was six months before I heard from him again.

A few years later, Bill showed up one day at my apartment in Venice, California. Again, he found me in the telephone book. I told him that I had tried to telephone him but got the same response as always: "a telephone that rings, but no one there to answer." Bill said that he moved around a lot. He had a friend with him that looked and acted mentally disturbed. I told Bill that I was engaged, and I invited him to come to my wedding. He gave me a puzzled look, congratulated me, and then said he was surprised I was getting married. Then he said, "I am no longer interested in women." He could see from my reaction that I was dumbfounded. He smiled and said, "I thought you knew." I had trouble believing him, but in keeping with his personality, he let me know that he had spoken and that the subject was closed. As we talked about my future wife, I got the impression that Bill felt that he had made a mistake by coming to visit me. Finally, he gave me his address and told me to send him an invitation to the wedding.

When Bill left, I was in a quandary. I just could not imagine that what he told me was true, yet I felt it might be. I recalled that during our visits to Japan, Hong Kong, and Australia, Bill never participated in any of the outings that involved finding women. Although we double-dated with my sister, Louise, and her friend, it was always my idea to go out together. Louise liked Bill, a lot, but quickly realized that nothing was going to come of their relationship. I thought about the parties in Los Angeles that Bill took me to; they were always heavily populated with a cascade of artistic types. Finally, I asked myself, "Why he was so surprised that I was getting married?" I was dizzy with speculation, and was out of sorts for days. I recalled Bill's reaction when I showed him the first letter I received from my dad while on patrol off Guam. I confided to him some things about my upbringing, problems with my stepfather, and sexual abuse by an older male family member. Although Bill was sympathetic and nonjudgmental, he said that he found my story interesting, as if to say, "Now, I understand you." I wondered if I had missed the major clue in his response.

Bill rarely spoke about his personal life, and I never knew if his folks were dead or alive. I knew so little about him after all these years, but he knew everything about me. I was disappointed by Bill's revelation. I realized that we had a one-sided friendship. It was not so much that he might be homosexual, but that I had shared my deepest secrets with him and he had not been open with me, until now. On the other hand, I am not sure how I would have reacted if he had leveled with me on board ship. Maybe he was not sure either. Perhaps he reasoned that after hearing my story about my childhood experiences with an older family member, revealing his sexual preference might have been too much for me to handle. Quite possibly, his admission might have ended our friendship on the spot, but I doubt it. I can still recall Bill's kind words of encouragement and support after learning of my childhood experiences. He helped me sort out some important issues, and I will never forget his loyalty and compassion.

The next time I saw Bill, he was living alone in an apartment in Hollywood. The telephone number he gave me worked, and I asked to drop by his apartment to give him an invitation to my wedding. He gave me his address. Bill looked gaunt, and he had a bad cold. He thanked me for the invitation. He said that he was not feeling well and suggested that we talk another time. As I left his apartment, I heard him mumble that he needed rest. Bill did not show up at my wedding, and I never saw him again.

Chapter Eight

My First Real Job: Living With Dad

When I was discharged from the navy, I agreed to live with my dad and his family in Los Angeles. It was a wonderful experience, and it gave us an opportunity to get to know each other better. Since my stepmother, Bertha, had passed a couple of years earlier, I slept in the same bed with Dad. The other bedrooms were fully occupied with my brothers and sisters. Dad and I had some wonderful late-night conversations. His openness was refreshing, and we became real friends as well as father and son. Dad confided in me the contents of his will and other matters that he thought I should know about. He also committed me to silence about his personal affairs and health problems that he had not shared with the family.

Unfortunately, after a few months, I became frustrated by my inability to find a job. Dad was not concerned and assured me that he would take care of me as long as I was out of work. Nevertheless, unbeknownst to him, I had another problem: I was lonely. I had no friends of my own in Los Angeles. Dad went to work every morning, and the children were at school most of the day. I found myself at home alone when I was not out job hunting. I told Dad that I thought I had a better chance of finding a job in San

Bernardino and that I wanted to give it a try. He was disappointed and told me that he was hoping I would stay with him. This was my thought, too, but I had been searching for a job in Los Angeles for several months. Since I did not have a high school diploma, I never got a serious interview for any job that I applied for in Los Angeles. Not wanting to abandon my dad, I asked him if he could get me a job with the cement finishing company where he worked. He refused to consider the idea and said that he did not want me doing that kind of work.

Me, 1960, After The Navy

Finally, I made my decision and moved back to San Bernardino. My grandmother was living alone, and she welcomed her favorite grandson moving in with her. In exchange for my room and board, I agreed to run errands, help clean house, and do some gardening work for her. I accompanied her to the bank to pay bills and helped her with shopping. During one of our outings, Grandy made me an offer that I could not refuse. She proposed to lend me money to buy an automobile so that I could chauffeur her to the bank and grocery shopping instead of us having to use taxis. With Uncle Johnnie's help, I decided on a ten-year old Buick Super four-door sedan. It was solid, plush, and in good running condition. This was a time when it was thought "cool" to give our cars names to reflect the driver's personality. We usually had the name painted somewhere on the body of the automobile. It was a big decision for me, and it took me several weeks to choose the name "Lost Soul" as my signature. Looking back on it all, it was a fitting description of how I saw myself at the time.

Soon after my return to San Bernardino, I ran into another high school friend at a neighborhood grocery store. Joshua was the first high school friend I had seen since I returned from the navy. He gave me the run down on what had happened to several of our classmates and mutual friends. He said that most were unemployed or worked at jobs they did not like. A few were in jail, and one had been killed in a car accident. Several of my female acquaintances, including his sister, had gotten pregnant in high school and had to drop out. He painted a picture much like the Statler Brothers' song "Class of '57." Joshua was one of the smarter guys in school, and he was from a stable and loving family. But now he looked unhealthy, and he smelled of alcohol. After our chat, he bought a bottle of whiskey and dashed off to join a friend waiting in a truck. His comments troubled me, and I changed my mind about looking up old friends and classmates. I figured that in time I would run into most of them.

Job Searches

It was as hard finding a job in San Bernardino as it was in Los Angeles. I mowed lawns, cleaned fishponds, and worked part-time as an aid at a downtown nursing home. I hated being adrift and without my own means of support. One day my cousin Cleopas told me that his dad had gotten a job for him with a construction company. I talked to Uncle Johnnie, but like my father, he felt that I was not cut out for that kind of work. After pressuring him for a couple of weeks, he agreed to talk to his boss about hiring me.

I started work on one of the hottest days of the year. Uncle Johnnie picked me up in his automobile around five o'clock the first morning, we started work at six. By noon, the temperature had shot up to 112 degrees Fahrenheit in the sun. The construction work was difficult for me but I was determined to hang in there. My task was to stack two-by-four boards from lumber piles near the road closer to a construction site. The workers took frequent water breaks and stood in the shade every half hour or so. I took a quick drink of water every few minutes and continued to work through the breaks. By lunchtime, I was exhausted. I barely made it to my Uncle's car before passing out from the heat. My Uncle poured water over my head and called my name to revive me. Several workers gathered around, and I heard one of them say, "I could tell this is not his kind of work. The guy never took a break!" I was sunburned, my muscles were sore, and I had trouble staying awake for the next two days. I was too embarrassed to return to the job.

I continued my weekly treks to the employment office to look for work even though my benefits had ran out. I thought about going back into the navy as an alternative. I missed the security, routine, and comradeship. One day at the employment office, an acquaintance mentioned a job posting by Patton State Hospital, a mental hospital located just outside the city. It had immediate openings for several Psychiatric Technician trainees. The duties were to monitor mental patients and to help the professional staff with patient care. The positions were permanent following the successful completion of a three-month training program. We both decided to apply.

Patton State Hospital, Patton, California

I passed the entrance exam and personal interview and was hired. My friend also took the exam but did not pass the personal interview. I am not sure why? According to the interviewer, my part-time work at a nursing facility and my having completed my military service were a "plus" on my application. New hires were offered a salary advance to purchase two sets of hospital uniforms worn by the psychiatric technicians (PTs). The uniforms were all white: shirts, pants, shoes, and belts, and could be purchased at the hospital employee store. Grandy volunteered to pay for my uniforms, so I was able to get my full salary. Thanks to Grandy, I had everything I needed for the job, including a new attitude.

The three-month training program at the hospital was tough. It consisted of a variety of college courses on health care, anatomy, and psychology, along with intense on-the-job training. We studied the different types of mental illnesses, treatment methods, and drug therapy. Special attention was given to understanding behavior modification drugs. We learned to look for overdose symptoms and to administer intramuscular injections. We went to class every day for a month or so, and then took ten half-day classes followed by actual work on a hospital ward. Each trainee was required to complete a term paper at the end of the course. My term paper was on "The Origin of Suicidal Impulses." I chose this topic because I had heard that two family friends had committed suicide when I was in my teens. Upon graduation, we received a psychiatric technician certificate from the California Department of Mental Hygiene. The training program was worth sixteen college credits toward a degree in psychology or sociology.

My first assignment after graduation was to the "ninety-day" observation ward. Patients were committed to the hospital by family psychiatrists or by local court orders after exhibiting psychotic behavior. Most of the psychological problems involved traumatic relationships with families or social adjustment issues. It was a sober feeling learning that I had experienced similar struggles as some of the younger patients. I could not help but wonder how I survived the psychological impact of a dysfunctional family while others did not. The answer would come, eventually.

There was relative calm on the ward the first week or so. Then suddenly, two patients erupted into violent temper tantrums. They were throwing chairs, screaming, and threatening to hit other patients. The nurses summoned the PTs to help restrain them before they hurt someone or themselves. I learned later that both of the patients had pretended to swallow their pills but had hidden them under their tongues and later spit them out. A nurse scolded one patient, and I heard her say, "Frank, you know this is what happens when you do not take your medication. Why do you do this to yourself?" The patient did not seem to understand what was happening to him. The other patient had several tablets in his pockets, including tablets that belonged to the first patient. There was concern that he had planned to use the pills to commit suicide. He was put on suicide watch.

On weekends, family members were allowed to visit. Refusing to see family members was a common reaction for some patients. Many resented having been admitted to the "psycho ward," while others were too confused or sedated to meet their visitors. It was amazing how many patients got depressed or went into temper tantrums when they learned that family members were coming to visit them.

Working on the Observation Ward was an interesting experience for me, but it was nothing compared to what we experienced on the ward for severely disabled children. Before we could work on this ward, a senior nurse took us to a large conference room and explained the types of patients we would care for. After a short introduction, several deformed and mentally retarded children were brought into the room for us to see. These children were categorized by the psychiatrists as cretins, morons, mongoloids, and severely deformed paraplegics. The misfortune of these children was horrifying to most of us. Next, they took us to see the bedridden disabled children. We had to observe the nursing care given to hydrocephalic patients. This was the most disturbing of all. A doctor explained that hydrocephalus is a condition where cerebrospinal fluid collects in the ventricles of the brain and causes rapid growth of the head and bulging forehead in infants. The children had heads that were several times larger than their bodies. They could not turn over by themselves. We had to feed these patients, and had to turn them over every few hours so that they would not get bedsores on their heads, which many of them already had. A nurse used some kind of salve to treat the bedsores every morning and evening. Despite their physical conditions, some children tried to smile and to talk with the nurses as we turned them over. Their utterances were always unintelligible.

The paraplegics, who were severely disabled, could not take care of themselves on their own. Some spastic patients could only communicate by flinging their arms or using their feet and eyes. I observed that the patients were sensitive to changes in their routines. They got upset if we would not allow them to watch television at the same time every day. It was as if their bodies responded to a certain time clock. Some became agitated when something was displeasing to them, even on television. The seasoned PTs were always able to figure out the problem, and they kept very good records for new orderlies. At times, I was appalled at what I considered rough treatment of some patients. Since I was not familiar with how things were done, I tried a gentler approach. The patients reacted negatively to my efforts because I had changed their routine. It was as if they saw the rough treatment as a sign that they were getting the kind of attention from the staff that they needed. Periodically, we had to help restrain patients that were combative. Once, a staff member threatened to turn off the television if a patient did not stop trying to hit him. Immediately, the patient showed that he had control over his limbs and stopped swinging his arms. There were other cases where patients seemed catatonic until they were asked to take their medications or go to the toilet. When threatened that they would lose their recreation-room privileges or visitor privileges, they would immediately change their behavior. It was remarkable to me that some patients that seemed oblivious to reality but always responded to incentives.

Patients on the "long-term" psychiatric ward were interesting to work with. Some were ambulatory and could engage in normal conversations with staff. Others were catatonic and bedridden. The functional patients—paranoids, schizoids, and mildly psychotic patients—were the most dangerous. In some cases, heavy medications were used to control potentially violent behavior. Still, we had to be on alert, constantly. Every day, at least one patient tried to escape from the hospital ward. Some patients would engage in conspiracies with other patients to try and trick the staff. For example, when a new staff member was assigned to the ward, the patients would size him up and hatch an escape plan. Once, a PT came to the ward to escort a patient to another ward. One of the more clever patients talked another patient into distracting the escort so that he could slip out of the door. He stood near the door pretending to chat with a third patient. The other patient was to engage the escort in a conversation once the door was opened. The clever patient gave himself away when a staff member noticed that he was standing near the door and wearing his best clothes.

The geriatric ward appealed to me the most, and I would have accepted a permanent assignment to this ward. It seemed that I was able to establish instant rapport with these patients. Most of them were chronically depressed, hypochondriacal, and terribly lonely. Some had not seen their family in years. Yet some patients had visitors two or three times a month. Our main task was to make sure that the patients ate their meals and got exercise during the day.

My first job on the ward was to take care of a patient that refused to get out of bed. Every morning he said that he was too sick to get up. The doctors confirmed that he was in good health but was very depressed. The medicine he was taking did not seem to help. We had to force him to get out of bed for breakfast, and then we locked the sleeping area to prevent him from going back to bed. One day I decided not push George to get up. I sat next to his bed and asked him why he was sick so often. He said that he did not know and that he had a pain in his chest. I asked him if he wanted me to rub his chest to make it feel better. He said yes. As I rubbed his chest, tears began to form in his eyes. I asked him why he was crying. He said that he did not know why. I told him that I was sure that he would get better and that we should take a walk. I helped him get dressed and took him to the dining room. He seemed more cooperative that day and did not try to get back in bed.

The next day I came to work, and George was sitting up in bed and waiting for me. He said that his chest was feeling better and that he would like to go to the dining room for breakfast. I helped him dress, escorted him to the dining room, and noticed that he seemed energized when I touched his arm. On the way to the dining hall, he started crying again and kept repeating that he wanted to see his son. I asked him to tell me about his son, but he could not remember his son's name or anything about him. I learned that his son and family would visit George every few months.

For about a week, I escorted George to the dining hall. Soon he started interacting with the other patients, and one day, he was sitting in the dining hall when I arrived at work. Each day, I would find the time to chat with him for a few minutes. About three months later, I received a note that my supervisor wanted to see me. He told me that George's family had written a letter to the hospital thanking the staff for helping George to improve. They had seen a remarkable improvement in his attitude, and they wanted to thank us for taking good care of him.

Another patient I was responsible for had a different problem. After lunch each day, he would return to the ward, take off all of his clothes, and lie on his bed, stark naked. When the staff asked him to cover himself, he would oblige, but when they left he would take the covers off again. One day I asked him why he insisted on lying on the bed naked. He said that he always slept in the nude. I learned from the staff that Ray was a model patient but had a serious neurosis. Apparently, he believed that the hospital was his real home, and he acted accordingly. His wife was a regular visitor.

I was sorry to leave the geriatric unit. I felt I was making a contribution to the patients there, and I believed that I was a source of comfort for some. Unfortunately, the work took its toll on me. The idea of people confined in a mental hospital for life was difficult for me to accept. I knew that most would never go home, and if they did, there was a good possibility that they would return.

Downhill Changes

I learned that the hospital had two rooming-house cottages on the grounds for single employees. There were six rooms to each cottage. Each room was furnished and had a private washbasin. There were two public showers and water closets at the end of the hall. I rented a room and bought linen, a radio, and a bookshelf. Living on the grounds was a boon, financially. It was cheap and I could walk to work. In addition, there was a cafeteria on the hospital grounds that served breakfast and lunch. Across the street from the hospital was a rustic bar-restaurant that also served lunch and dinner. During the evenings, it was packed with people from the hospital and the local community. Overall, I was satisfied with my decision to move to the hospital grounds. On weekends, I would stay at Grandy's house in town. Usually, I would drive back to Patton on Sunday afternoons.

During my second year at the hospital, several administrative changes did not go over well with the employees. Beyond firing several PTs for unknown reasons, the hospital was under pressure to provide a different approach to serving the mentally ill. Most of the employees, including administrative staff, were unhappy about the changes which included the decision to eliminate the periodic rotation of PT staff to different wards and to assign them permanently to specific wards. I was assigned to the long-term patient ward. I was not happy about this change, and I wondered if I could endure the routine of working on this ward year after year.

Not long after the changes began, a close colleague committed suicide in his room on the hospital grounds. Some wondered if his death had something to with the changes made at the hospital. Those close to him were interviewed. I told the police that a few weeks before the shooting that Jim had bought a gun and invited several of us to his room to see it. He said that he had always wanted to own a gun and was planning to visit his parents in Laguna Beach, California, that weekend and show it to them. The following Monday, the hospital administration informed the employees that Jim did not make it home but had killed himself in his room over the weekend. The gunshot wound was to the temple.

Jim's apparent suicide shocked me. He was a high-energy person and seemed to like the work he was doing at the hospital. I recalled that during the training program, we read each other's term papers. He liked my paper on suicide and agreed that suicide was the wrong solution to life's problems. I will always believe that Jim's death was an accident. I believe that he was experimenting with the dangerous game of Russian roulette and accidently shot himself. As administrative procedures changed at the hospital, so did the social climate in and around the hospital. The bar across the street changed hands, and many new faces started showing up. The new customers were rowdy and turned on by drinking parties, marijuana smoking, and experimental sex. Some of these activities found their way to the employee rooming houses on the hospital grounds. The rooming houses were like an after-hours bar and similar to a frat house. I was not immune to some of these activities, and I found myself tolerating things that I had always believed were wrong and destructive. Finally, I started experiencing the same kind of anxiety that drove me to leave home at sixteen. Every day became a struggle. I needed desperately to escape the hospital social and work environment.

Worldliness

I will never forget the events that brought things to a head. After a party at a staff member's house, a colleague asked me to drive him and his girlfriend home. He insisted that I drop him off first. I did not think too much about his request until later when his girlfriend directed me to a remote location so we could have sex. She wanted to have sex with a black man, and he agreed to help set it up by insisting that I drop him off first.

A couple of weeks later, I was having a beer with some colleagues in the bar, when a PT accused me of "playing with his mind." George became verbally abusive and invited me out for a fight. The fight lasted two minutes and his eye was badly swollen. I felt sorry for him and helped him back into the bar. I asked him why he wanted to fight me. He said that he wanted to "connect" with me but that I always ignored him. George seemed like a nice guy but I felt that he wanted something more from me than friendship. Apparently, he got tired of my failure to respond to his overtures, and the alcohol caused him to react hostilely towards me. This was not the only incident that I had to deal with in this regard.

The positive side of these experiences is that, eventually, they helped me understand and define my own sense of morality. Consequently, I had a hard time sustaining close friendships with those whose moral persuasions were so different from my own. It was burdensome having to avoid sending the wrong signal, especially to someone that I enjoyed being with socially. Once again, reminiscent of my teenage years, I folded into myself and distanced myself from social interaction with certain colleagues and bar clientele. I moved back to Grandy's house in the city. As a commuter, it was easy to explain why I did not have time to socialize after work. My frustrations allowed me to think about the unthinkable: finding another job.

A Cry For Help: Mother To The Rescue

During one of my weekend visits to Dad's, I talked about my disillusionment with my job. Dad seemed to have difficulty comprehending the seriousness of my situation, but he listened quietly. Finally, he said, "Well, son, I think you should do what you have to do." This was my problem—I did not know what to do, and he gave me no hint about what I should do. I was becoming increasingly frustrated and decided to mention my problem to my mother. I arrived at Mother's house late one afternoon, and I noticed the house was unusually quiet. The shades were drawn, and Mother was lying on the couch staring at the ceiling. I asked her if she was all right. She said that she was just thinking about her life. After making sure she was really OK physically, I told her how unhappy I was with my job at Patton. After

My Biological Mother, Mary

listening to my story, she said, "Why are you afraid to find another job and make new friends?" I told her about the difficulty I had finding a permanent job and that I did not want to go through that experience again.

Mother sat up on the couch and told me that I could "master" my fears if I believed I was doing the right thing. Then she said something to me that was as if a bomb dropped in my lap. Mother looked at me hard and said, "Son, you are blessed with two character traits that I admire in you. You have integrity and you have courage." I sat there stunned as Mother reminded me that despite all the unfortunate things I endured from her and the men in her life, I had did not given up, and when the time was right, I had the courage to break away and go out on my own. Mother recalled how she had felt when I sent money home while in the navy and mentioned my willingness to help her financially once I found a job at Patton. I felt that something was seriously wrong with her. She had never talked to me this way before, nor since my childhood had she shown interested in my feelings about life. I remember thinking, "Who is this person? Is she my mother?"

The sun was fading, and it was becoming darker and darker in the house. The atmosphere fit the situation as Mother poured out her heart to me. She said that when I arrived, she had been thinking about her life and the troubles she had caused for herself. She had many regrets, but she never thought she would end up alone in life, without a husband or someone to love. The worst part, she said, was that she was responsible for her situation. She told me that my father was someone she had pushed away because she hated being controlled by a relationship, and that she had lashed out whenever her independence was threatened. At last, Mother's behavior began to make sense to me. The combative behavior toward my stepfathers, her mixed feelings about her children, and her disappearances on weekends told the saga of a free spirit trapped by the bondage of carrying for offspring. Finally, Mother said, "You know, son, insisting on being my own person has left me alone." She told me that I was much like her, but she thought I was still young and destined to do some good things in this world. Finally, she said, "Fear of doing what is right can force you down the wrong path." We hugged, and I left energized and encouraged by our talk. At the same time, I knew that I had a lot to do if I was going to live up to her vision of me and my future. First, I had to get a high school diploma if I were going to find a good-paying job. The next day, I visited the San Bernardino Adult Evening High School office. The registrar looked up my records and gave me an accounting of my high school credits. She told me that all I needed was one semester of US Government and one semester of California State Government to complete the requirements for a high school diploma. She noted that I had done well in high school and that I had earned extra credits from "electives" that I had taken, and that if I had stayed in school, I would have had enough credits to graduate midterm. I was able to take the two courses simultaneously, which meant I had to attend classes every night during the week. Monday, Wednesday, and Friday I took US Government, and Tuesday and Thursday, California State Government. The courses complemented each other, and I received "A" grades in both courses.

The Evening High School graduation ceremony was low-key. There were five graduates present, and we had a Valedictorian. It was an important night for me. Now, at twenty-three years old, I had a high school diploma. I was very happy because I had finally graduated from high school. I recalled being rejected as a pre-OCS candidate because of no degree. At the same time, I wondered if my life might have been different if I had taken and passed the GED exam while in the navy. I had applied for several positions that required a GED certificate, but I did not have one.

Us Post Office

I started looking for a new job immediately. While scanning the classified section of the *San Bernardino Sun* newspaper, I saw an advertisement that said the US Post Office was hiring distribution clerks and letter carriers. The minimum requirement was a high school diploma. There were also points allowed for applicants that had completed military service. I took the test for "distribution clerk," passed it, and accepted a job offer. My starting salary at the post office was more than my current salary at Patton Hospital, and the post office was closer to home. I resigned from the mental hospital, giving the proper two-week notice.

My Friend Jake

My first friend at the post office was a guy named Jake. He was a couple of years older than me, he was savvy and smart, and he reminded me of the old salts in the navy. We went through orientation together and practiced taking the street tests together. New employees had to pass a city street test within the first three months. While preparing for the tests, we decided to take a break. Jake took me to Las Vegas, Nevada, for my first visit to that city. He rented a hotel room near one of the big casinos, and we spent the weekend gambling and eating good food. We also drove to San Francisco together, toured the California wine country, and returned via the Pacific Coast Hwy. I had lived in California most of my life but never had the opportunity to tour the state.

Not surprisingly, Jake was broke frequently and often had to borrow a few bucks from me a few days before payday. He always paid me back on time. Jake said that he lived with a woman and that they had a couple of kids but they were not married. One day Jake invited me to a club just outside town. I discovered that Jake was part of a Country and Western band; he played the guitar and had a good singing voice. At one concert hall, Jake introduced me to Country and Western singer Bobby Bare. During his singing gigs, Jake displayed a confidence and vibrancy not seen in his work at the post office.

Jake was crushed when he failed the final city street test. I was not surprised, given how often he missed our practice times. He was given two opportunities to retake the test, which extended his job a couple of months. Unfortunately, he still did not pass and, finally, had to be let go. I think Jake failed the tests because he was too busy socializing with friends. I warned him several times that he was not studying enough, but he was sure he would pass. For a while, Jake showed up at our favorite coffee shop to keep in touch. Eventually, he distanced himself from his former postal colleagues and soon disappeared from the scene. I was disappointed because Jake was a good friend. His adventurous spirit was his downfall. I ran into him by accident a few years later. He was working at a supermarket in the northern part of the city. He seemed embarrassed to see me, and after a brief conversation, I got a strong impression that he was not interested in renewing our friendship. When we separated, I knew we would never see each other again.

I enjoyed working at the post office because there was very little stress except during Christmas time. On the other hand, I disliked the "swing shift," which was 3:30 p.m. to midnight. It seemed that I was working when everyone else in town was out having fun. When the opportunity came, I changed my hours to the "graveyard shift" (midnight to 8:30 a.m.). The day shift was reserved for those who had seniority. One morning as I was punching out on my time card, a colleague remarked that he was surprised that Jerry, an older clerk, had been working at the post office over twenty years. I checked out the seniority list that was posted near the time clock. It did not surprise me that I was at the bottom of the list. However, I was stunned to learn that Jerry had started to work at the post office in the year I was born and that we were doing much the same kind of work. I began to understand why several colleagues had commented to me that they could not understand why I had chosen the post office as a career.

More Caregiving

During this period, I was having a difficult time trying to be responsive to my mother's side of the family. My Uncle Emeal had been in a car accident near Santa Maria, California, and he was paralyzed from the waist down. His injuries were so serious that they could not move him for two months. I was obliged to drive Mother and Grandy to Santa Maria during my days off. Although I had a full-time job like my other relatives, none were willing to take Grandy to see my Uncle. Finally, we were able to move Uncle Emeal to the Veterans Hospital in Long Beach, which was much closer.

At the same time, Grandy was also having some serious health problems resulting from a stroke she had in her late fifties. I remember the Sunday morning that it happened. As usual, I went over to her house to accompany her to church. She was still in bed. I woke her up, and she discovered that she could not talk properly. The stroke had disfigured her face, and her mouth was no longer in its proper place. One of her eyes was also off-center. I panicked and bolted to get my mother. Fortunately, Grandy escaped without major paralysis. Mother and Aunt Queenie massaged her face every day until her mouth returned to near normal. Grandy was also suffering from hardening of the arteries in her feet, which caused a burning sensation. We all took turns massaging her feet during visits.

As the years passed, the burning sensation in Grandy's feet became more intense. The doctors diagnosed her as having hardening of the arteries. Grandy did not believe the doctors. She was convinced that a jealous person had put a "hex" on her. She started visiting women who claimed to have special powers to reverse hexes. I put countless miles on my automobile taking Grandy to see these individuals. I waited in the car for hours while these charlatans tricked her out of her money. In addition, there were times when I had to search Grandy's house for hidden objects that might be a source of the hex. One day Grandy invited a woman into her house to look around. Of course, the woman claimed she had found an egg full of Grandy's hair under her bed. Grandy believed that this was proof positive that someone was trying to harm her. I went to Uncle Johnnie for advice on how to handle the situation. He counseled me to avoid criticizing Grandy's efforts to find relief. As always, Uncle Johnnie gave me good advice.

Despite the money Grandy spent on a cure for the hex, she was never short of funds. I assumed that her funds came from Papa's Social Security and life insurance benefits. She and Papa had contracted to have a new house built on their property before he died. Grandy was determined to follow through with the commitment. She had a new house built on the property and at the time, it was the nicest house on the street.

One day I telephoned Grandy to see what time I was to pick her up to go shopping. She did not answer the telephone, so I drove over to her house. When I arrived, the front screen door was unlocked. Leaving the screen door unlocked was unusual for Grandy, even when she had visitors. I walked in and saw her lying on the sofa. I thought she was asleep. I tried to wake her and discovered that she was no longer with us. She had died of a heart attack several hours before I arrived.

This was a sad day for the whole family, especially for me. My grand-mother was my greatest supporter. If I needed anything, she was always there to support me. Mother was shattered by the news, but my Aunt Queen took the loss the hardest. She had to be sedated, and she was never quite the same after that. According to Grandy's Will, the house went to Aunt Queen, the oldest child. Aunt Queen refused to live in the house, and at first, wanted nothing to do with the house, so Mother and I rented it to help pay the mortgage. Unfortunately, we had trouble with each tenant and decided not to rent it again. Mother suggested that I move into the house, and she and I paid the mortgage on the house for years until it was paid it off.

With Grandy gone, responsibility for my uncle fell to me. I managed his finances and took his disability checks to the hospital for him to sign. I opened a bank account for him and paid his bills each month. I visited him every two weeks to give him money to buy toiletries and other things he needed. The hospital did not allow patients to have more than twenty dollars in their possession. Each visit to the hospital was an ordeal for me.

Uncle Emeal was convinced that he would walk again. He fell out of bed several times trying to prove it. Soon, his mental faculties began to decline, and he became uncooperative and hostile to the hospital staff and visitors. During one visit from my mother, he cursed her, and she refused to visit him again. To ease my frustration over the situation, I scheduled my visits to the hospital on Saturday mornings; and on Saturday afternoons, I drove to Los Angeles and spent the night with Dad and his family. This strategy helped reduce the stress on me.

Chapter Nine

My Intellectual And Spiritual Renaissance: My Friend Joe

After a year or so at the post office, I decided to join the office bowling league. I enjoyed ten-pin bowling, and it became one of my favorite sports outings. One day, I decided to go practice at a bowling alley just a few blocks from my mother's house in Muscoy. Sanhi was an older bowling alley but was popular with the better bowlers. I saw a letter carrier that I had seen at the post office practicing, alone. Although we had never spoken, I introduced myself and asked if I could join him. We had a lot of fun and decided to have a bite to eat in the restaurant afterward. We became fast friends. Since we did not work the same hours, we arranged outings in advance. We usually met at different bowling alleys to practice bowling and have coffee. Despite our close friendship, Joe and I had very different lifestyles. We rarely saw each other on weekends. He spent his weekends visiting casinos in Las Vegas, Nevada, and Gardena, California. He was very good at math and was convinced that he had learned a few mathematical theories that would help him win at card games. I spent my weekends in Los Angeles with my dad.

Joe was a voracious reader and had a book with him just about every time we met. It seemed that he was interested in every topic under the sun, but his focus was philosophy, mathematics, and chess. He was also a body builder and spent a lot of his time bulking up and then slimming down. Joe tried to interest me in bodybuilding, but I was an avid handball player and was not about to give that up. Joe taught me how to play chess and introduced me to the world of philosophy. In my mind, he was so intelligent that I could not understand why he was working at the post office.

During one of our chess games, Joe asked me if I had gone to college. I laughed and told him that I had just finished high school a couple of years before. He did not believe me. I explained that I had dropped out of high school and joined the navy. He said that he would have never guessed it. He asked why I had not taken some college courses at the local college. I did not see much chance of getting into a college. Nonetheless, Joe kept coming back to this theme, and every time we met, he urged me to check out San Bernardino Valley College (SBVC). Seeing my trepidation, he promised to help me with my courses if I found them too challenging. He said that he had completed two years at the University of Michigan and that he had every intention of going back to finish. Joe suggested that since I was working the midnight shift, I could take some college courses after I got off work in the mornings or before I went to work in the evenings.

Finally, I decided to pick up a registration packet from the SBVC registration office and look at it. Joe guided me through the registration forms and even selected the courses I should take. My first two classes were English Grammar, commonly known as "Bonehead English," and English Composition and Literature. Joe helped me understand writing concepts and reviewed my weekly homework. I got an A grade on my book report and a B+ grade in the class. The next semester, I took two courses: English Literature and World History. I received an A grade in one and a B+ in the other.

I did not know that college could be so much fun. It was a sobering experience learning how little I knew about so many things. I regretted dropping out of high school, but I was sure that I probably would not have gone to college at all if I had stayed in school and not joined the navy. In addition, I could not recall any of my relatives mentioning that a family member had gone to college, although some were definitely smart enough.

Joe helped me see that I had not taken advantage of the opportunities to complete my education while in the navy, nor immediately after my discharge, and he pointed out that I could do something about my situation. In addition, he convinced me that my good grades were no accident. I could tell that Joe was destined to be a teacher. He introduced me to various issues of science, history, and philosophy. As a result, I bought books to help me understand how to think logically and to recall things that I had read and heard. One day Joe and I argued about a historical fact. He got so frustrated by my comments that he suggested that I go to the library and read Will Durant's books, *The Story of Western Civilization* and *The Story of Philosophy*. Durant's works on history and philosophy were fascinating reading.

Reading these books while visiting my uncle in the hospital provided a good escape. Joe was the only one I could talk to about my caregiving burdens. Once, Joe convinced me to take a trip somewhere to clear my mind. He suggested that I take a drive to Yosemite National Park for a few days. I had never been to Yosemite. I talked Joe into going with me. It was in the early spring, and the park was almost empty. With the backdrop of light snow on the trees and ground, the park scenes were awesome. Joe's friendship and encouragement during this period were fundamental to helping me make it through this difficult time.

My Friend John

To gain experience on the job, my supervisors assigned me to work on the "pouch rack" to learn about moving bundled sacks of mail from post office to post office. Several colleagues warned me that John, who was in charge of the pouch rack, was difficult to work with and that he was a religious fanatic. True to form, the first night John and I worked together, he asked me about my religious affiliation. I told him that I was a Baptist. John said that he was a Christian. I responded that I was a Christian too. John replied, "But you said that you were a Baptist; now which one is it?" Our relationship went downhill from there. My reaction to John's comments was visceral. He had embarrassed me, and I went home that morning determined to set him straight. I found Grandy's Bible and started reading it.

When I was young, I was obliged to attend church with my grandmother. I enjoyed Sunday school, but having to sit through two-plus hours in worship services was difficult for the young people. The most exciting thing I can remember about church was the trip to the Baptist Youth

Retreat in Big Bear Lake, California, when I was twelve years old. The retreat was open only to baptized young people. I remember spending weeks listening to Grandy's gospel music waiting for a sign that I should be baptized. It did not come. Finally, I pretended that I had gotten the call and asked to be baptized. No one questioned my confession. Four of us were baptized that day. I learned later that they had fudged their calling as well.

My grandmother was pleased that I had been baptized, and she convinced my mother to let me go on the retreat. The retreat was exciting. We stayed in log cabins with four bunk beds. The experience was great—we sang around the campfire at night, studied the Bible during the day, played games, took long walks, and ate well. It was the first time that I spent more than one night away from home. Although I went to church a few times while in the navy, my interest in religion and spiritual matters was practically nonexistent. In addition, while trying to cope with the social environment at Patton, the thought of seeking spiritual guidance to deal with my frustrations never crossed my mind.

My discussions with Joe had introduced me to alternative philosophies to Christianity. Nonetheless, I believed that I was a Christian because I had grown up calling myself a Baptist and I attended the local Baptist church. I spent days trying to find information about the Baptist church to counter John. Unfortunately, the Bible I was using did not have a Biblical index. I began by looking at the first few books of the Old Testament. I knew about famous Bible characters but very little about doctrinal issues that divided Christendom.

Failing to find any reference to the Baptist church, I turned to my *Webster's Dictionary*. The dictionary listed John the Baptist and the Baptist church. I cited my research and proudly told him that Jesus's disciple John was a Baptist. John was disappointed at my response and asked me to look at the text again. He said that John the Baptist and Saint John were two different people. Although John was less arrogant this time, I could not forget his cocky and smug attitude a few days before. I understood why some people did not like the man, and I was determined to bring him down. I knew the next month was going to be hell. It was some time before I realized that John was directing me down a predetermined path.

As the weeks went by, I noticed that John also had a sense of humor and was not the pariah that I had thought. Instead, several colleagues respected him and came to him for advice about religion and church doctrines. John seemed to have an answer for everything. I began admiring him from afar. Although my feelings toward him began to change, I was determined to get the best of him on this religious issue. I admit that it was all about ego. I studied the Bible every chance I got. Soon, I was intrigued by the Old Testament writers' insight and wisdom, and their understanding of human nature. The faith and reverence of Bible characters such as Abraham, Joseph, Isaiah, Solomon and his father David inspired me. I spent a lot of time soaking in the wisdom of the Books of Psalm, Proverbs, and Ecclesiastes, and looking up the New Testament scriptures that John had cited.

My new interest in religion fascinated Joe. He said that he was raised Catholic, but he had stopped attending Mass while in college. He considered the Bible largely historical and did not know much about the doctrinal issues dividing the different Christian faiths. Moreover, for him, "organized" religion had a bad reputation. Consequently, Joe brought me books and articles that described the many evils perpetrated in the name of religion. He also encouraged me to read books that questioned the deity of Jesus and the existence of God. I believed God existed, and I was not convinced that organized religion was a bad thing. I found myself in a two-front war against Joe and John.

Despite Joe's rejection of theistic philosophy, he helped me understand the historical debate between faith and science. I was reading books and discussing ideas that I had never encountered before. It did not escape me that none of the literature provided by Joe talked about the positive aspects of religion. Joe said that he had difficulty comprehending something that he could not see or prove. I reminded him that he believed in many scientific theories that could not be proven. I pointed out his blind acceptance of mathematical formulas that he used to help him win at cards in Las Vegas. I was sure that faith had as many random successes as his math formulas in the gambling world. Furthermore, I could not understand how someone could argue persuasively that God did not exist given our own existence and the remarkable laws of physics and biology, as well as those of the universe. Joe reminded me that he was an agnostic, not an atheist. He said that he did not know if God existed or not. This was the first time I understood the difference between the two terms.

For a while, I was a complete skeptic about everything. I used some of Joe's arguments to put John off balance, and some of John's arguments to deal with Joe. On occasion, they were in basic agreement, such as the universe having structure and design. John reasoned that because the universe had design, it followed that its design must have a purpose. Joe did not dispute this, and he agreed that the universe had a coherent structure and in a sense was purposeful in nature. However, John went further and argued that everything contained in the universe, including human beings, had a purpose for its existence. John cited Biblical references that claimed the universe was designed and held together by an eternal spiritual force that is sustained and personified by the deity of Jesus Christ. I had never heard anything like this before, and I challenged John to show me where these things were found in the Bible. He cited several Bible passages to support his argument:

> In the beginning was the Word, and the Word was with God, and the Word was God. He was with God in the beginning. Through him all things were made; without him nothing was made that has been made. In him was life, and that life was the light of men (John 1:1-4, NIV).

In another place, John cited the mysterious passage,

> For by him all things were created: things in heaven and on earth, visible and invisible, whether thrones or powers or rulers or authorities; all things were created by him and for him (Colossians 1:16-20, NIV).

John argued that the physical universe was created by God and for God, and that we can know God's purposes for creating man. He quoted Solomon's keen observation: "Fear God and keep his commandment, for this is the whole duty of man" (Ecclesiastics 12:13). John had a good grasp of science and philosophy. He postulated that since we know that the universe did not always exist because it is getting older, and it is expanding from a central point; thus, a beginning is required. All this is acknowledged by modern science, he said. By understanding that the universe has design and purpose, it follows that, by necessity, all things in the universe must have a reason for being here.

The most interesting conclusion that John drew from this thesis was that human beings were qualitatively different from all other created things. Humans have the ability (we can test it) to ask and seek answers to the questions: Who am I? Where did I come from? Why am I here? Thus, humans have a basic need to discover their purpose for being here. He concluded that our cognitive ability to understand science, philosophy, and spirituality connected humans to the universe in a different way from other things. All this resonated with me.

I have always felt that human beings were special. In elementary school, I observed that there were things uniquely associated with human beings: they built hospitals to care for the sick, schools to teach the young, factories to make things, and statues of themselves and others, and they worshiped things higher than themselves. They also tilled crops, grew food for themselves, cared for other living creatures, fed them, healed them, and improved on certain aspects of nature to make their own lives easier. No other animal, bird, or insect could do what humans could do, yet we could do just about everything they could do—even fly, swim, and dig holes in the ground. I was convinced that man was different from other creatures and that there was no limit to what man could do. Joe thought it was reasonable to assume that man was a special creation. He accepted that humans have the gift of self-awareness and can understand and manipulate the world around them in ways other living organisms cannot.

On the other hand, Joe could not accept that the Creator of the universe had revealed his plan for man in a book. Joe encouraged me to take a college course on philosophy so that I could understand other points of view. The next semester, I enrolled in a morning Humanities class at SBVC. I was exposed to a lot of new ideas, including the "Theory of Evolution" and the "Big Bang Theory." However, I was more intrigued by the writings of Plato, Aristotle, Descartes, Pascal, and Hegel.

My discussions with Joe and John affected me deeply. Although the three of us worked at the post office, I was never able to bring Joe and John together for a discussion or debate. Eventually, I had to accept Mao Zedong's view that "objectivity is a myth," and that in any discussion or argument, we must inevitably "lean to one side." As a result, I agreed to study the Bible with John. My studies introduced me to a view of religion that neither Joe nor I had talked about in our discussions. Joe focused on the philosophical writings about religion, East and West, and the different theories of creation. Most dealt with the negative impact of religion in the world and lauded the insight of ancient and modern philosophers. John talked to me about the nature of God, faith in Jesus Christ, and the

Christian way of life. He was smitten by the Gospel and talked about the life-changing power of Christian love and the peace he found in developing the spiritual side of his nature. He argued that what sets Christianity apart from other religions is that it focuses on the two aspects to human nature: physical and spiritual. Like the physical side, the spiritual side can be taught and trained, and it can ultimately become the leading aspect of our basic character, without denying the physical aspects of man. This spiritual transformation comes through faith in Jesus Christ and communion with the Holy Spirit, and it is expressed in our love for our fellow human beings and all of creation.

On the question of life after death, my conversations with Joe about matter and energy supplied the concepts I needed to deal with this question. If it is true that all things in the physical universe are either matter or energy (we did not talk about gravity), then living organisms are no different. Since matter and energy are interrelated, and cannot be created or destroyed, I wondered what happened to the life force that leaves the body at death. According to Genesis, God formed Adam out of the dust of the earth, and "breathed life into him and he became a living soul." Solomon proclaimed, "All men die and the body turns to dust, but the soul returns to Him who gave it." What happens to the energy of life that leaves the body at death? We know something leaves, whether it is the "spirit" or "soul" of the man, our "life force," or the part of us that thinks, believes, and trusts. When the dead are examined, we know that something is missing. Where do these missing elements go? Science still has not determined what part of the physical body houses the energy of life and releases it at physical death. I thought it logical that our life force still exists somewhere in the universe and is not destroyed. If our spirit continues after our physical death, how we live in this life has to be connected with it in some way. Although I do not believe that anyone is all bad or all good, I have met some mean-spirited people, and they died that way.

Finally, I thought about Pascal's conclusion that it was a good wager to believe in God: If we believe in him and he exists, what have we lost? If we do not believe in him and he does exist, we have lost everything. However, it was not the wager that persuaded me; it was the idea that there was something of God in us all, and that we are intimately connected to the universe. To me, it was no accident that I felt this way. It was the culmination of my self-awareness and my seeing that all human beings had similar dual natures. I believe that Christianity requires a thoughtful consideration of the facts about the universe, its nature and design, the uniqueness of humans, the person of Jesus Christ, and the realization that there is a "First Cause" or "Creator" of the universe that is eternal, outside time and space as we understand it.

The New Testament Church

John talked about his small group of New Testament Christians that had dedicated their lives to worshiping God and caring for each other the way the early Christians did. He cited Biblical examples of brotherly love, burden sharing, community outreach, and spiritual living. John believed that sharing our faith proves that we are our "brother's keeper." I wanted to see who these people were. I thought to myself, "Who could resist such a testimony?" My first surprise was the size of the congregation. There were about twenty people present. Nonetheless, they welcomed me with a great degree of warmth. They spent an hour on Sunday mornings studying the Bible. This was followed by a worship service. During worship, they sang, prayed, took Communion, and listened to a speaker that preached about brotherly love. Worship lasted about forty-five minutes. After church, they invited me to a potluck dinner at one of the member's homes. There were lots of food and nonalcoholic drinks. I enjoyed myself and got a chance to meet John's wife and children. I continued to study with John at his home, but it was several months before I agreed to visit his church again, even though I was impressed by what I had seen and experienced.

One day I was bowling with Joe at Arrowhead Bowl, and I saw a member of John's church who was bowling alone. I went over and spoke to him. He invited us to join him and said that he had wondered if he would ever see me again. I was surprised that he remembered me. I had visited the church just once, and several months had passed. I agreed to stay and bowl a game with him. Joe bowed out. Rollin was a quiet, patient man with a rugged face and outdoorsman's physique. We seemed drawn to each other in a special way, and his kindness toward me was an important factor in attracting me to their church.

The deeper I got into my religious studies, the more I tried to understand the spiritual side of human nature that John talked about. How to translate these spiritual ideas into practice was a mystery to me. As I was skimming through the Bible one evening, I found a passage in the Old Testament that intrigued me. The prophet Micah wrote, "He has showed you, O man, what is good. And what does the Lord require of you? To act justly, to love mercy, and to walk humbly with your God" (Micah 6:8). This was such a lofty concept, so unselfish in nature, that I found it difficult to believe that these words emanated from the thoughts of man without inspiration from God. I had discovered an outlook that mirrored my concept of what a loving God would want of us.

The idea of being fair to everyone, being willing to forgive, and believing that God existed and cared for me inspired me to study further. It was not until I understood the coherent theme of the New Testament that things began to make sense. I saw that everything related to our purpose in life is tied to how we treat our fellow man, and to our acknowledgement of a Creator. The love and compassion displayed by Jesus Christ in his "Sermon on the Mount" in the Gospel of Matthew, and his prayer to his father, God, in the Gospel of John, chapter 17, were mesmerizing. I decided to visit John's church again. The spirit of love and respect for each other was still present among the members. Another thing that attracted me to John's church was its simplicity. Over the years, I had been visited by a host of door-knocking religious groups and had attended different churches with friends. However, this was the first time I encountered a Christian group that sourced all of its practices to the Bible itself. I was encouraged to study the Bible for answers myself, and not to rely on all sorts of pamphlets and church documents that dictated what I should believe. I discovered that such terms as "fundamentalist," "orthodox," "liberal," "conservative," "progressive," etc. were alien terms to the Scriptures. I became leery of applying political terms to expressions of faith.

I never talked to John about my negative childhood experiences. Yet what I was learning spoke directly to my problem of forgetting and forgiving the damage I felt at the hands of my mother and stepfathers. It finally occurred to me that my folks raised me the only way they knew how. Papa was brutal with his corporal punishment, and it seems that Mother took her cue from him. I am not sure how Shorty was raised, but for some reason he felt compelled to separate me from his circle of affection. He could not accept me even as an extension of his affection for my mother, and he did not try to placate her by being nice to me. I wondered whether his treatment of me had been dictated by how he was treated as a child.

I started looking to the Bible for examples of forgiveness and how to deal with troublesome issues. One day I was studying the Bible and my eyes fell upon the passage, "Bear with each other and forgive whatever grievances you may have against one another. Forgive as the Lord forgave you" (Colossians 3:13). I decided to give this idea a try. Mother was the first to notice the change in my disposition. Her most telling comment was her admission that she was surprised that I had not abandoned the family long ago. She repeated her remarks to me that day I visited her and found her reflecting on her own life, and she helped me see the rightness of my commitment to persevere with my family all these years. It was comforting to know that my mother had seen the positive results of my newly found faith.

Mother and Shorty had gone their separate ways several years earlier. As if I were being tested, one day Mother asked me to drive Shorty's kids to San Jose so that they could spend the day with him. She said that Shorty had developed a bad case of glaucoma in both eyes and wanted to see the children before his sight was gone. I agreed to drive them to San Jose. As we were leaving, Shorty told me that he was having trouble using the eye drops the doctor gave him for his eyes. He asked me if I would put several drops in his eyes for him. His request touched me deeply, and I felt compassion for him. The regrets over my so-called "lost childhood" and resentment toward him seemed to dissipate.

My Christian Family

Becoming a Christian increased my circle of friends dramatically. I was encouraged by the number of people who truly wanted to be at peace with God and man. Jim and Marlyn Crampton were members of the church and became my "spiritual" Mom and Dad. They mentored me in the faith and displayed the practical aspects of Christian love as a family. Their home was a refuge for me. Often when I wanted to get away from the routine of work and school, I drove over to Jim and Marlyn's to relax. I was always welcomed no matter when I arrived. On Sundays, I was a regular at their lunch table. Jim and Marlyn not only taught me about living a Christian life, but also were good examples of a close-knit family that loved and respected each other. Periodically, I would overhear their discussions about issues on the job, and certain frustrations with building their new home. A wonderful thing I learned from Jim and Marlyn was to let my faith shine through my attitude and behavior rather than through argument and debate. The idea of "organized" religion took on new meaning for me. It provided a support system that promoted deep and loving relationships with others. I learned about compassion, and I lost that haunting fear to open my heart to strangers. Everything about being a Christian has something to do with how we treated other people. I believed that I was well suited for this kind of life. I reflected on my childhood burdens of caregiving, working with the mentally ill at Patton Hospital, seeing to the needs of my grandmother,

Me And The Crampton Family

managing the business affairs for my uncle, etc. I realized that I was living a life of service, and my new faith helped me to see the intrinsic value in sharing the burdens of others. I explained my feelings to Joe, but I could not persuade him to come to church with me and see the wonderful things I was experiencing.

Mother's Reaction To My New Faith

Mother was intrigued by my new faith. She asked me what we did during worship services. I asked her to come to church with me and see. She promised that she would go. A few weeks later, she telephoned me suggesting a date. I was speechless. Mother had not gone to church, except to funerals, for as long as I could remember. We arrived at the church building just in time for Sunday school. Mother seemed interested and admitted that she did not know that I knew so much about the Bible. During the twenty minute break between Sunday school and worship services, Mother disappeared for several minutes. I found her behind the church chatting with three men. They were smoking cigarettes. The scene was amazing for me. I had often heard that smokers have a lot in common and that many important decisions were made during cigarette breaks. She said that she was happy to see that I was not part of a group of "crazies." She said the church reminded her of the one she attended as a young girl. I was glad to have Mother's validation. From then on, I became the family expert on Bible issues.

Zoleta: A Challenge To My Faith

Dad wondered if my new religion was preventing me from visiting him on weekends. The fewer visits had nothing to do with my new religion. I had a problem with Dad's live in girlfriend, Zoleta. She did not like me, and she made it difficult for me to like her. From the beginning, I tried to get along with Zoleta for Dad's sake, but the more I saw of her, the more difficult it was to put up with her haughty attitude. She tried to make me feel like an intruder and complained to Dad that I was trying to turn the other children against her. I cannot recall having a civil conversation with her. When I visited, she would storm around the house and do her best to show that she was in charge. In truth, she was in charge, most of the time.

Dad was concerned about raising his three younger children without a mother. I think that Zoleta used this as her hold over my dad. She was constantly saying that if it were not for her, the younger children "would be a lost cause, like the older ones." She made sure that Gloria, Carolyn, and Johnnie had everything they needed, especially if it meant buying nice gifts for Christmas and fancy clothes for school. In truth, Zoleta was attentive and caring to the three younger children, and they loved her for it.

None of the older children believed that Zoleta's concern for the younger ones was genuine. Since I did not live with Dad full-time, I could not see the whole picture.

Zoleta tried to exploit a mistake I had made when I sold the Corvair that Grandy had bought me. Dad was impressed by the number of trips I had made between San Bernardino and Los Angeles without the Corvair breaking down. I had put over 109,000 miles on the Corvair in four years from chauffeuring Grandy, and visiting Uncle Emeal and my father. I decided that the Corvair was too small, and I started to look around for a bigger automobile. A colleague suggested that I might want to look at a used 1957 Chevy that he had seen for sale at a Chevrolet dealership in town. He and I test-drove the Chevy, and I loved it. It was cool-looking and had a powerful engine. I bought the car, and the next week I drove it to Los Angeles to show my dad.

Dad's response was not what I expected. He wanted to know what I had done with the Corvair. I told him that I had traded it in. Dad was angry and hurt. I forgot that he had mentioned to me that if I decided to buy another car, he would like to buy the Corvair from me for my sister Gloria. This was the first time that Dad scolded me, and it did not feel good. He gave me cash money to buy back the Corvair from the dealer. I prayed that the dealership had not sold the Corvair. It had been a week. When I told the dealer what had happened, he laughed and said that I could buy it back at the same price. Happily, the dealer agreed to keep the Corvair on his lot until Dad and my brother could drive to San Bernardino to pick it up.

Miss Zoleta had a field day over this incident. She ranted and raved about the situation as if I had betrayed the family. She claimed that I had no regard for my dad's wishes or Gloria's needs. Dad knew differently and was not concerned about Zoleta's opinion of me. After the car was safely in Gloria's hands, he was back to normal and as affectionate as ever. He was pleased that I had managed to buy back the Corvair. I do not think he expected it. I made no excuses for my actions, and I did not argue with him about the car.

Zoleta tried her best to sow discord between Dad and me, but nothing she tried worked. One day I overheard her asking my father if I had asked him for any money. She seemed oblivious that I was working full-time and that each time I visited my dad I brought him a gift. Once, I got tired of her shenanigans, so I pasted a piece of paper in a corner of the living room, near the ceiling. She noticed the paper, as I knew she would, and stood in a chair to see what it said. I had written, "Why are you looking up here, stupid?" Zoleta was outraged. I denied putting the paper there. She looked at me and said, "Do you think I am a perfect fool?" I calmly replied, "Not a perfect one." She stormed out of the room screaming, "I am going to tell your father!" It was not a nice thing for a new Christian to do. Dad never said anything to me about my relationship with Zoleta. I think he enjoyed knowing that at least one of his children could handle her. Although I did not like Zoleta, I never spoke ill of her to my dad.

Chapter Ten

College Or Bust: Daring To Go Against The Tide

I was burning the candle at both ends and more, by working the midnight shift at the post office, taking courses at SBVC, faithfully attending activities at church, and visiting my Uncle in Long Beach and my dad in Los Angeles. All this took its toll on my health. My energy levels dropped, and I was tired most of the time. One day Mother told me that my sister was having surgery and that the family was asked to give blood in advance. My blood sample was rejected. The nurse told me to see my doctor and have a blood test. According to the doctor, the iron in my blood was low and I was anemic. He asked about my health history and suggested that I take vitamin B-complex shots for a few weeks. Finally, he told me that I needed to decide between work and school. About the same time, I read in the newspaper that the GI Bill had made it through the US Congress. The bill offered financial assistance to military veterans who wanted to go to college. I learned that I was eligible for the program. I talked to Joe and several of my co-workers about quitting the post office and going to school full-time.

The colleague that I respected most on the night shift offered me good advice on a variety of subjects. Responding with his usual wisdom, Harold said that "a door had been opened" and that I had no excuse but to walk through it. He helped me calculate how much money I needed each semester. We determined that drawing out my four-year contribution from the post office retirement system, along with the GI Bill benefits, would be enough for one year of college. Harold suggested that I start looking for a part-time job and take the leap. Harold was old enough to be my dad, and in many ways, he reminded me of him. His final message to me was, "If you don't quit this place and go to college, I will never speak to you again." I could see that his concern for me was genuine. I decided to follow his advice. Once again, I was in the right place, with the right people, and heard the right message. Joe said that I had taken the logical course, and John congratulated me for stepping out in faith.

I looked into the job possibilities in the new Inland Shopping Center, as Harold had suggested. I got a job at Sears as a part-time salesclerk. They assured me that they would adjust my working hours to fit my college schedule. It was a perfect situation for me. I recalled that I had dropped out of high school for an unknown future in the navy; now, I was leaving a career job at the post office for an uncertain future.

My family could not believe that I was leaving a good government job to go back to school. Mother was convinced that I had lost my mind, and our relationship deteriorated. Her concerns were understandable. She was depending on me to help with the mortgage payments on Grandy's house. I was disappointed by my mother's attitude toward me. She had been so supportive of me when I sought her advice about leaving my job at Patton. Unfortunately, she was not mollified by my promise to give her money each month. My father was proud of me and held me up as an example to the other children. We all knew that Dad's motive was to shame the other kids into finishing school. Uncle Johnnie supported my decision, as always, but even he found this decision a bit irrational.

I resigned from the post office and started to work at Sears without a break. The Inland Shopping Center was brand-new and smelled of fresh paint and cement. This was a sharp contrast from the dismal and stuffy smell of the post office. My first job was to work with other new hires, inventorying stocks and organizing the storage rooms before the store formally opened. We also attended a training program to learn how to sell

Sears merchandise. Sears had its own approach to sales. We were told not to pressure customers to buy things, but also not to let them out of the store without suggesting a purchase.

I was assigned to Men's Furnishings. I sold shirts, ties, men's underwear, and T-shirts. When the doors opened, the rush of customers was maddening. We spent as much time restocking shelves as we did selling clothes. I was glad that I was working part-time and not full-time. For the first few weeks, it was more work than I had expected. I was amazed over the number of people I saw from my past. I reestablished contact with dozens of my former schoolmates. The other salesclerks could not believe that I knew so many people, and at times, they thought it unfair when my friends would only buy from me.

I was good at sales and seemed to have the personality for it. Several times, I was named best salesclerk in my section. Unfortunately, part-time salesclerks could not cash in on the bonuses for exceptional sales performance. But my performance did not go unnoticed by management. One day the personnel manager called me to the personnel office. This was an uncertain time because several salesclerks had been called to the personnel office and subsequently let go. The personnel manager asked me if I was interested in joining the Sears management program and coming on full-time. I thanked him for the honor but declined. He asked me to come and see him if I changed my mind. I was flattered by his offer, but my commitment to getting a college education was firm. I had given up a full-time job and sacrificed a potentially secure post office career to attend college. I was determined that nothing would stand between me any graduating. Later, when I transferred to UCLA, Sears offered me a part-time job in one of their stores in Los Angeles. I decided not to commit myself until I had settled in.

San Bernardino Valley College

I majored in psychology at San Bernardino Valley College. Dr. Blume was head of the psychology department and an excellent teacher. His class "The Psychology of Personality" is what hooked me on psychology. We did a lot of reading about personality development. He introduced the class to the writings of Carl Rogers, Eric Fromm, C. S. Lewis, and Viktor Frankl. I was deeply touched by Frankl's book *Man's Search for Meaning*, which talked about the importance of faith in dealing with desperate situations. This class was a great complement to my understanding of political philosophy and history.

Mr. Moore And The Debating Club

One day, a political science professor, Mr. Moore, asked me if I were involved in any extracurricular activities at school. I was not. Working part-time, taking a full load of courses, participating in church functions, dating, bowling, and meeting my friends in coffee shops left me with little time for involvement in extracurricular activities. Mr. Moore suggested that I get involved in campus activities of some sort if I intended to transfer to a four-year college. He was very popular on campus and considered the brightest of all the professors. He encouraged me to join the SBVC debating team. He said that I would make a good addition to the team. The idea piqued my interest.

The first question we debated was "Should the United States continue to support South Vietnam militarily against North Vietnam?" No one in the club wanted to take the "pro-involvement" stand. Mr. Moore urged me to take the pro stance, though I had not focused on the Vietnam issue. I did some research on the issue and was ready when the time came. At first, the number of people that showed up for the debate was intimidating. The room was filled to capacity. After listening to the opening statements of my opponents, which were long on rhetoric and short on facts, I felt that I could handle the situation. I started my comments by pointing out that I had been to Asia and knew something about the region. This disarmed my opponent, who had only an intellectual understanding of the area. I also expanded the debate by talking about the spread of Soviet communism in Eastern Europe and how the US Marshall Plan and containment policy had saved Western Europe from totalitarianism.

My opponent was at a loss for words when I began quoting from the Soviet Union and the Peoples' Republic of China government statements supporting the North Vietnam takeover of South Vietnam and Marxist-Leninist publications calling for the overthrow of capitalist countries including the United States. I reminded my opponent of the suppression of democratic institutions that followed takeovers by Marxist Leninist regimes in Eastern Europe and North Korea. These examples grabbed the audience, and I could feel that the crowd was moving to my side. After the debate, my opponent congratulated me and said that I almost persuaded him to change his views. Mr. Moore also congratulated me on an effective presentation. He said that the debate gave the club a shot in the arm. Mr. Moore's class was my first introduction to political science. He was a marvelous teacher, and I thought about going into teaching because of him. Nonetheless, I stayed with my psychology major.

Chapter Eleven

African-American History: A General Awakening

I graduated from San Bernardino Valley College with honors and received the SBVC Faculty Association Scholarship. The scholarship gave meaning to the popular song of the times called "The Impossible Dream," written for the 1965 musical _Man of La Mancha_. The following summer, I enrolled in two night courses at the University of California, Riverside (UCR) campus. The civil rights movement was in full swing and I wanted to understand more about the intellectual roots of the movement. This was my first exposure to African-American literature and history. We did not study about the contribution of black Americans to American history in high school or at SBVC. I was impressed by the number of books on the history of black people in America that I had never read or even knew existed. Although I had read excerpts from James Baldwin's _Notes of a Native Son_, Ralph Ellison's _Invisible Man_, and several works by Martin Luther King, Jr., I knew very little about the philosophies of Frederick Douglass, Booker T. Washington, W. E. B. Dubois, Malcolm X, and philosophers and civil rights activists. It was clear to me that my social environment offered few opportunities for me to learn about the civil rights movement and black

American history. Outside of church, I could count my black (and white) friends on one hand.

My experiences in the US Navy, Patton State Hospital, US Post Office, and Sears offered few opportunities to introduce me to American intellectual history. In the US Navy, I served on three destroyer escorts. Each ship had a crew of about a hundred eighty sailors, and there were no more than five or six blacks on board each ship. There were two blacks in my starting class at Patton, but I was the only one that stayed with the program. At the post office, I was a clerk, and the majority of blacks working there were either letter carriers or mail handlers. Most were older than I was and rarely had time to chat with clerks. I had only a few close friends in the navy; and during my teens, my caregiving responsibilities limited my social contact at school. On the other hand, I had more than enough relatives living in San Bernardino and Los Angeles to interact with on a daily basis.

At Sears, I was the only black salesclerk in my division. At SBVC, I did not have much in common with other students since the average age of student body was at least six years my junior. Nonetheless, I figured that I would meet a number of black students closer to my age in the UCR Black Studies program. It did not happen. There were twenty students in the class; five were black. We had some wonderful classroom discussions, but we were all commuting students and, at ten o'clock in the evening, no one wanted to stay after class to have a cup of coffee. I never met any of my fellow students beyond the campus.

While at UCR, I worked part-time at Sears and as a substitute schoolteacher in San Bernardino. Demographics had changed since I was in high school. I was amazed at the number of schools where the student body had become almost completely white, black, or Mexican. Although there was no obvious forced discrimination that I could see, the neighborhoods generally dictated the student body makeup. On one occasion, I was teaching at a predominantly white elementary school in the northeast of the city. A fifth grader came up to me, and in an innocent yet curious way, said, "I have never seen a colored teacher before." He was fascinated by me, and was the first student to raise his hand when I posed questions to the class. Even as a substitute teacher for elementary and junior high school in San Bernardino, I had only scant contact with regular black teachers. Most were new to the area, had families, and were not interested in expanding their circle of friends to substitute teachers. It is no wonder that when I told Mother that I had met my future wife, Nora, at UCLA, she responded, "What color is she?"

My Friend Greg

One day at Sears, I had to prepare a refund for a customer. Since I was only part-time, I had to get the refund authorized by an assistant division manager. I asked a young man named Greg, the assistant division manager, to sign the authorization. When Greg signed the refund, I noticed that his handwriting was very neat and that he made an effort to make it so. I told him that I had studied handwriting analysis while working at Patton. Greg was interested in hearing more, and we agreed to talk during our next break. We hit it off quickly, and met in the Inland Center Mall for coffee regularly. Greg was about twenty years old. He was tall, fit, and well dressed. During our discussion, I noticed that he was interested in public affairs and social issues.

Greg has a good memory, and most of what follows is his impression of our early relationship, with only a few tweaks from me. One day, Greg asked me if I had an extra room in Grandy's house that he could rent. He said that he wanted to move out of his parents' house in Yucaipa, California. He explained that he was taking classes at SBVC in the evenings and that it would be more convenient for him if he were living in San Bernardino. I discussed the possibility with my mother and she suggested that since we had not known each other very long, I should let him sleep in the attached furnished garage formerly occupied by one of my cousins. Greg agreed to the arrangement.

Greg grew up in Yucaipa, a small town about fifteen miles from San Bernardino. Yucaipa had few blacks, if any, living there. He was active in school sports and had only encountered blacks in games against teams that had black athletes on them. He had no opportunity to interact with blacks socially or develop friendships with them. Despite his general ignorance of blacks, Greg was not concerned about moving into a predominantly black neighborhood. There were a few whites living in the area, so I was not concerned about him being rejected or mistreated. Initially, Greg's parents were not happy about him moving in with me. Finally, Greg introduced me to his mother. After a short conversation, Greg's mother decided that I might be a good influence on Greg and moderated her concerns.

I introduced Greg to Joe, and soon we became a threesome at Sambo's, our favorite coffee shop in town. Greg and I saw eye to eye on most things, including religion, and of course, our speculations about Joe's mysterious absences. By this time, Joe had left the post office but was not working. Yet he always had a lot of money. Sometimes Joe was gone for several weeks, and Greg and I never knew how to reach him. Periodically, we confronted Joe about his absences and accused him of being secretly married or working for the FBI. We went so far as to make up stories about seeing Joe in strange places. Joe seemed to enjoy our interrogations. The three of us enjoyed speculating, analyzing people, discussing social ideas

One day Mother suggested that Greg move out of the garage and into one of the bedrooms in Grandy's house. Greg had gotten to know my family, and they all liked him, especially my mother. She thought he was courteous, intelligent, and handsome besides. Mother gave all of my friends "handles." Greg was my "good-looking" friend and Joe was my friend with the "pretty eyes." She referred to one of my black friends as the "smoky black" one.

Greg felt that he had been accepted as one of the family, and he would accompany me when I visited my folks. A few months after moving into the house, Greg began pointing out the obvious fact that the house was becoming run down and showing signs of years of bad maintenance. He proposed that we find a nice apartment together. Greg found a two-bedroom apartment on Arrowhead Avenue north of Baseline that we could afford. It was within our work and school commuting limits. Baseline Avenue and H Street enclosed the northeast quadrant of the city and was the unofficial "ethnic dividing line." It seemed that no one was trying to change the status quo, although San Bernardino High School, which was fully integrated, was in the northeast.

Greg recalls that when we entered the apartment manager's office and asked if we could see the vacant apartment, the manager appeared nervous. It was clear to us that he did not want to show us the apartment. He claimed that he would have to talk to the owner of the complex first. Greg was offended by the agent's demeanor and insisted that the man tell us why we could not show us the apartment. Feeling pressured, the agent managed to ask us a few questions about our relationship and work status. We could see that he was thinking that there was some kind of illicit reason for our wanting to share an apartment together.

The agent's reaction was no big surprise for me. By the sixties, the benign racial situation in San Bernardino had changed significantly. The city had grown apart racially and was very different from the city I had known growing up. Although there were no so-called ghettos in San Bernardino, there were frequent gang fights between blacks and whites, Mexicans and whites, and blacks and Mexicans reported in the newspapers. In addition, it was becoming a haven for drug pushers.

Greg was annoyed with the agent's line of questions but kept his cool. I was impressed by Greg's fortitude and his desire to take the lead in dealing with the agent. I spoke only when spoken to and kept the agent off-balance by just staring at him. Greg answered the agent's questions calmly and finally asked the agent, "Is it a question of skin color?" I was shocked by his comment, and the agent sat back in his chair in horror. After a long pause, the agent asked us to complete the application, and without contacting anyone, he gave us a move in date. I got the impression that the agent had not seen his actions as racist until Greg raised the subject. Greg was very proud of himself. I was proud of him, too. We had succeeded in integrating northeast San Bernardino.

The apartment was great. It was new and had a garage and swimming pool. Greg claimed that the new apartment was more conducive to studying and to his mental health. We enjoyed the welcome change and joked with each other about the experiences that we had gone through. One day, I complained to Greg that his stringy hair was stopping up the bathtub and that he needed to make sure he cleaned out the drain after his shower. He responded that my short black curly hair looked like bugs on the floor and suggested I get rid of them after I showered. We got a good laugh out of it. Nonetheless, we were both conscientious about keeping the apartment clean. The kitchen was always spotless since we rarely ate at home.

Greg and I spent most of our spare time together. We were aware that we were a curiosity factor when we went shopping together at the local supermarket. We were convinced that our neighbors assumed that we were living together for reasons other than economics. These assumptions were not limited to our neighborhood. A colleague from Sears showed up at Sambo's one day and saw Greg sitting by himself. Greg was waiting for Joe and me. The person asked if he could sit with Greg. Somewhere in the conversation, the guy implied that he was aware of Greg's relationship with me and thought Greg could do better—in other words, drop me for him.

It took Greg a half hour to figure out what had happened. When Joe and I showed up, Greg was laughing hysterically.

Greg and I remained close after I transferred to UCLA. Whenever I visited San Bernardino to see my family, I made sure I spent some time with Greg. At Greg's wedding, there was one event that had a lasting impact on Greg's relatives and his new wife. Greg's three-year-old niece was asked to carry the bride's bouquet down the aisle. When she saw all the people, she became frightened and froze. I noticed the people trying to encourage the little girl to bring the bouquet forward, but she would not move. I left my seat and gently approached the little girl. I took her hand and escorted her down to the front of the church. Greg told me later than his family remarked how special that event was to them, mainly because of the stark contrast of a tall black man leading a trusting little blonde-haired child down the aisle by the hand. He said that it spoke volumes to the people present at the wedding. Greg and I continue to maintain our brotherly

Greg's Wedding Party: Unknown, Me, Greg, And Joe

relationship, although my travels have separated us more often than we would like. Despite our lives diverging because of our work and separate travels, we manage to see each other as often as we can. Our friendship has been one of the highlights in my life, and I will always cherish the times we spent together. Just as fate brought Joe into my life to awaken me intellectually, Greg enriched my life by being the first person that I could share my life story with without regret, and I know the feeling was mutual.

Chapter Twelve

Women In Love And Guy Friends: Women In Love

It was not until I joined the navy that I learned about managing boy-girl relationships. My shipmates talked openly, and often intimately, about their girlfriends and love interests. They also shared their experiences and offered advice to the younger sailors. At sixteen years old, their suggestions were immensely helpful to me. After I got out of the navy, I started seeing a girl who had pretensions to become a singer. I liked her a lot, but she was more interested in her singing career than settling down with one person. I always felt that she was looking past me for someone more attractive or experienced. Our relationship got complicated once I left Patton and started working at the post office. I had mixed feelings about spending my weekends with her in nightclubs. In truth, I had trouble understanding why she wanted to be with me. We were so different in disposition and social interests. She was less flexible, almost domineering, and could vacillate between being charming and cold. I was just the opposite. She always knew where I stood and had no trouble discerning what I liked and disliked. Neither of us drank much when we were out, so that helped our relationship. We were able to talk about our differences, only because I would always give in to her requests.

I continued to see her for a few months after joining the post office, but my social contacts there piqued my interests as well. I wrote a couple of songs for Jasmine to sing at her gigs, and we recorded a duet single record together. The A-side was a peppy song about a guy falling in love with a girl and taking her before a court to plead for her love. It was called "The Motion." The side B, however, was a ballad written by me, and personal. I wanted to express my dreams of falling in love. I was unhappy with my love life, and I was certain that Jasmine was not what I wanted in a lover. The lyrics included the words:

Heaven sent a star
Down from up above.
It touched our hearts
And taught us how to love.
The star of love, happiness, and desire
Joined two lonely flames as one sacred fire.
That star will always, forever be,
A secret, between you and me.

I do not know what happened to the recordings. Jasmine told me that another company bought the record company and that no one could find the recording.

During our visits to different nightclubs, Jasmine flirted with anyone she thought might help her singing career. Occasionally I would sing a couple of peppy opening songs for her, but I was not very good. Jasmine could sing, and she knew how to work the crowd. I suppose it paid off on at least one occasion when she succeeded in getting us a slot to appear on American Bandstand as background dancers. It was fun but a lot of work. We practiced before the event, but she really was not a good dancer. Finally, I told Jasmine that I could no longer spend time with her because I was having trouble balancing work and school. It was partly true. I was working at a new job, taking college courses, on the post office bowling league, visiting my uncle, and driving to Los Angeles a couple of weekends a month to see my dad.

After breaking up with Jasmine, I found myself trapped in a relationship that proved even more troublesome for me. I got entangled with a girl that was devilish, to put it mildly. It all began when Mother telephoned me and asked me to drop by and give her friend a ride home. Although Leeta was my age, I had never seen her before. I should have known what was coming when Leeta refused to give me her address and said that she would show me the way to her house. We had sex the first night in the car in a parking lot near her house.

I started dating Leeta, and that was a mistake. Leeta wanted to marry me and have my baby. I was not interested in getting married, and I was certain that if I were, it would not be to Leeta. For one thing, she drank too much. A couple of times she showed up at the apartment intoxicated and brought a bottle of scotch along. She did not mind that I did not drink. Leeta showed her true colors when she introduced me to her circle of friends. They seemed surprised that we were together, and one of them said so. Most were heavy drinkers, and often argumentative and combative toward each other at parties and barbecues. After a ruckus at one of the parties, I told Leeta that I was calling it quits. I did not like her drinking or her friends. She was furious and promised to cut down on her drinking and drop her friends. I stayed with my decision.

One day I was cleaning out my car and found a pair of Leeta's panties under the front seat in my car and another pair deep in the glove compartment. I confronted her about it, and she admitted that she had put her underwear in my car. She said a friend told her that if she hid the underwear in a place where I spent a lot of time, I would never leave her. I had waded through enough sorcery with driving Grandy to her fake healers. Leeta's involvement in this kind of activity unsettled me to the core. I was straightforward with Leeta about why I did not want to see her anymore. She was upset and even threatened to slash the tires on my car. Fortunately, she never did anything except to complain to my mother that I had mistreated her. I could not believe that I had gotten entangled with someone willing to use sorcery to sustain a romantic relationship with me. I told Joe what had happened. He was the only one I trusted with this information. Joe was astounded by my story. He was also puzzled by my apparent preoccupation with having a girlfriend. He did not think I could fit one into my busy life without giving something up. He was correct. In addition, I had started attending church activities with my friend John and had agreed to bowl in two leagues. In addition, I refused to give up my handball games twice a week with my friend Al Ramos.

One night at Arrowhead Bowling Alley, I saw a tall, lovely black woman bowling several lanes away. I asked a friend to introduce us. Beatrice was poised, intelligent, and sexy. We chatted during the evening, and I learned that she was a single parent and had two children. Beatrice told me that she was looking for a partner to bowl with in an upcoming mixed doubles tournament. I agreed to bowl with her. She was a good bowler and we made a good team. Although we bowled together, my romantic interest in her fizzled the night she asked me to drop by her house to pick her up for bowling practice. She was intoxicated and said that she wanted to take our relationship to the next level. Until that night, I was thinking the same thing. I left her house very disappointed. Nonetheless, we continued to bowl together until the season was over. She asked me to take her home after bowling a few times, but I refused, claiming that I had to meet someone else.

One night Beatrice started drinking heavily at the bowling alley. She got angry with me for not paying attention to her, and she quit bowling in the middle of a game. She left her bowling ball, shoes, and bag on the lane and walked out. My friends wanted to know if we had broken off our engagement. I learned that night that Beatrice had told several bowlers that we planned to marry. Her antics that night ended our relationship, and I surmised that she eventually understood why.

Shortly after my abortive relationship with Beatrice, I started dating a girl that I met on campus at SBVC. Theresa seemed like a very nice girl. Although she was not very pretty, I convinced myself that she was worth a look. Theresa had many good qualities. She was intelligent and kind, and was a practicing Christian. Her parents were ecstatic that I was dating their daughter. I was probably the first person that had dated her seriously in a long time. It turned out that we had very little in common, and it was obvious to everyone that saw us together. I took Theresa to church with me a couple of times and introduced her to some of my Christian friends.

Billie Bunn, a Christian lady that I admired, took me aside one day at church and told me that she thought Theresa was a nice girl but that she could see we were very different. Billie said that she hoped I was not thinking about marrying Theresa. My roommate Greg made similar observations, except Greg was more colorful in describing Theresa. Greg thought that Theresa had an abnormally large mouth and that her eyes were too far apart. Although Greg's vision was failing, his description of her was essentially correct. She was not an attractive woman. I had no illusions about that, but I continued to see her. I never introduced Theresa to my family because I was sure Mother would have disapproved, and that she would have given Theresa a handle that could prove embarrassing.

After transferring to UCLA, I continued to see Theresa, but it did not take long for our relationship to end. Theresa had also transferred to a college near UCLA. One day I invited her to a reception and dinner honoring the Thai ambassador to the United States. When I picked Theresa up for the dinner, I was surprised that she was not dressed for the occasion. She was wearing jeans and an old sweatshirt. She said that she had forgotten we were going to a reception and dinner. I had to wait for her to change clothes. To make matters worse, she yawned throughout the dinner and finally dozed off. I noticed that she was distracting the ambassador. I looked at her and realized that she was fast asleep. I was horrified! I moved to wake her, but the ambassador suggested politely that I should not disturb her. It was obvious to me that Theresa was not interested in the dinner conversation, and it was obvious that she did not care to fake it. We did not see each other much after that.

I had started seeing Veronica, my mother's close friend and neighbor, while still dating Theresa. Veronica was a couple of years older than me. She was intelligent and very attractive. She had two young boys. One weekend Veronica and I drove to Los Angeles to see my dad. He was recovering from a heart attack. My sisters and brothers in Los Angeles liked Veronica and treated her as one of the family. Their response led Veronica to believe that I might be interested in a long-term relationship with her. She wanted desperately to remarry.

Uncle Johnnie was opposed to my budding relationship with Veronica. He thought she was unstable and had some kind of personality flaw. I made it clear to Veronica that I saw her as a friend, not a romantic interest. She tried to enlist Mother's help to win me over. I was not surprised. It must have been clear to all my girlfriends that my mother had a lot of influence on me. Mother liked Veronica and believed that we would be good for each other. I did not think so. I felt that she was in the dumps too often. Eventually, Veronica became seriously depressed. She was hospitalized, and her children were place in foster care. Mother encouraged me to visit her in the hospital, but I decided it was not a good idea. I did not want to give Veronica the wrong impression and disappoint her further. A couple of years later, I learned that Veronica had been admitted to a mental institution, and that she died shortly thereafter.

Guy Friends

As a single guy, I collected a variety of male friends of all personality types. It seems that I had a unique facility to get along with everyone, young and old. My genuine openness often became a problem. It was stressful trying to accommodate the variety of invitations to lunches, dinners, and parties. Fortunately, my new friends were of a different type than those I had worked with at Patton Hospital. Occasionally, I complained to Greg and Joe that trying to deal with their different personalities and invitations was stressing me out, and that I had trouble disengaging with friends that required more attention than I could give them. My comments reinforced Joe and Greg's argument that I should be more discriminating in selecting my friends. They described my associations with my different girlfriends as disastrous, and my associations with my male friends as "unhealthy." Greg was put off by the backslapping, snuggling up, off-colored gesturing, and beer drinking of my bowling friends. He argued that many of my bowling friends were closet homosexuals and that their amorous behavior toward one another implied it. I was disappointed by his characterizations and rejected his and Joe's suggestion that I quit bowling with them. I was a people person and being with friends was a stress reducer for me despite my complaints. Plus, I had no problem with physical contact with men. Like in the navy, we knew where to draw the line.

Victor was my favorite bowling friend, and a hugger. He was at least fifteen years older than me, married, and he had a grown son. Joe and I first met Victor during a Sanhi Bowling Alley "King of the Hill" tournament. Victor, barely a 150-average bowler, became the King of the Hill by dethroning a 200-average bowler. It seemed that every ball Victor rolled in the runoff was a strike that night. He noticed us cheering him on and came over to thank us. Joe and I dubbed him "the King" after that. Victor defended his crown for three weeks and drew quite a crowd. He seemed to bowl better when he had supporters. Since we bowled on the same league, Victor and I got to know each other. He invited me to his home a few times for dessert and coffee after bowling. Unfortunately, our close relationship provided additional fodder for Joe and Greg,

Joe and Greg said that I was too enamored with Victor and that my relationship could easily fall into their so-called "unhealthy" category. Nonetheless, they both like Victor and chatted with him on occasion. During one of our discussions about my relationship with Victor, Joe made a compelling argument that Victor's tendency to hug me after each strike was sending the wrong message. Greg accused me of seeing Victor as a sub-stitute father figure. In a sense, my dad and Victor were similar. Both men were successful construction workers, and neither had finished high school. Moreover, they had difficulty relating to their children. However, this is where the similarities stopped. My dad was a loner and had very few friends. Victor was outgoing and transparent. He liked people and social activities. He played tennis, bowled, and was part of a billiard team. Because of Joe's comments, I decided to limit my social contact with Victor. A few weeks later, VJ, Victor's son, pulled me aside at Sanhi bowling alley and asked, "What is going on between you and my dad?" I had no idea what he was talking about. He said that his dad was upset because I had stopped talk-ing to him. He wondered if his father had hurt my feelings in some way. I told VJ that I liked his Dad a lot, that I had nothing against his Dad. I confessed to being preoccupied with work and school. VJ was relieved and asked if I could find the time to come by the house to see his Dad. I asked him if his dad had told him to talk to me. He said, "No, my mom did." Finally, VJ said told me that I was like the son his dad had always wanted. He explained that he and his dad had lost their special relationship after he decided to drop out of college and to get married. He said that his dad never finished school and did not want the same to happen to him. His dad had established a college fund for him, and his refusal to finish college was a big disappointment to the family. VJ's comments came as a surprise to me, but it explained why Victor was always curious about how I man-aged to work full-time and take college courses at night. I was sorry that I had jeopardized our relationship because of Joe and Greg's suspicions. Fortunately, I was able to repair my relationship with Victor. This taught me a lesson about being overly concerned and influence about what others think, even close friends.

Despite the near fiasco with Victor, Greg and Joe helped me come to grips with the burden I had taken on with male friends, girlfriends, church members, and colleagues at work. They were correct in arguing that I needed to be less generous with my time. I spent many hours listening to my friends tell me about their problems when I should have been studying or getting some rest. Greg and Joe thought that my behavior indicated something missing in my emotional character. They saw that I was always on the giving end, and that few of my friends seem to offer any positive contribution to my life that they could see. This was not true. I was convinced that I needed my friends as much as they needed me.

Church Folks

Besides my outings with Joe and Greg, I spent a lot of time at church socials. I attended Sunday school and worship services on Sundays and Bible Study class when time permitted. There was something special about getting together with friends of shared values and beliefs. We counseled one another and reinforced each other's resolve to be a better person. This is where I believe so-called organized religion has its greatest appeal. My church families provided a view of marriage and family that I had heard about, dreamed about, and talked about from childhood, but never experienced firsthand. Several of my Christian friends provided my first real example of an ideal family. Jim and Marlyn's relationship always came to mind. Their relationship demonstrated that as husband and wife they were true friends, and they seemed to know each other's heart and soul. It was obvious that the love and respect they shared was their common bond. Jim preached at church on Sundays and taught adult Bible Study. I had lunch with them almost every Sunday after church, and sometimes I visited them on Saturdays when I did not want to drive to Los Angeles to see my dad. I saw in their example the kind of family life I wanted should I ever get married.

Billie and Doug's family also provided some useful information about married life. They had five children that were under twelve years old. Their closeness was emblematic of what I missed growing up and often dreamed about in a family. Occasionally, I joined them on Wednesday night for dinner before attending Bible Study. It was a joy to see them sitting together at the dinner table with their five children and discussing everyday activities. One evening one of the young boys asked why it felt good to climb trees. His dad promised to explain it to him later. I think my decision to have dinner with my family as often as possible, before going out to my clandestine meetings in the evenings, stemmed from my experiences with these families.

Friend Of Friends

Looking back over my life, I was compelled to respond to people who seemed interested in me or that seemed to need my company. I suspect that my caregiving responsibilities had inculcated in me the notion that I was, in fact, my brother's keeper. It was always difficult for me to turn people away, and I had no problem sharing my time with the underdogs and the unpopular. At the same time, I refused to compromise my values. I believe my romantic involvement with Beatrice, Theresa, and Veronica can be seen as part of my caregiving fixation. Each of these women needed someone in their lives, especially Beatrice and Veronica, who were single parents. Although I resisted being snared by them into unhealthy relationships, I spent a lot of time just listening to them lament their mistakes in life.

I am confident that I can trace some of my feelings to my mother. She cared deeply for friends and family. She demanded that I take good care of my brothers and sisters, and I did. Despite her petite size, she was afraid of no one, not even the white sheriff in rural Mississippi in the 1930s. When the sheriff took her to the Monroe city limits and told her that the town was not big enough for the both of them, mother sneaked back into town to collect her frightened friends. Although her wrath was fierce toward her children, our love and respect for her knew no bounds. I am convinced that I owe my compassion, independence, and risk taking to Mother. After I left home, Mother's example of strength and resolve followed me. I did not run from a fight, and I threw my protective net around my friends as she did with her relatives and friends.

On the other hand, there was a downside to my willingness to entertain strangers. Although I was never homophobic, managing a normal friendship with homosexuals was often problematic. It was difficult to show comradely affection without it being misinterpreted. Several friends were convinced that I was vulnerable because of my dysfunctional childhood. This is what Joe and Greg warned me about. They saw my friendliness to strangers as an open invitation to certain personality types that was bound to cause misunderstandings. During an interview at a graduate school, a student adviser whispered to me that he had read my personal history and would like to drop by my hotel room that evening for a chat. Another student adviser who overheard his comments warned me about the ruse. Sure enough, late that night the advisor identified himself as he knocked on my hotel door. I did not answer.

At the same time, some people interpreted my friendly manner as naiveté or even as harboring a sinister agenda. Many of my high school classmates saw me as standoffish, as thinking that I was better than they were. Most never knew what was going on in my family life. Early in my navy life, several shipmates thought I was rejecting them because I did not seek to join their exclusive club. Dad's girlfriend, Zoleta, impugned my motives for wanting to spend time with my dad. She thought I was after his money. She could not fathom the depth of our love for each other. A colleague at Patton Hospital was convinced that I avoided him because of his sexual preferences. In fact, I did not know his sexual preferences until he confronted me about it. These were just a few painful examples of people misreading my motives and behavior.

The problem was manifested in the clearest terms by the comments I received from a friend and mentor toward the end of my career at the CIA. Randy wrote to me to share some thoughts about my personality when he learned that I was writing an autobiography. He said that he had always been mystified by my tendency to reach out to strangers. He confessed that he could never allow so many people into his life. Randy said that he had tried to understand me the whole of our career together. In his letter, he wrote that he and a mutual friend had discussed me:

> When Terry was here, we talked a lot about you, and with probably a sense of far more mystery about you than you two could ever have about me. You are really an enigma, Odell, and I've never met anyone who could explain you to me. Some guesses, yes, some wild speculation, yes, even some allegedly wildly true stories, yes, but nothing that gets to your nub, nothing that gets to your core, not even anything that gets under your skin. For many of us, you are a lot like looking at a picture, but we simply can't even get past the varnish.

I suppose that Randy, like Joe and Greg, thought I was painting over a flaw in my character, when I was only being me. Nevertheless, Randy had some praise for me. He mentioned that he was always impressed by how I related to foreign officials. He noted that when they were reluctant to meet with American officials, I could make it happen. He recalled that a certain Russian diplomat was asked why he agreed to meet with me after turning down invitations from other US officials. To his surprise, the official responded, "Mr. Lee is willing to listen to our views while standing up for his own; we can trust him to be honest." The diplomat went on to comment that he did not trust people that would not stand up for their country. I learned that an account of this exchange found its way into an official report.

Chapter Thirteen

The Great Leap Forward: My Friend Bob

One night while studying alone at Sambo's Restaurant, I noticed a guy sitting at the counter by himself. I had not seen him in Sambo's before. He was reading a textbook, and he looked in my direction several times but avoided direct eye contact. About two weeks later, he showed up at Sambo's again. He sat right next to me, introduced himself, and said that he noticed we had the same study schedule. Bob said that he was a junior at the California Polytechnic Institute in Pomona (Cal Poly) and had just moved to San Bernardino. There was an instant connection, and neither of us got any studying done that night. We agreed to meet at Sambo's at the same time the next week.

My chats with Bob were different from my talks with Joe and Greg. Bob was a serious college student and an Air Force ROTC recruit. He wanted to become a fighter pilot. He reminded me of some of my former navy friends, and I was immediately drawn to him. He had big dreams and was positive he would succeed. However, Bob was not happy at Cal Poly and was thinking of transferring to another school. He asked my advice on things and I was happy to pontificate. I introduced Greg and Joe to Bob.

Greg was suspicious of Bob and thought that he might be a pothead. He said that he did not like Bob's eyes and urged me not to trust him. Bob noticed that Greg did not care for him, but he never said anything to me about it. I got the impression that they just did not like each other. Joe, on the other hand, enjoyed discussing architecture and physics with Bob. One evening Bob told me that he was transferring to UCLA because he'd had enough of Cal Poly. He said that he had been accepted for the fall quarter and that he was moving to Santa Monica in a couple of weeks. Although I was happy for Bob, I was disappointed that he was moving away.

Just before Christmas, Bob showed up at Sambo's looking for me. He was excited about UCLA and was convinced that I would be happy there. He urged me to transfer from UCR. Bob said that he had already talked to his brother, Dan, who worked in the Financial Aid Office at UCLA, and that Dan would help me get a part-time job and some financial support. I did not realize how serious Bob was until he told me that I could room with his brother starting in the spring quarter. He said that he was moving in with his girlfriend. He seemed determined to get me to leave UCR and join him at UCLA.

Overall, several factors made a move to Los Angeles an attractive idea. I could put some distance between Mother and me. Our relationship had become strained after my decision to leave the post office and enroll in college full-time. In addition, Leeta was still a problem. She would show up at places looking for me. In addition, I was also becoming convinced that Greg and Joe were right that I was collecting too many unhealthy characters as friends. Finally, I would be closer to my dad.

The negatives were leaving my friends Greg and Joe, and moving from a hometown that I loved. They were not serious ones, since UCLA was just over an hour away from San Bernardino. I prayed for wisdom to make the right decision, and the courage to carry it through. I checked with the UCR admissions office and learned that I would have no problem transferring to another University of California campus, if there was space. My grades at SBVC proved very helpful. After talking to Dan by telephone, Bob was right on the mark about financial aid and job possibilities for me. Joe and Greg were cool to my idea about transferring to UCLA but did not try to dissuade me. Mother was not happy but resigned to the fact that she could no longer control my life. Ken, a member of my church, had gone to UCLA, and he encouraged me to take the leap. I mentioned the possibility to my dad, and he was excited by the idea. The most significant encouragement came from an unlikely source: a bowling teammate.

My Friend Jack

I first met Jack while substituting on a bowling league at Del Rosa Bowl. One evening he asked me what I did for a living. I told him that I was working part-time and going to college. He wanted to know why I was not home studying. I thought it was an odd remark since we barely knew one another. I was polite and told him that I had finished studying and that bowling was my outlet. I asked what he did for living. He said that he was a salesman. Each time I saw Jack, he asked me how school was going. He seemed genuinely interested in what I was doing. When I told him that I was thinking about transferring to UCLA, he was excited by the idea. He said his son was a student there. Jack offered to write me a recommendation letter. He also said that he would like to arrange a dinner at his house so that I could meet his son.

I was surprised by the size and elegance of Jack's home, which was in the Del Rosa area of San Bernardino. His wife greeted me at the door. She noticed that I seemed in awe by the size of the house. She smiled and said to me, "Jack didn't give you that door-to-door salesman story, did he?" It turns out that Jack was the head of the NASA Space Survival division at Aerospace San Bernardino. His wife told me that I was not the first person that Jack had lied to about his profession. She said that Jack spoke of me often, and wanted to help me in any way he could. Just then, Jack came downstairs with a big smile on his face. He was very pleased that he had fooled me for over a year. He handed me the recommendation letter written on NASA letterhead. It mentioned my high character and offered that I was a good candidate for a financial scholarship to the university. He also mentioned that he was contributing a hundred dollars to help me buy books.

I learned that night that Jack graduated from the University of Colorado with a PhD in nuclear physics and that as a young scientist he worked on the follow-up programs coming from the Manhattan Project. Jack said that he had taken an interest in me because he believed that I was a serious-minded young man trying to better himself. He was impressed that I had decided to go back to school at age twenty-six; the age he earned his PhD. It was from Jack that I first heard the phrase "Don't let a good mind go to waste." A couple of years later, Jack had a heart attack and decided to retire to the San Diego area. I will always remember his kindness, generosity, and sage advice.

My Roommate, Dan

I did not meet Bob's brother until I got an acceptance letter from UCLA. Dan and I hit it off right away. He was different from Bob in both demeanor and outlook. Dan was a first-year graduate student at the UCLA Business School, had a motorboat, and was a member of the UCLA Karate Club. I was pleased to have Dan as a roommate, but I was unhappy with the living arrangements. The bedroom in the apartment was small, and the twin beds so close together, it was as if we were sleeping in the same bed, much like the Navy bunks. I could see why Bob had wanted to move in with his girlfriend. We agreed that we should get a bigger place.

Dan wanted a place closer to his girlfriend who lived in Pacific Palisades. In a matter of weeks, he found us a large two-bedroom apartment on Pacific Avenue in Venice, about two blocks from the beach. Unfortunately, he did not want to commit to the landlord without talking to me, and by the time we could move, the two-bedroom apartment was gone. We settled for a one-bedroom apartment in the same building. It was twice the size of our old apartment. The bedroom had lots of closet space and was large enough for twin beds, two chests of drawers, and two nightstands. The dining room and kitchen were just the right size for two people that did not cook. There was enough space in the dining/living room for two desks so that we could study without getting in each other's way. The apartment building also had a swimming pool in the courtyard, although it was just two blocks from Venice Beach.

Dan came through by identifying different financial-aid packages and explaining repayment arrangements, and he walked me through the Federal Student Loan Program. With the college loans and part-time work, I had no trouble meeting my expenses. My dad was proud that I was paying my own way. He saw me as a good example for the rest of the family and frequently referred to the fact that I never asked him for anything. The reason that I never asked him for money was twofold: I did not think he could afford it, and I did not want him to think that he owed me something for not being there while I was growing up.

My mother had always been careful to honor my dad and say good things about him. I never felt that he had abandoned me. Once, Dad asked me about my school expenses. I told him that I had it covered with the GI Bill and money I had saved while working full-time. I lied. If it had not been for the student loans and part-time work, I could not have managed the costs. It turned out that my dad had substantial savings and would have gladly helped me if I had come to him.

Dan and I got along well as roommates. The only problem we had was Dan forgetting when it was his turn to clean the apartment. Finally, I suggested that we clean it together. It worked out better since Dan seemed to prefer team efforts. Bob and Dan often had trouble getting along. Once, Bob refused to come over to the apartment to see me because Dan was there. He suggested we meet at a coffee shop. Bob showed up with a black eye. He said that Dan deliberately hit him during karate practice. Although I was convinced that Bob was exaggerating, Dan could be a little rough. Once they talked me into going to Karate practice with them, and the coach told Dan to relax and not be so aggressive, not just with Bob, but with others as well.

Periodically, Dan complained that I went out to dinner with Bob but was always too busy to go out to dinner with him. This was just coincidence. I enjoyed Dan's company a lot. However, he had a serious girlfriend and he was not around very much. In fact, Dan was less complicated than Bob, and more laid back. He liked movies and parties, but also had no trouble staying at home watching TV and eating popcorn. Bob was often too reflexive and quiet. He could be happy sitting for hours in a coffee shop just staring out the window and saying nothing. If we went to a movie, Bob would rarely want to discuss the plot.

My Job In Watts

Dan used his connections to get me a part-time job. The first job was with a local tutorial service in downtown Los Angeles. The job lasted two months. The client got into an argument with the lead tutor and wanted him fired. The other tutors quit in sympathy, effectively ending the program. Dan came through again with a lead on another job. UCLA was funding an educational program to work with minorities in Watts. My teaching credentials came in handy. I was hired right away to tutor high school dropouts preparing for the GED test. The classes were held in a large trailer on the east side of Watts near Compton. Most of the students had dropped out of high school for reasons other than academic failure, and had gone to work to support their families. It was challenging and fun, but a long drive from UCLA.

One day a couple of students in the program complained that the concepts they were learning were not relevant to their lives. We discussed what it meant to be educated in America. Finally, one student blurted out, "How would you know since you are a foreigner?" Several students chimed in with a hearty "Amen!" I was taken aback by their assumptions and asked them to guess my home country. The majority thought I was from Jamaica. They had difficulty believing that I was born in Louisiana and grew up in San Bernardino, California, just forty miles from where we were meeting. Ironically, they were not deterred in thinking that I was different. Although laughing at themselves for thinking that I was a foreigner, they suggested that I was "bourgeoisie" and born with a "silver spoon" in my mouth. I seized the opportunity to tell them my story about dropping out of high school, going into the military, and realizing that I needed to go back to school. They were stunned. They realized that I had gone through some difficult times as well. One man, who had been silent during the entire discussion, finally spoke up. He commented that the discussion pointed out just how isolated they were from the real world. Addressing the others, he said, "It is shameful that you brothers think that an educated black man has to be a foreigner."

Church Fellowship: A Bust

I had trouble finding a church in the Los Angeles area that fit my comfort level. None seemed to have the warmth and family-style environment that I was used to in San Bernardino. I will never forget the encounter I had at a church in our fellowship located near my apartment in Venice. The church had a membership of around seventy-five people. The average age of the congregation was around fifty. I visited the church three Sundays in a row. The first two Sundays, only the preacher and another member introduced themselves and engaged me in a conversation.

The third Sunday, another member of the congregation approached me and asked if I was a Republican or Democrat. He never asked my name.

I said that I was neither. He responded that most of the members were Republicans and that I should know that. I told him that I was looking for a church home where I could get involved and strengthen my faith. He suggested that I might be comfortable going to another church. It was evident that some white Christians had an aversion to worshiping God alongside Christians from different racial, cultural, or ethnic backgrounds. I suspect that since then, many of these folks have died believing that they were right in feeling this way. It was not lost on me that this was also a problem in the early Christian church obliging the Apostle Paul to comment:

> You are all sons of God through faith in Christ Jesus, for all of you who were baptized into Christ have clothed yourselves with Christ. There is neither Jew nor Greek, slave nor free, male nor female, for you are all one in Christ Jesus. (Galatians 3:26-28)

The preacher overheard my conversation with the member and apologized for the man's comments. He said that the congregation was conservative and feared change. The location was a problem for them, he said. The members deplored the changing environment in Venice, California, and feared that it might bring liberals, revisionists, and leftists into their congregation. The preacher said that I was welcome to stay, and that I should not be dissuaded by the member's political talk. Nonetheless, I decided not to go back to that congregation. Fellowship was important to me, and this church seemed more interested in politics than the Gospel of Jesus Christ. I suspected that this congregation did not believe in the God they claimed to worship and serve. From then on, I went to church only when I visited San Bernardino a few weekends a year.

The Automobile Salesman

In order to save gas on my trips to San Bernardino, I traded in my gas-guzzling 1957 Chevy for another Corvair. This time I ended up with a lemon, One day the owner of a Chevrolet dealer in Santa Monica saw me in the waiting room studying for an exam. He came over and introduced himself. He said that he had seen me in the waiting room at least once a month and wanted to know what was wrong with my car. I told him that my Corvair was leaking oil, smoking, and stopping on me a couple of times a week, and that his mechanics could not find the problem. The owner said that he admired me for bringing books along so that I could study while waiting for my car. He asked me about my background, noting that I was a little older than most students at UCLA. I told him that I had been in the navy, worked for a few years, and decided to go to college on the GI Bill. After our chat, he walked over to a salesman and said something to him. The salesman came over to me and said, "It's your lucky day." He asked me to follow him outside and said, "The boss wants you to pick out a new car." He said that it was no joke. The salesman asked me to try out the new Camaro. I did not like the sports feel of the Camaro, so I tried the Chevelle Malibu. It was perfect. Finally, he asked me if I had a job and any credit. I told him that I had a part-time job as a tutor for athletes at UCLA. He said not to worry, that he would take care of everything. The dealer arranged the financing, and I agreed to pay a certain amount each month. The salesman said that I should increase the monthly payments if I got a better paying job. They took the Corvair as a trade-in, and an hour later, I drove away in a brand-new Chevelle. This confirmed for me that there really are people in this world who want to help other people, with no strings attached. This man took a chance on me, and he was not disappointed. When I showed up at school in a brand-new automobile, many of my friends thought I had a lot of money. I figured no one would believe my story so I told them that my dad bought it. Ironically, my family had trouble believing the real story, as well.

Chapter Fourteen

Friendships And Politics

A man of many companions may come to ruin, but there is a friend who sticks closer than a brother. (Proverbs 18:24)

Friendship must be a bold force if it is to survive time and distance, or it can lose its attraction, like two magnets set too far apart. —Odell Lee

My Friend Max Mayer

Besides Bob and Dan, the first person I met at UCLA that got my attention was Max Mayer. He was active in the UCLA Veterans Club. I read in the *Daily Bruin* school newspaper that the Vets Club was meeting to elect a new president. I arrived at the meeting late, and the election was already over. Max was the new president. Several vets were giving him a hard time about establishing too many rules. They wanted to make the club a purely social club with a loose structure. Max argued that the club's real purpose was to act as a support group for vets on campus. He reminded them that the club had been created to provide guidance and counseling to vets as well as to organize social activities. Max made a persuasive argument when he pointed out that some vets were entering college for the first time and needed help adjusting to campus life. I admired Max's determination to give the club a real mission. I saw him as a man with a plan. I spoke up in Max's defense and argued that if we were going to make a difference, the club needed a clear mandate and structure. After the meeting, Max thanked me for my support. I decided to join the club and volunteered to help organize club activities, including tutoring those having trouble in certain subjects.

Of all the friends that I have had in my life, Max was the most loyal, sincere, and unchangeable. I have never met anyone quite like him. Max was a former marine and had a brown belt in Karate. He exuded compassion

My Friend Max Mayer

and selflessness, and was deeply concerned about environmental pollution and social justice issues. We had friendly discussions about these issues, especially whether or not the pollution problem could be solved in the future by technology. Our most contentious discussions were the existence or nonexistence of God. Max claimed that he was an agnostic and, therefore, uncertain about the God issue. I read many of the books Max recommended on agnosticism, but as with Joe, I was unable to get him to read books that supported Biblical theology, Jewish or Christian. From my point of view, Max based all of his arguments on books that condemned religion and never considered religion or spirituality in a personal way. He was fond of repeating clever-sounding ideas of scholars that believed religion was one of main sources of pain and sorrow in the world. I argued that nonreligious people, including scientists, have caused just as much suffering in man's inhumanity to man. I mentioned the invention of war machines, biological weapons, and the atomic bomb. Despite our polar-opposite views on the existence of God, we shared the desire for a better world. We just disagreed on what was necessary to make it come about.

I trusted Max so much that I even let him talk me into smoking marijuana for the first time. I got sick afterward and vomited all over my car. We did not know if it was the marijuana or too much beer that caused me to get sick. Nonetheless, I never tried marijuana again. Another time, I agreed to let Max hypnotize me. This was a major test for me. I did not know what would happen, but I was willing to let Max have absolute sway over my thoughts and feelings. Although the hypnosis did not work, this was just another example of my deep trust in him. In short, Max is the brother I always wanted. He was someone to talk to when I was down and I could trust him completely. There were two occasions when he literally rescued me from harm's way. One weekend at UCLA, I had a sudden attack of acute bronchitis, and I could hardly breathe. I telephoned Max. He dropped what he was doing and drove across town to pick me up and take me to the UCLA Medical Center in Westwood. He stayed with me in the clinic until I was treated and able to go home. Once I was settled at home, he telephoned several times during the next few days to make sure I was all right.

The next time Max came to my aid was years later when my wife and I lived in Paris, France. Max was visiting us for a few weeks and trying to decide if he wanted to move to France as well. One morning, I woke up early with a strange feeling in my abdomen and back. I went to the bathroom to urinate and apparently passed a kidney stone. The pain was excruciating and I collapsed. Max helped Nora get me to a taxi and to the American Hospital. He did not leave the hospital until he was sure that I was out of danger. There were times that I was there for Max too, and I am sure he remembers those times. Over the years, our paths have strayed and crossed many times, but our deep affection for each other has never wavered. I confess that I owe this to Max, who has always stayed in touch. He has chewed me out often for not writing or telephoning, and has wondered if I appreciated our friendship as much as he did. This is another issue that we have debated over the years. As with most issues, Max is wrong about this one, as well. I love the guy, and he knows it.

My Friend Charles Stephens

One day I was leaving the Ackerman Student Union building at UCLA when I saw a guy debating with a group of students about the United States' role in the Vietnam War. Charles was a staunch supporter of our involvement in Vietnam. He was arguing that Communist totalitarianism was poised to take over all of Southeast Asia. Charles was the president of a small international relations club called the Thomas Jefferson Club (TJ Club). He was willing to debate anyone on the subject. The club's motto was "Dialogue, not Diatribes." No matter what other students said to Charles, he never got angry and he never yelled at them. He seemed self-assured, and he believed history would prove him right.

As I was standing there listening to Charles, two students turned over the club's table and scattered the literature on the ground. The two students were members of Students for a Democratic Society (SDS) club. SDS was a pseudo-Marxist-Leninist-oriented group that was violently opposed to US military involvement in Vietnam. I was surprised by the behavior of the SDS students, who frequently touted their love for free speech and social equality. I decided to write a letter to the editor of the UCLA Daily Bruin about what I had witnessed:

"Editors:

This is my first quarter at UCLA, and I am impressed with the prevailing atmosphere that lends itself to discussion and debate. However, I am somewhat disappointed with the attitudes of some of the participants in these discussions. A few weeks ago, I observed a heated discussion between a member of the Thomas Jefferson Club, a club that supports the current American foreign policy, and a group of about thirty students who advocate our immediate withdrawal from Vietnam. It is not the thirty against one that concerns me; it is the tactics of debate that the thirty used. I am an advocate of free speech and dissent, and I support the elimination of war as a method of settling disagreements between nations. Even so, I would have been embarrassed to be numbered among the thirty who confronted Charles Stephens that day. I was amazed at the derogatory statements and the verbal attacks on Stephens' person. Unfortunately, the riotous behavior of this group of students overshadowed the worthwhile purpose of the discussion. What was equally tragic was the group's intolerance of Stephens' position. Any defense of the United States' involvement in Vietnam was either interrupted or shouted down. Many claimed that anyone who writes a pro-Vietnam article either has been bribed by the administration or is just another mouthpiece for its lies. Any rejection of the authorities cited by the thirty was met with a rash of harsh statements such as "Fascist," "Bircher," or "murderer," or booed hysterically. At one point, I feared the imminent destruction of Stephens and his table. It seems to me that there is something lacking in the peace movement. They don't seem to desire a critical evaluation of all evidence pertaining to the Vietnam issue. The most flagrant characteristics that seem to be missing are those enduring qualities of tolerance and understanding from which peace derives its meaning. I fail to see value in any movement that allows instinct to run riot over reason.

—Odell Lee, Soph., Psychology

The article had an unexpected impact on campus. Several professors in the Political Science department used the article for discussion about democracy and freedom of speech. I was amused when I overheard a student say, "That girl Odell is really sharp. Just about everyone in class agreed with her article, even a few of the more radical students."

The next day after the article appeared, I went to the TJ Club table and told Charles I had written the article in the *Daily Bruin*. Charles wanted to hug me. He showed me that he had posted the article on his display table. He said that he had photocopied it and sent copies to friends. We chatted for a while, and Charles told me that he was in the UCLA PhD program. I also learned that Charles was an avid handball player. Four-wall handball was my favorite sport. We arranged to play a game that very evening. Eventually, I joined the Thomas Jefferson Club and began writing articles explaining the position of the club on domestic issues, campus violence, and the Vietnam War. The idea was to demonstrate that the Thomas Jefferson Club was not a right wing–sponsored club but an international-relations club interested in debating international issues. SDS responded to each of my articles, and we had a lively debate.

SDS, BSU, And Me

Charles was getting tired of being castigated by the leftists on campus. He told me that he had decided to get involved with a national association of students that supported US involvement in Vietnam. I let him talk me into becoming president of the TJ Club. It was a big move for me. A few weeks before, I had been appointed to the ideology committee in the Black Student Union (BSU). The announcement did not escape SDS and the black students on campus. At the time, there was concern among black students about the growing influence of the Black Panther Party organization on the BSU. SDS wrote an article in the *Daily Bruin* questioning my motivations for membership in the BSU and the TJ Club. They admitted that they were puzzled by it all and called for me to explain myself. I was able to answer them in several articles in the Daily Bruin. I outlined my views on the civil rights issue, which mirrored the BSU's position and attempted to show that the TJ Club was not a right-wing club. SDS responded to my article by saying that they would "withhold judgment" on my personal politics, but noted that the TJ Club's position on Vietnam "spoke for itself": if the

TJ Club is for military involvement in Vietnam, it is supporting a right-wing cause. Some BSU members echoed SDS's observations, believing that the political philosophies of "left" and "right" were fixed and that their adherents agreed on all political and social issues. They also subscribed to the idea that "liberal" was just a euphemism for leftist and "conservative" was one for rightist. They averred that there was no place for a "mixed" view of politics as in economics; you are either a liberal or a conservative. Most Black Student Union members could care less about my membership in the TJ Club. They knew that I was teaching high school dropouts in Watts and tutoring several minority athletes on campus. No one ever confronted me about the issue when I showed up at meetings and at the BSU table during lunch at the Ackerman Student Union building.

One day while I was on a trip back east, there was a confrontation between supporters of the Black Panther Party and members of Ron Korenga's group US during a BSU meeting on the UCLA campus. A black student was shot dead during the meeting. Several of my friends were concerned that I was the one shot. The issue had nothing to do with me—I was not the chairman of the BSU Ideology Committee, and I had joined only a few weeks before the tragedy.

Our efforts to change the image of the TJ Club were only partly successful. We organized a debate on the Vietnam War and invited all sides. Charles was instrumental in getting the Thai ambassador to the United States and the United Nations, Anand Panyarachun, as our featured speaker. SDS and other antiwar groups were invited to debate the TJ Club and others in Royce Hall on campus. The night before the debate, SDS students destroyed all the displays and props for the debate. They were caught in the act. The trashing of the exhibits happened the night before the visitors, including leftist speakers, were to arrive on campus. SDS refused to apologize and claimed that the students had a right to oppose "warmonger propaganda." Like many pseudo-Marxist-Leninist-led organizations, SDS believed they were defending students from being exploited by "capitalist reactionaries." Therefore, they arrogated to themselves the right to dictate what students heard and understood.

In my letters to the *Daily Bruin*, I mentioned the danger to public education when the self-appointed "leaders" of tomorrow, left or right, were allowed to determine what students saw and heard. I argued that SDS and other groups with one-sided ideologies were afraid of scholarly discussion and feared that their position would not prevail in open debate before the American people. It was clear to me that SDS could not subscribe to Thomas Jefferson's observations that "error of opinion may be tolerated where reason is left free to combat it." Nor would they have supported Jefferson's proclamation, "I have sworn upon the altar of God, eternal hostility against every form of tyranny over the mind of man." SDS sealed its own fate by its arrogance and its refusal to condemn the attack on the displays. As a result, the organization was banned from all University of California campuses for fifteen months. The decision of the UCLA Student Council and the UC Board of Regents was unanimous.

The Gang Of Four And My Visit To Vietnam

One day Charles mentioned to me that a member of Congress was trying to pull together a group of students to make a fact-finding trip to Vietnam. Charles said that he had submitted my name and sent them information about me. When they discovered that I was black, they were very interested. I decided to get some advice on whether or not I should accept the invitation. I went to Professor Simon Serfaty, who was very popular on campus. The political science students loved his presentations and his personality. I approached Professor Serfaty and told him about the invitation. He was aware of the TJ Club since the brouhaha with SDS was all over campus. Serfaty said that he could not tell me what to do, but that he would go on the trip if he were given the opportunity. He offered some additional advice. He said that I should keep in mind that what I said and did might stick with me for years and affect my future if I was interested in politics. He mentioned that some people have regretted their position on issues while in college and that their articles and interviews have come back to haunt them later in life. I thanked him for his advice and counsel. I decided to go on the trip.

When we assembled in Washington, DC, for briefings and visits to offices of a couple of congressmen, I learned that the other students had arrived several days before me, and they seemed to know each other. I felt that I was an outsider right from the start. We were a strange group. Robert was from Indiana University and the son of an army general. The two others were Romanians students that had immigrated to the United States. Daniel was a student at Brooklyn College in New York, and Octavian was enrolled at San Francisco State College in California. They were all staunch anti-Communists. Daniel was an outspoken critic of the anti–Vietnam War movement and traveled around the United States opposing the philosophy of leftist students groups. He talked about what it meant to live under communism and how he did not want that to happen to the South Vietnamese. Octavian was low-key and seemed to parrot Daniel's comments. I did not think Octavian was interested in the Vietnam War and thought that he had come along only to support Daniel. Robert was the most intelligent, and he had suspicions about my true political leanings. He was also puzzled by the philosophy of the TJ Club.

One evening Robert commented to me that the TJ Club's philosophy seemed "left of center." He said that the only point he agreed with was the club's position on Vietnam. Robert was confident and self-possessed. He subscribed to the view that nothing that seemed liberal or leftist was worth considering. He scoffed at the "Dialogue, not Diatribes" slogan, and said that I was naive to believe that leftists were interested in rational dialogue on Vietnam. Robert did not believe in dialogue on the Vietnam War either.

Officials from the State Department and the Pentagon briefed us and gave us press credentials, travel funds, and military ID cards. These items were to facilitate our travel and transportation around Vietnam. According to my ID, my rank was equivalent to major in the army. Having been in the military, I thought major was a high rank to bestow on mere students. I commented about it to the other students. My comments did not go over well. Not one of them shared an equivalent rank with me.

Our first stop before Vietnam was a visit to a military hospital where we saw wounded soldiers that had been medevacked to Japan. It was not a pretty sight. Many were badly wounded. Those who were alert spoke to us about their experiences on the battlefield. There was a consensus that they believed in their cause. We had dinner that evening with the commander of a military base and discussed what we could expect to see during our trip. It was an informative discussion, and Robert proved quite knowledgeable about the military aspects of the war. We arrived in Vietnam at Tan Son Nut Airport in the late afternoon. Our Vietnamese welcoming party did not show. Thanks to Robert's quick thinking, we hitched a ride on a military shuttle that was leaving for downtown Saigon. Our hotel was near one of its stops. Our welcoming committee showed up at the hotel about an hour after we had already checked in. The trip had all sorts of logistical problems. We were to stay for four weeks, but most of the plans for us were ad hoc. Our Vietnamese hosts invited us to a few receptions and introduced us to several Vietnamese college students. The Vietnamese students showed little interest in us and had difficulty relating to our purpose. We got together as a group only twice, once at a picnic and another time to take photographs. Our trips outside Saigon were carefully orchestrated as much for our safety as for what we were allowed to see. Nonetheless, we saw that Vietnam was a beautiful country.

We had lunch frequently at the US Officers' Club in Saigon. The soldiers and sailors were intrigued by our visit to Vietnam. One Saturday afternoon we had just finished a wonderful lunch when we heard a loud commotion in the kitchen. It was loud enough to get everyone's attention. Some officers were concerned because they had been obliged to leave their weapons in the foyer outside the club. Suddenly, the kitchen door opened, and two Vietnamese dressed in white coats and porting broom sticks burst through battling the biggest rat I had ever seen. The rat was fighting back. It snared and leaped in the direction of his attackers then fled into the restaurant. This caused pandemonium in the restaurant. Officers were yelling, jumping on the counters and tables, and asking for their guns. I took my cue and jumped on a table too. Finally, a Vietnamese hit the rat with the stick and he fell still. No one moved. They thought it was possible that the rat was playing dead. The Vietnamese scooped the rat up and put it into a burlap sack. There was a big applause for the victors, and they bowed graciously. One of the officers said that he wondered what the enemy would think if they had seen high-ranking American officers jumping on tables and fleeing the restaurant. He admitted that big rats were aggressive and had no qualms about attacking humans if they got in their way. I was glad that the officers were not allowed to bring their guns into the club.

About a week or so after our arrival, we discovered that much of our schedule did not come off as planned, and we had a lot of time on our hands. I was bored, and I decided to arrange for a trip to the countryside. I approached a colonel in the Officers' Club and asked him if there was any way we could get to see more of the country. He suggested that we visit the Joint United States Public Affairs Office (JUSPAO) and talk to the colonel in charge. I decided to go over and talk to him. The colonel briefed me on JUSPAO's mission in Vietnam. I explained why I was in Vietnam and that I wanted to see more of the country. He asked if I had any press or military credentials. I had both. He said that a contingent of Japanese journalists was being ferried to Phu Bai and up to Hue the next day. If I could get my things together, he would see that I got on the airplane. I mentioned my trip to the other students, but they were not interested. They said they were expected to visit a school the next day and wanted to stay with the planned arrangements.

I took the plane from Saigon and flew to Phu Bai. I was the only American passenger on board. The Japanese journalists were in Vietnam for a fact-finding trip and tour of the old city of Hue. The pilot of the airplane was an American by the name of Bill Barton. He asked me where I was staying. Since I did not have a room, he suggested I get a room at his hotel, where most of the American civilians stayed. He offered me a ride into the city. At the hotel, I met several other Americans. Tom, a US Information Agency (USIA) official, asked me what I was doing in Vietnam. I told him that I was a student at UCLA and was there on a fact-finding visit. He seemed intrigued. Later that evening, Tom asked if I was free for the evening. He asked what kind of ID I had because he wanted to invite me

My Lane Trip With Japanese Journalists To Phu Bai, Vietnam

to a party on a military base nearby. I showed him my US Army civilian ID and my press credentials.

Tom introduced me to the general, who welcomed me to his party. The general was a social butterfly and introduced me to each of his fifty or so guests. Finally, he asked me to sit next to him during dinner. I got the impression that the general suspected that I was more than I claimed to be. I also got the impression that my USIA friend was more than he claimed to be. Later that evening the general told me to be ready at 7:00 a.m. for a short helicopter ride to Hue. He said that his Vietnamese counterpart had invited him to a traditional festival at the old temple in his honor. The USIA official was also invited but said that he would drive to the festival. The next morning I was put on the general's helicopter and whisked away. I had never been on a helicopter before. I thought I had left my stomach on the landing field. It was such a bizarre ride. There were seven of us in the helicopter: the general, his aide, two pilots, two gunners, and myself. The gunners sat with their feet outside the helicopter and pointed their guns at the ground. There were two escort helicopters that maneuvered to the left and right of our helicopter. The helicopters changed altitudes every two or three minutes to avoid ground fire. From the air, the old city of Hue was a beautiful sight to see. There was the old temple, the old city, and a countryside that had thousands of bomb craters. The terrain looked like the moon with a green carpet. We landed just outside the city and drove to the temple in military jeeps.

The festival was exciting, colorful, and long. The general told me that he would be leaving the festival early but that he had arranged a tour of I Corp (pronounced "eye core") for me. That afternoon, we drove to Quang Tri, where we spent the night. The next day I toured the outskirts of the DMZ. I took lots of pictures and talked to American soldiers assigned to South Vietnamese units along the border with North Vietnam. The next morning I was invited to visit a Vietnamese controlled military base where a Viet Cong soldier was being interrogated. My guide asked if I wanted to watch. A red flag came up in my mind. I could just see, years from now, newspaper headlines mentioning me watching a Vietnamese being tortured. I declined the offer and suggested we see something else. I told my American guide that I was not there to report on the Vietcong but on whether or not the United States should continue to support the South Vietnamese struggle for independence.

The next day we drove around the countryside for a closer look at the bomb craters. At one point, we had to push the jeep through one of the craters because we could not get around it. The general's aide informed me that he had arranged for me to have dinner in Buon Ma Thuot with the commander of the US airbase there. The same pilot that flew us from Saigon to Phu Bai flew me to Buon Ma Thuot. The aircraft was small and had only six seats. At Buon Ma Thuot, we drove to an airfield that had helicopters of all kinds parked on a landing strip. I learned that it was a staging area for upcoming military operations. I was given a short briefing on North Vietnamese and Vietcong activity in the area. That night after dinner, we were jolted by incoming recoilless rifle rounds. We were escorted to an underground shelter. The soldiers did not seem worried and served coffee and snacks during the bombardment. The shelling lasted for a couple of hours.

There was a command center in the shelter, and I could hear soldiers communicating enemy locations to US Navy aircraft carriers off the coast. The planes from the carrier were given targets and locations to bomb. We could hear the navy jets swooping over the base and bombing enemy positions. The next day, I noticed that several helicopters had been destroyed. That afternoon, I flew back to Phu Bai hen on to Saigon. I met the students at the hotel and they wondered where I had been for a week. I told them that I went to the DMZ. They were obviously jealous.

I got back just in time for a briefing by the mayor of Saigon. It was a command performance since it had been scheduled from the day we arrived. The mayor thanked us for coming to Vietnam and hoped that when we returned to the United States, we would tell the American people about the Vietnam people's desire to be a free democracy. After the briefing, we were invited to a cookout in Cam Ranh Bay, near Nha Trang. The weather was perfect and the food was delicious. Most of the guests were Vietnamese officials and college students. Later that night, I had a violent attack of diarrhea. I knew exactly what had caused it. A Vietnamese gentleman suggested I try the Vietnamese version of a spring roll called popiah. It was filled with raw vegetable and fish. None of the other students tried the popiah.

The next morning we were scheduled to visit a Vietnamese school. I told our hosts that I was too sick to join them. A day or so later, a US embassy official who said his name was "George" knocked on the door to my hotel room. He flashed his embassy credentials and said that he had come to take me to a doctor. I asked him who told him that I needed a doctor. He said that he was just following orders. He drove me to an American civilian doctor. The doctor saw me right away. He examined me and gave me an injection. I was put to bed, and I stayed at the clinic for next six hours. Before leaving he gave me another injection. The injections got rid of most of the pain and slowed down my trips to the toilet.

A couple of days later, I joined my fellow students again for a night trip into the countryside to observe a Phoenix Unit night operation. I was not sure what the unit was about and had trouble getting a clear explanation. I learned later that it was an intelligence operation to eliminate the Viet Cong infrastructure. We were paired with an American soldier that was part of the unit. My guide said his name was Jim. He picked me up at the hotel early that evening, and we went out with his Vietnamese unit. It was pitch black—I could not see a thing, and I did not hear any gunfire. Jim and I were the same age, and we had a long chat during the outing. He refused to tell me his last name or where he was from in the United States. We returned to Saigon very late. Jim suggested that I spend the night at his place because of the curfew. We chatted late into the evening. The next morning Jim took me to breakfast at a local restaurant and drove us around the outskirts of Saigon for several hours. Just before lunch, Jim got a message on his walkie-talkie that I was invited to a dinner party at the home of an embassy official that wanted to meet me. That evening Jim dropped me off at the home of the embassy officer. I did not know anyone at the dinner; I was not sure why I was invited while the other three students were not.

The dinner party was quite interesting, and a couple of civilians got into a serious debate about US support for South Vietnam. As curfew time was approaching, most of the guests left. Our host insisted that I stay the evening with two other guests. After most of the guests left, it was clear that my host had an agenda. The conversation was just short of an interrogation. He did not believe I was who I claimed to be, and he urged me to come clean. Despite his intrusive questions, he had a good sense of humor, and I enjoyed the evening.

The next day the USIA official drove me back to my hotel, and I rejoined my student friends. They were not happy with my "going it alone" mentality. I told them that I was not happy with them wanting to sit around the hotel or hang around the Officers' Club when we had no scheduled meetings. Octavian agreed that they could have done more to see the country. The embassy had organized a reception for the four of us at the deputy chief of mission's (DCM) residence. Suspicions about me intensified when a US embassy courier arrived at the DCM's reception and asked for me. He delivered a note from the Thai ambassador to Vietnam inviting me to visit the Thai embassy. The ambassador's note requested that I visit the embassy to finalize my "official visit" to Thailand. Robert, Daniel, and Octavian were surprised and wondered why they were not invited. I was as surprised as they were about the invitation.

During my visit to Thai embassy, I learned that the Thai ambassador to the United States had arranged the visit for me. I recalled that I had made a courtesy call on Ambassador Panyarachun in Washington, DC, to thank him for speaking at UCLA on behalf of the TJ Club. During the visit, I told him that I was leaving on a trip to Vietnam. The ambassador suggested that I take the opportunity to visit Thailand while I was in Southeast Asia. I told him that I would try to arrange a short visit before returning to the United States. I had no idea that the ambassador had communicated my itinerary with his government and requested an official invitation for me to visit Thailand.

My Vip Visit To Thailand

A week later, I left for Thailand. I was shocked to discover that George, the US embassy official that had taken me to the doctor ten days earlier, was seated next to me on the airplane. He said he was going to Bangkok for a couple of weeks of Rest and Relaxation (R&R). He suggested that I have dinner with him and his wife one night in Bangkok. I accepted his invitation but told him that as a guest of the government, I was not sure about my schedule. George wanted to know how my trip to Thailand had come about. I told him my story. He promised to give me a call at my hotel. The coincidence of his presence on the plane, in the seat next to me, did not escape me.

When the plane landed in Bangkok, the passengers were asked to remain seated until a VIP guest disembarked. The flight attendant came to my seat and asked me to escort her to the exit. A limousine drove up to the airplane and parked next to it. I was able to step from the stairs directly into the limousine. The minister of information was waiting in the limousine, and he gave me a bouquet of flowers as the limo moved toward the VIP lounge. The press and photographers were assembled in the VIP lounge.

Although they took pictures of my arrival, I was instructed to ignore them because they were there to meet someone else. The arriving VIP was South Vietnam's vice-president, Nguyen Cao Ky. He was transiting Bangkok on a return trip from Europe.

My registration at the hotel was taken care of by an aide to the information minister. I was booked into a small suite and given a schedule for the evening. My driver picked me up at the hotel around 7:00 p.m. and drove to the Oriental Hotel for dinner and a show. There were about ten Thai officials present. A traditional Thai dance troupe performed for us. The star attraction was a beautiful Thai dancer. My hosts watched me carefully as I swooned over the beautiful dancer. To our surprise, her identical twin sister joined her during the dance. Even the minister of information had trouble focusing on the two women at once. After the show, we had a wonderful Thai dinner in the hotel.

The minister of information gave me a schedule that included a fifteen-minute meeting with Thai Foreign Minister Thanat Khomen. Also, there were passes for private visits to several tourist sites and shrines. My visit was for ten days with lots of free time on my own. The minister told me that I was free to use the limousine and driver full-time for my stay. He said that he had given my driver a copy of the schedule so that I would not miss any appointments. Finally, the minister said that he was retiring for the evening but had arranged for me to see the Bangkok nightlife. I declined the invitation because I was exhausted after the flight, late show, and dinner. I think the minister was pleased that I decided to call it a night. Every day I visited a different tourist site, including the Reclining Buddha and the palace. I was able to take a couple of trips to the Pattaya Beach area. I had a lot to time on my hands for exploring the city and countryside.

One day I left my hotel to take a walk. A man approached me and said that he knew that I was an "important person" and wanted to make sure that I had a good time in Bangkok. The man waved at my driver who was parked nearby. I took this to as a signal that the stranger was no threat to me. He was carrying a large picture album and showed it to me. He said that he could arrange for me to have anything in the book that I wanted. The book was filled with photos showing every sexual act that one could imagine—women with women, men with men, threesomes, and animals. I was stunned by some of the photos. I told him that I was not interested. He gave me his card and said to call him if I changed my mind. He said that there was no need to worry because he and his people were very discreet. All that day I had trouble getting these photographs out of my mind. That evening I had my first dinner outing with George, my embassy friend from Saigon. I told him about the man approaching me outside the hotel. He was not surprised and told me that Thais had a different view of these kinds of things. He suspected that my hosts sent the stranger to me as a token of their hospitality. He did not seem bothered at all, and he offered no suggestions on how to handle the situation if I was approached again. He laughed when I told him that I had already decided that I was not going to do anything that I might regret later. I remarked that someone took those pictures and that I did not want to appear in the photo album in the future.

My meeting with the foreign minister went well. My driver dropped me off at the Ministry of Foreign Affairs (MFA) where I was met by an aide and ushered into the foreign minister's private office. The foreign minister wanted to know what students on college campuses thought about his government's support for the United States in Vietnam. He said that his government was concerned about the threat of communism to the Thai kingdom and, while Thailand sought peace with its neighbors, it felt obligated to support the South Vietnamese struggle for independence. The meeting was aired on national TV. The sound bite made it appear that I was head of a large delegation of students doing a fact-finding tour for American colleges.

The second dinner I had with George was different. His wife, a Thai woman, joined us for dinner. They had seen the TV coverage of my visit with the foreign minister. I got the impression that they were satisfied I was legit once the saw me on TV. That night we visited a couple of jazz clubs after dinner. It was a great evening. Throughout the visit, my driver was courteous, knowledgeable, and helpful. I invited him to join me for lunch at the tourist sites, but he refused. He said that he could not leave the limo unattended. I was reminded by a foreign ministry official that I should tell the driver when he could leave for lunch. I learned that the driver had not eaten lunch the first two days of my visit. I apologized to the driver.

One day the driver showed up in a Mercedes that had no air-conditioning. He asked if I preferred the Mercedes to the Cadillac. I told him that I preferred the Cadillac because it had air-conditioning. He seemed disappointed. It finally dawned on me that he was freezing in the Cadillac. I suggested that he turn the AC to low. There was no way that I would voluntarily give up of use of the Cadillac. It was much too hot and humid driving around in the Mercedes. About a week into my visit, Octavian, the student from San Francisco State, showed up at my hotel unexpectedly. He asked if he could stay with me. He said he was fed up with Vietnam and "this stupid trip." He told me that Robert had returned to the States just after I flew off to Thailand and that Daniel was still in Vietnam and planning to stay as long as possible. Octavian's arrival turned out to be a good thing. He was easy to talk to, good company, and much more worldly oriented than I was. He talked me into exploring some places that I would have never gone alone. He seemed to have an instinct for finding the interesting nightspots and singles bars in Bangkok. The areas we visited reminded me of my US navy days in Japan.

Return From Southeast Asia

Returning from Vietnam, Charles and I were invited to the Airlie House in Virginia to take part in a seminar on US military involvement in Southeast Asia. After the arrival reception, Charles and I went to our sleeping quarters. We had to share a room with two other people. While dressing for the evening meal and seminar, I looked in the mirror and asked Charles to come and look at what I saw. Charles came over, and I said, "Do you see this? I am a big black token." Charles was mortified, but he knew it was the truth. There were at least seventy people there, and I was the only black.

During cocktails and cigarette breaks, the only people who talked to me were people I had met before. When I walked in the room, I got surprised looks, and the crowd parted before me—implying, from my point of view, that they thought I was out of place. Nonetheless, others eventually came over to introduce themselves. Our sponsors arranged for our group to get as much exposure as possible. I appeared on local television talk shows in Los Angeles and Washington, D. C., and gave speeches at conservative security conferences around the country. I used my words carefully, I was always mindful of the advice I had received from Professor Serfaty. Nevertheless, some of my comments that appeared in conservative newspapers were inaccurate, and they always mentioned that I was a "Negro." My talks dealt with comments I had heard from American soldiers and civilians working in Vietnam. Ironically, my reputation as a black student leader against violence on campus seemed a novelty to some, and I received several invitations to speak on the subject. I even received an invitation to speak at the prestigious "Town Hall of California" discussion group about nonviolence, which was a relief for me. I was tired of discussing my trip to Vietnam.

Chapter Fifteen

Finding Nora, My First Love: Love At First Sight!

When I returned from my trip to Southeast Asia, I had to re-register in school. I do not know why, but the dean of women's office handled the process. As I entered the office, I noticed a beautiful woman sitting at a desk facing the entrance. She was the only person in the office. Nora greeted me with the most precious smile I had ever seen. It was love at first sight. I imagined walking down the aisle in matrimony with this woman even before speaking to her. I had never felt such a strong attraction to anyone before. Finally, I introduced myself and explained that I was re-enrolling after a leave of absence. Nora said that I had come to the right office, and she gave me some papers to complete and sign. I completed the papers, and she went over them to make sure everything was in order. After leaving her office, I was sobered by the thought that such a beautiful woman could not possibly be single. I had neglected to check her finger for a wedding band or engagement ring.

I met Charles for lunch later that day and told him about Nora, and said that I felt strongly that I was going to marry this girl. Charles laughed at my comments and said that he would drop by her office to check her out. That evening, I mentioned to Dan that I had met the girl of my dreams. He responded that he had met a girl that he thought would be perfect for me. He said that he would introduce her to me when I came by his office. We had no idea that we were talking about the same woman. Dan met Nora shortly after her arrival at UCLA. Both worked in the admin building. When I went off to Vietnam, I left my Chevelle with Dan, and he drove it to school periodically. One day he took Nora to lunch in my car. He told her that the car belonged to his roommate and that his roommate was rich. Dan promised to introduce us when I returned from Vietnam.

Just after New Years, I was in the dean of finance's office when Nora dropped by to share some leftover Christmas candy with his office staff. Her office was just across the hall. She was just as beautiful and poised as when I first met her a few weeks earlier. I got the same déjà vu feeling that I had when we first met: I could see us married. The dean introduced us, and we acknowledged having already met. I was glad for the introduction, because with my preoccupation about having a future together, I had trouble remembering her name.

Fearless

The next week, Charles and I were having lunch in the UCLA Terrace Room restaurant. Nora and a friend entered and began looking for a seat. I pointed her out to Charles. He commented that he thought Nora was one of the most beautiful women he had seen on campus. As fate would have it, the only seats available in the room were at our table. Nora and her friend came to our table, and Nora asked if they could join us. Her presence was magical. Charles was smiling and could not contain himself. They thanked us for allowing them to join us. They began a deep discussion and generally ignored us. I noticed that Nora was not wearing a wedding ring. I was convinced that this was no coincidence. I decided to craft a strategy to pursue her.

As I was leaving the Ackerman Student Union that day, I saw the "Spurs" group selling Valentine cards. They viewed themselves as a campus delivery service and charged fifty cents to hand carry a Valentine card to anyone on campus. I decided to make my move. I sent Nora a Valentine card with the text message:

> My Dear Nora,
> Please be my Valentine.
> I love you, but I am afraid.
> Fearless.

The following Monday, I went to Nora's office to confess having sent the Valentine card. She was not there. I offered to leave a message with Mary Jane, the assistant dean of students. Immediately, Mary Jane summoned the dean of women and said excitedly, "This is Fearless!" Dean Nola Stark recognized me as the president of the TJ Club and asked me if I had seen the UCLA *Daily Bruin* that morning. She said that Nora had responded to my Valentine card in the "Personals" column. The response read, "Dear Fearless, don't be a coward. Your Valentine."

Encouraged by her clever reply, I left a note asking Nora to have lunch with me between 11:00 a.m. and 3:00 p.m., any day from Monday through Friday. I left my home telephone number and asked her to call me around 6:30 that evening. Dean Stark promised not to give me away. Nora telephoned me that evening and we chatted for several minutes. She agreed to have lunch with me the next day. I suspect that she was under pressure from the dean to follow up with me.

I picked Nora up the next day, and the first thing she said to me was, "I have been in this car before. Are you Dan Abram's roommate?" Only then did I realize that Nora was the girl Dan was trying to fix me up with all along. I took her to a small café in Westwood. I was very nervous but was determined to discover as much as possible about this fascinating woman. We talked about our backgrounds, and I was surprised to learn that she had been born and raised in Mississippi. I had often thought that I wanted to marry someone with Southern values. Nora had finished her bachelor's degree in business at Alcorn College before coming to California. She was relaxed and seemed surprised that I was interested in her. Frankly, I was beside myself. I had not felt this way about a woman, ever, and my desire to have her increased every time I saw her.

Tying The Knot

The courtship was very fast. Our dates were long and we talked a lot. Nora knew that I was in love with her. On the third date, I told her I that I loved her, and proposed. She did not respond immediately, but I got the impression that she was flattered by my proposal and that a "yes" response was coming. We disagree on how many dates we had before she said yes to my proposal. I remember her saying yes on the fifth date; she still says it was not that quick.

Nora invited me to her apartment for dinner one evening, and her sister, Lela, joined us. I am positive that Lela was there to give me the once over. I liked Lela right away, and I thought the feeling was mutual. The following weekend, Nora invited me over to a family cookout at her brother's home in Los Angeles I met her brother Buford, his wife, Marie, and their two children, Tony and Jeffrey. Lela was there with her husband, Shirley. The family treated me as a special guest and shared with me some family pictures, including several of Nora as a child growing up in Mississippi. I felt very comfortable with the family, and I assumed that Nora had told them of my marriage proposal, although no one mentioned it.

A few weeks later, I broke the news to Mother. I told her all about Nora and promised to bring her to San Bernardino for a visit. Mother was happy for me but had one question. She asked, "What color is she?" Dad was extremely excited and could not wait to meet Nora. I got the impression that having his oldest son married meant something special to him. Both sides of my family loved Nora and were always disappointed whenever I visited them and did not bring her along.

Nora organized a birthday surprise party for me that year and invited all my UCLA friends: Max, Charles, Dan, Bob, and a few others. I was especially pleased that she had invited my brothers and sisters on my father's side of the family. They all showed up. Max suggested that we take a family picture together. It is the only photograph we have of all my siblings on my father's side of the family. Understandably, Dad became emotional when we presented him a large copy of the photograph.

The party took a comical turn when it was time to present the birthday cake. Nora brought out the cake for all to see. Unfortunately, it was in bad shape. Somehow, maneuvering in her friend's kitchen, she dropped the cake just before I arrived. After a conference with the attendees, it was decided that she should present the cake anyway. With lots of laughter, I cut the cake as if it was in fine shape. Nora and I were married three months later at her brother's home in Los Angeles. I was blessed to have my mother and father present at the wedding. As far as I can remember, my mother and father had never attended a function together, on my behalf, except of course, at my conception. There were no more than twenty guests invited to the wedding. Since Nora's mother and father could not make it to the wedding, Buford gave her away. Andrea Hill, Nora's best friend at UCLA, was her maid of honor. My roommate, Dan, was my best man.

Nora, Given Away By Her Brother Buford

Nora And My Wedding Picture

Our wedding reception was held at the UCLA Recreation Center on campus, thanks to Dean Stark. Charles presented us with a remarkable wedding gift: a two-week stay at his family's home in Mexico City and a weekend at their country house in Tepotztlan, Mexico. Charles's brother met us at the airport in Mexico City and drove us to the family home. The house was beautiful! A ten-foot wall surrounded it, and when the gates opened, there were several peacocks walking around the very large garden area. The house was staffed with a full-time housekeeper, cook, and gardener. We also had use of his family's Mercedes for forays out of the city. We drove to the small country house in Tepotztlan, some sixty miles away. We spent a weekend there. It was very romantic. There was a spectacular swimming pool in the front yard. A small waterfall flowed down the mountain. We could see it from the master bedroom. Every evening the caretaker lighted a fire in the fireplace for us. He also did some shopping for us. Because of Charles's generosity, we had a first-class honeymoon.

Charles, Nancy, And Dan (My Roommate And Best Man)

Nora (My Bride), Me, My Mother, Mary, And
My Father, Beebe Charles

The Full-Court Press

After our honeymoon, we returned to the States knowing that I should get a better paying job. Money was tight, and we agreed that if I could graduate early, I might be able to earn some extra money to supplement our income before going off to graduate school. I enrolled in five courses the following winter quarter. I petitioned to use the sixteen credits that I had received from the training course at Patton State Hospital. The five courses, along with the sixteen credits, provided the required one hundred eighty credits I needed to graduate in March instead of June. The downside of it all was that all sixteen credits could only be transferred over as C grades. This brought my overall grade-point average down at bit. But I did not mind since I had a high grade-point average and had been admitted to the doctoral program in international relations at Johns Hopkins University. In addition, I received wonderful news from the fellowships that I had applied for to graduate school. I was awarded the Woodrow Wilson Fellowship, the Danforth Doctoral Fellowship, the American Political Science Doctoral Fellowship for Black Students, and the Ford Foundation Doctoral Fellowship for Black Students, among others. I was accepted to every university I applied to except one, and I received fifty-two unsolicited admissions to graduate programs at schools in the United States and Canada. All the invitations included a letter congratulating me on the number of fellowships that I had won. I was most proud of a letter from the University of California Board of Regents congratulating me on the "unprecedented" number of fellowships, which they said "honored" the University of California. I graduated from UCLA with departmental honors in political science and was named "UCLA Honor Senior." I received a precious gift of a leather-bound yearbook with my name printed on the cover, with an insert that read,

HONOR EDITION OF THE SOUTHERN CAMPUS is given by the Associated Students of the University of California, Los Angeles, to the men and women of the senior class who have best distinguished themselves as Californians in scholarship, loyalty, and service to their alma mater. Beginning with the number one in the year of our Lord, nineteen hundred and twenty-four, it is each year limited in number, of which this is number 923.

I had narrowed my graduate school choices to Stanford University and Johns Hopkins University. Both schools accepted me into their PhD programs with a four-year fellowship. After much discussion with my political science professors, I was persuaded that continuing my education on the east coast would broaden my perspective on international affairs. It was a good move. I believe that if I had chosen to stay in California and attend Stanford University, I would not have made the contacts in Washington, DC, that influenced my decision to focus on foreign affairs and intelligence work.

My Friend Ron

I was still taking care of Uncle Emeal's financial affairs and visiting him every few weeks at the Veterans Hospital. Seeing that I would soon be going to graduate school out of state, I discussed my situation with Uncle Johnny. I explained to him that I was going off to graduate school on the East coast and that I needed to find someone to manage Uncle Emeal's affairs, and to visit him at the VA hospital when necessary. In addition, anyone that replaced me would have to deal with his angry moods and his distrust. I told him that Uncle Emeal once refused to sign a check needed to pay a bill, but that he relented when he thought I was not coming back to see him. Since I did not have a power of attorney over my uncle's estate, I had to rely on persuasive techniques to get him to cooperate. Uncle Johnnie suggested that I see Ron Skipper, a young lawyer in San Bernardino, who had just opened his law practice in town. Uncle Johnnie said that I should remember Ron from high school. The name was familiar, but I could not remember the face. Ron was the quarterback for the San Bernardino High School football team when I was there. Uncle Johnnie said that one of his lawyer friends at King Brother Law Offices was trying to help Ron get on his feet.

Ron did not remember me at first, but I remembered just about everything about him. After all, he had been our local high school football star. Ron brought me up to date on his new practice and talked about his life after high school. Ron said that he had married Wanda O'Brien. I remembered Wanda. All the boys in high school had a crush on Wanda. Of course, as expected, she was the girlfriend of the school's quarterback.

Uncle Emeal In Veterans Hospital With Visiting Celebrity

Ron mentioned some people he was still in contact with after high school: Danny Castro, Junior Howard, Don Sampson, and others. I knew just about everyone he recalled. The more we talked, the more we realized how much we had in common. Our paths had crossed many times before.

Ron's demeanor and professionalism impressed me, and his "can-do" attitude was encouraging. Ron agreed to prepare the paperwork for the "guardianship" that made it possible for me to manage my uncle's affairs from a distance. Mother promised to take care of any local issues and to visit Uncle Emeal on a regular basis. Uncle Emeal agreed to sign the papers, and a member of the hospital staff witnessed it. Ron was a godsend. Our friendship blossomed in leaps and bounds. When my wife and I moved to Paris, France, a few years later, Ron and Wanda were our first visitors. They have graced us with visits to just about every place we have lived outside California, including Washington, D. C.; Paris, France;

Singapore; New York; and Brussels, Belgium. We once invited Ron and Wanda to join us for a boat trip up the Congo River. Unfortunately, they could not make it. It was the only time they did not visit us while we were overseas. Whenever we return to San Bernardino for a visit, Ron and Wanda provided a home away from home. Their generosity and kindness have shown no limits.

Chapter Sixteen

Twist And Turn On My Road To The Cia: Graduate School

In graduate school, my concentration was international relations, Asian area studies, and American foreign policy. Other required courses were International Economics and a foreign language. The first go at my dissertation was "The Nixon Doctrine in Asia." During my second year, I attended the Institut d'Etudes Politiques de Paris (Paris Institute of Political Studies), in Paris, France, to research the similarities and differences between the American and French foreign policy approaches to Southeast Asia. After reviewing my research and my detailed summary of several chapters, my then adviser, Professor Robert Osgood, urged me to change the focus of my dissertation topic to discuss the impact of the so-called Sino-Soviet split on US foreign policy in Asia. The consensus was that my observations would contribute to understanding the Sino-Soviet split itself. My new dissertation was "The Impact of Marxist-Leninist Ideology on the Foreign Policies of Communist States—China and the Soviet Union." Using Chinese and Russian Communist party documents, public foreign-policy statements, and reports of actual behavior in the international arena—particularly examples of Chinese and Soviet intervention in Korea, and Soviet intervention in Eastern Europe, and elsewhere, I challenged the traditional assumption of Western foreign-policy experts that insisted on decoupling Marxist-Leninist political ideology from Soviet and Chinese foreign-policy decision-making. If my challenge were successful, it would raise serious questions about our understanding of Sino-Soviet relations. .

Family Tragedy

After graduate school, I was hired by a company to support research projects and feasibility studies in Asia and Australia. This job was exactly the kind of work I was looking for, but I did not want to be away from my family after Nora became pregnant with our first child. During one my trips to Japan, I was devastated to learn that we had lost our first baby and that Nora was in the hospital. I returned home immediately. The doctor's concern for Nora overshadowed the tragedy of losing our child. It took several months before she was back to normal. I resigned from the research company to look for a job that would keep me closer to home. Prince George Community College hired me to teach in the Veterans Upward Bound Program and to teach a special class called "Introduction to the Social Sciences." I introduced students to the core requirements for academic majors in the social sciences. Unfortunately, after two semesters I was discouraged by my students' apparent lack of interest in their studies. Several students chose to be absent during planned tests, and they complained about having to take the test when they returned to class the next day. Others seemed more interested in socializing than studying. I did not enjoy failing students, so I began to look for another job.

A Johns Hopkins alumnus that worked for the Asia Foundation, a nonprofit organization, mentioned to me about an American spice-extraction company looking for someone to open and manage a satellite office in Singapore. He said that the company president would be visiting Washington, DC, in the a few weeks and would be available to interview candidates for the job. I was unsure if I would qualify for the job since I knew nothing about spices, but I agreed to contact the company for an interview. During the interview, the president said that his company intended to establish an office in Southeast Asia to begin marketing oleoresins (water- and oil-soluble flavor extracts) and natural food colors made from a variety of spices such as chilies, cloves, nutmeg, hops, turmeric, and black peppers. I admitted to knowing very little about spices. Nonetheless, after reviewing my resume and discussing my interest in international affairs, the company president thought I might be a good fit the job. He offered to arrange an interview for me with his company's human resource staff and his board of directors. My main competition, he said, was an in-house employee who had traveled to Southeast Asia on several occasions and was familiar with Indonesian and Malaysian spice growers and suppliers. However, the employee had little marketing experience, and he had never lived overseas. On the other hand, I had no knowledge of the spice-extraction business and was concerned as to whether or not I could handle the job. The president reminded me that the job would be largely marketing and support of their purchasing staff. He was confident that with my knowledge of Southeast Asia, I could do the job. Moreover, if accepted by the board of directors, I would enter a four-month training program on spice extraction and processing at the company's home office in Michigan.

Marcus And Me In Singapore

Our pediatrician convinced us not to give up on having children and Nora got pregnant a few months later. Unfortunately, problems developed a second time. In the seventh month, Nora was hospitalized with a second case of toxemia. There was a serious risk that we could lose both Nora and the baby. The doctors at Georgetown University Hospital worked wonders. Marcus was born by Caesarian, and I was allowed to observe the process through a glass door. We did a lot of praying, and the prayers and support of our church community at the church of Christ in Falls Church, Virginia was overwhelming. Marcus arrived stronger than expected, and Nora's health began to improve almost immediately after delivery. Marcus weighed only two pounds and fourteen ounces and had to remain in an incubator for four weeks. Because of the fine work of Dr. Gerber (yes, his name was Dr. Gerber), we avoided another painful experience. Instead of reflecting on the tragic incident that took our first baby, Melissa Joy, we concentrated on how blessed we were that our son had survived. We decided to settle on a family of three.

New Job Overseas

Shortly after Marcus was born, we learned that I got the job with the spice-extraction company. I traveled to the home office and met with the human resource person and the board of directors. The final phase of employment required an interview with a local psychologist. The psychologist explained that it was company policy to have psychological profiles done on the executive staff. Two remarkable events occurred related to my visit with the psychologist. At the end of our session, the psychologist asked me why I had accepted this job. He said that he was concerned that I might become bored working for this company. Immediately, I thought this was his way of saying that he would not recommend me for employment because I was "overqualified." However, he signed off on my acceptance paper and said that I should think about his comments. I explained to him that I would be opening an office overseas for the company and that I doubted that I would have time to be bored. He said that he did not know this and withdrew his comment. Finally, he said, "You know, they really want you for this job."

I showed up for work the next day and I was ushered into the president's office. He asked me about my visit to the psychologist. I told him that everything went well and that we had a good talk. The president asked if I knew that the psychologist had a fatal heart attack shortly after I left his office. I was stunned. As far as I could tell, the psychologist showed no sign of being ill during our talk. The president said that it was a very sad situation. He said that the psychologist was recovering from a previous heart attack and that he decided to take some time off. When the psychologist did not show up at their vacation spot that evening, the family was concerned and asked a neighbor to go by the house and check on him. Apparently, the psychologist had been in the process of packing his suitcase when he had another heart attack. This one was fatal.

Orientation And Training

The company orientation program was comprehensive. I spent the first month working with the front-office staff learning administrative procedures and shadowing the company vice-president and the purchasing manager. Next, I worked in the laboratory for several weeks, learning how to evaluate the properties of different spices, and how to use the gas chromatograph to measure residual extraction chemicals in spices. The third phase placed me in the company extraction facility for several weeks. This was a "hardhat" area, and I was supplied with proper safety clothing and steel-toe shoes. I observed the process of extracting oleoresin and natural food colors from various spices. Special chemicals and steam were used to dissolve the flavor buds of chilies, garlic, hops, cloves, nutmeg, and other spices. In a similar process, the natural color was extracted from such spices as turmeric and red peppers. The oleoresin and colors were processed in either water- or oil-soluble form, and mixed depending on the planned use. For example, we mixed color extracts from turmeric, red peppers, and other spices to get the butter color for margarine. In some cases, the color was removed from spices designed for such products as mayonnaise and clear sauces.

In the extraction facility, I had lunch with the extraction-plant crew every day at the same time. One day, a worker asked where I was born. I told him where I was born and grew up. "But you have a foreign accent," he said. The other workers agreed, and none seemed to believe that I was American. One worker told me that he had never seen a "person of color" working in the front office, unless he was a foreigner. All agreed. Finally, one of the workers asked the personnel officer if I was an American. Only then were they satisfied that I was telling the truth. I thought it curious and humorous; there was nothing I could do to convince them that I was born in the USA. This incident reminded me of my earlier experience working in Watts, California, while a student at UCLA. My GED students assumed I was from a Caribbean nation because of my alleged accent. My demeanor was also an issue during my overseas experience. While I was living in Singapore, one visiting sailor embraced me because he thought I was from Senegal; and while representing the United States at a reception in Europe, I was often mistaken for an African diplomat, especially when speaking a foreign language. But in Africa, I had a different experience. Our housekeeper told me one day, "You are not like us even though your skin is the same color." I asked him to explain what he meant. He said that he had looked in our refrigerator and noticed that we ate different food. He said, "You eat the same food as white people." Apparently, in his view, we are what we eat. On other occasions overseas, I was viewed by African diplomats as just another rich American.

Republic Of Singapore

After my orientation and training, we moved to Singapore. A week after our arrival, the company vice-president arrived, and we left Singapore for a month visit to Indonesia and Malaysia. He helped me to "hit the ground running" by introducing me to clients and Indonesian officials, and having me tour spice extraction facilities in Java and Sumatra. My family was ensconced in a nice hotel in Singapore. Nora was tasked with finding us an apartment to rent and learning about the city. I was not happy about leaving her in Singapore, alone, after only a week. Nonetheless, she managed to take care of our housing problem while caring for our six-month-old baby. When I returned, she had found a nice apartment, arranged to purchase additional furniture, hired a permanent babysitter, and made a few helpful friends in the business community.

Finding office space in Singapore, filing work permits, hiring staff, and calling on potential clients proved quite taxing. In addition, I traveled to Indonesia at least twice a month to oversee the operations of our two extraction plants that we ran jointly with the Indonesia Agricultural Ministry. During my travels, I put together a pictorial album for the company to show how certain spices used by the company were grown, how they looked at different stages of maturity, and how spices were harvested. On the marketing side, I negotiated the company's first contract with the Singaporean government to provide spice oleoresins for use in sausages and other food products.

The company provided me with a state-of-the-art mini-laboratory, including a gas chromatograph to test the parts per million of extracting solvents remaining in our natural food products. My work also took me to Australia, the Philippine Islands, Hong Kong, Taiwan, and Bali where I met clients, negotiated sales, and resolved quality-control problems concerning our products. I visited several agricultural areas to evaluate potential proprietary spice-growing opportunities, including a two-week visit to Papua New Guinea, arguably the most primitive country in the world.

Papua New Guinea was an experience that would test my patience and resolve. The government hoped to interest our company in establishing a spice-growing area to provide cash crops for the local population. I was met at the airport by a government official who escorted me to my hotel. The next day, I was surprised when an Australian government contractor arrived at the hotel to escort me around the country. During my first visit to the agricultural ministry, I was informed that since I would be traveling to some remote areas, it was best that a "white" person accompany me to the interior regions. They explained that because I was of Negroid origin,

Visit To Black Pepper Plantation In Sumatra, Indonesia

the local population, also black, would look upon me as a potential threat because I did not speak their language, described as "one talk." He said that blacks that did not speak the same local village dialect were greeted with suspicion. There were over three hundred dialects spoken in the country. Apparently, the country was always under threat of tribal wars because of women being kidnapped, and neighboring tribes stealing farm animals (mainly pigs, which are revered there). More than once, the skirmishes were so intense that the Australian army had to intervene to help the Papua New Guinea government restore order.

I was very happy to have the Australian contractor with me as we visited the areas. Many of the locals, both men and women, were dressed in scant clothing and the men usually carried axes or clubs. Semi-nudity was prevalent throughout the hinterland. Women wore only skirt-like dresses, and men wore loin clothes that often did not cover all of their genitals. The locals stared at me very hard and seemed ready to pounce if I showed interest in their possessions, especially their women. According to my Australian guide, during World War II, a contingent of black American soldiers and airmen were stationed in the country. He said that the country used to be so backward that the locals were astounded to see black men driving tractors and flying airplanes. Nonetheless, I was permitted only scant association with the villagers. In the end, I determined that the soil in the areas identified for cash crops was unsuitable for the types of spices we wanted to grow there.

Living in Singapore was a wonderful experience for my family. The people were friendly, the social activities were exciting, and the restaurants were fantastic. We found a wonderful church community and were able to establish close fellowship with local worshipers. We were active in Rotary International, the Singapore American Club, and the Singapore International Petroleum Club. I served as the Singapore American Club's food and beverage chairman for six months, vice-president and administrative chairman for one year, and acting president for nine months. During this time, I helped oversee major renovations to the club that included a new parking structure, and tennis and squash courts. I studied the Chinese language for two years and learned to play golf and squash. I was a social fixture at parties given by American companies and the American embassy, and at functions hosted by the Singapore government. We participated in the American Club bowling league, and we were members of a softball team sponsored by American companies. Our uniforms were full replicas of our US baseball teams' uniforms.

Nora and I met some wonderful friends in Singapore. My best friend there was Charles "Dick" Bowers, the administration counselor at the US embassy. Nora introduced him to me at a going-away dinner party for another American Foreign Service officer, Felix Bloch, whom I first met while a graduate student at Johns Hopkins University. We often vacationed with Dick and his wife, Karin, and their two children. The four of us vacationed together on Rawa and Tiaman, two resort islands off Mersing, Malaysia, in the South China Sea. Dick and I arranged our work schedule so that we could have lunch together at a Chinese restaurant every Wednesday to practice our Chinese language skills. Life was good. The downside was that Singapore was a long way from home. Nora's father became seriously ill while we were there, and the trip back to the United States took over twenty-two hours.

When the company made a decision to move the Singapore office to Jakarta, Indonesia, in order to be closer to our spice suppliers and extraction facilities, Nora and I had to make a difficult decision. The living conditions in Jakarta were less than ideal when compared to Singapore. In addition, Marcus was just turning four years old, and we wanted to get him acclimated to his home country. We decided that it was best for our family if I resigned from the company and we returned to the United States. Fortunately, when word got around that I was job hunting, I received several offers from my American contacts in Singapore. I accepted a job with an international petroleum supply company that was looking for a person to manage its office in New York City.

New York City, New York

Living in New York was an exciting experience. Our apartment was in a new building near Fifty-fifth and Broadway, and only a short walk from Carnegie Hall and the Theater District. Soon after our move to New York, Nora got a wonderful job working in the business division at CBS News. We placed Marcus in a nearby preschool, and Nora dropped him at school before walking to her office. My office was located on the East side of town, and I took a bus or subway to work. My job was to manage an office that involved contacts with foreign petroleum-supply firms located in

New York. I had a substantial budget for business outings at restaurants, Broadway plays, and memberships in sports clubs to entertain clients. Also, we attended a church on the Upper East Side that had an active outreach program to the local community. I taught part-time on Saturdays at our Learning English through the Bible program at the World Trade Center.

Despite our love for New York, I was increasingly unhappy with my job. Often I had little expertise available to support negotiations with foreign companies interested in leasing petroleum-drilling equipment from our company. It was as if the home office was more interested in having a high-profile presence in New York than running an effective office representing their business interests. Consequently, there were just too many unproductive meetings to my liking. After two years I was ready to move on, and I starting applying for jobs in different areas of the country, including several international research companies in Washington, DC, and California. Nora was unhappy about the prospects of leaving her job in New York, but agreed to move if I found a better job.

One evening a representative from the Central Intelligence Agency (CIA) called on us at our home in New York. He told us that I had "come to the agency's attention" and that I was someone they needed for an unspecified job. We were stunned. I was positive that I must have been vetted by a CIA person during my visit to Vietnam several years earlier, or maybe even during my three years in Singapore. These were the only places that I could think have where I might have met someone working for the CIA that had gotten close enough to evaluate my background. The officer pointed to my international experience, academic credentials, foreign languages (French, Spanish, and rudimentary Chinese), and personality traits, which he said made me an ideal candidate for their organization. He also said that the agency had been making an effort to increase their staff of minority intelligence officers for covert field operations. In this regard, he said that I had come highly recommended. Nora and I were intrigued as the agency officer outlined the job and what I would be doing. The offer seemed more attractive when the officer explained that Nora would be aware of my activities where possible, and where appropriate. Nora and I agreed to consider the opportunity and get back to him. He left his business card with us.

Been There, Done That!

I was definitely a "people person," and I seemed to have no trouble making contact with strangers and selling products, and I was good at learning foreign languages. However, I had never considered working for an intelligence organization. I remembered a conversation I had with then CIA Director Richard Helms while in graduate school at his first speech to an academic audience. During our chat, Director Helms asked if I had ever considered working for CIA. Not surprised by my negative response, he said, "You ought to think about it. I think you have what it takes." Several years had passed since my conversation with the director, so I do not think this played a role in the CIA approaching me.

My interest in foreign affairs dated back to junior high school when I won a geography contest. I was interested in foreign cultures and languages, and dreamed of traveling abroad. In addition, I was savvy streetwise. Despite his antipathy for me, my stepfather, Shorty, schooled me in techniques for braving back alleys and the importance of keeping secrets, and to "think out of the box." These concepts helped me to understand covert activity and to maneuver in potentially dangerous situations at a young age. I recognized that intelligence tradecraft training was similar to some of the tactics I had learned from Shorty. In addition, Mother impressed upon me the importance of self-reliance and taking responsibility for my actions. I believe her positive (and negative) examples gave me the confidence to work independently without fear or fretting—something I had to do in Singapore and Indonesia in business. I learned the value of leadership and teamwork in the US Navy, and I found comfort in comradery. Finally, I discovered that my years in the navy and at the post office would count as qualifying years toward government retirement. The cards seemed tilted toward the CIA as a possible profession.

Chapter Seventeen

The Central Intelligence Agency: A Culmination Of Experiences

Changing jobs meant giving up a lucrative position in New York for a risky life in intelligence collection. The recruiting officer arranged for me to visit Washington in order complete the necessary paperwork. My background check took several months, followed by a polygraph. I completed a battery of psychological tests that confirmed I had the necessary character traits for covert intelligence work. Finally, I was commissioned as an intelligence officer. At the same time, unbeknownst to Nora, CBS was planning to renovate the Evening News Division in New York and relocating its staff to Washington. Nora was offered a job in the Washington office working for Dan Rather, former anchor of CBS News.

Field tradecraft training was intensive and exhaustive. New case officers had to demonstrate an understanding of intelligence sources and methods. I need not discuss the particulars of my training in detail since there are so many books available that adequately describe the training case officer in detail (see Annex). In addition, there are some very good books that explain espionage terminology and the morality of espionage. For example, Fred Hitz's book *The Great Game: Espionage in an Age of Uncertainty*, James

Olson's *Fairplay: The Moral Dilemmas of Spying* and Floyd Paseman's *A Spy's Journey: A CIA Memoir* are excellent reads. During my career, I had personal contact with these authors. Also, I would recommend Robert Ludlum's *Tristan Betrayal*, Dusko Popov's *Spy Counterspy*, and Victor Cherkasin's *Spy Handler: Memoirs of a KGB Officer* for those interested in agent handling and counterintelligence operations.

In general, my duties as a case officer involved human intelligence collection (HUMINT). Essentially, a case officer in the Directorate of Operations (National Clandestine Services) is tasked with collecting information important to US government security and economic interests. Our job is to assess a person's character in order to determine if they can "handle" keeping secrets, by worming our way into his or her circle of friends and winning his or her confidence. Obviously, we want to find those individuals who are willing to spy on their country or on groups hostile to the United States and its Allies. Once recruited, agents are trained in basic intelligence tradecraft to collect information discreetly and to avoid being discovered by local counterintelligence organizations. Both the case officer and his agent must have a keen sense of their surroundings, be familiar with surveillance detection, and have convincing cover stories for their "status" (why we are in a certain location) and "action" (why they are with certain persons or asking certain questions). Finally, training is provided for producing intelligence in a format that can be readily used or interpreted by case officers and CIA analysts.

There are a variety of covers employed to meet foreign nationals. These include operating under alias and under "nonofficial cover" or "official cover." To facilitate opportunities to meet targets, I attended diplomatic receptions, social gatherings, foreign-policy forums, and trade shows in several different modes. In this regard, case officers must be adept at role-playing and at vetting individuals using a variety of established methods. Once fully recruited and polygraphed, it was incumbent on the case officer to monitor and manage agent operations. Depending on the information desired, technical officers are brought in to assist with specific training and tasking. In most cases, an agent's life is in his case officer's hands. Our job is to protect him from making mistakes that can get him arrested for unauthorized association with foreigners, which will certainly lead to imprisonment or the death penalty. Therefore, agents are provided with primary and secondary clandestine communication plans or devices

Me And Me

to arrange secure meetings. It is extremely rare for a case officer to involve himself in direct intrusion into a foreign ministry building or military base. We recruit locals to do this kind of activity. Imagine the consequences of a foreign official caught searching a government office in another country.

There are several reasons a person will spy for a foreign intelligence organization: people volunteer their services because they have an identity of interest with a certain government, or they are concerned about what is happening in the world and believe the CIA can do something about it. Some individuals believe that passing information to another country will help put pressure on their own country to change policies, or they might want to earn favor hoping to relocate to the United States.

On occasion, it may be necessary to approach an individual with a "cold pitch." This approach is direct, discreet, and not without preparation and evaluation of potential success or possible blowback. Money is usually an important factor in cold pitch. On the other hand, revenge has proven to be the least desirable reason to recruit an individual. An agent will have a different agenda and may want to use CIA as a tool to accomplish personal ends. Finally, in some cases, an individual might turn down a recruitment pitch, however presented, but will want to continue a social relationship with the case officer. In this case, the individual will jealousy guard the case officer's identity. We do make friends, sometimes, lifelong friends.

Some Uncommon C.I.A. Operations.

I had many interesting adventures as a case officer, some exciting, some not so exciting, some dangerous, and some not so dangerous. The most difficult job an intelligence officer has is maintaining his or her cover. In many cases, we must work at a cover job during the day, and engage in our clandestine work at night or on weekends. If the cover job requires a full day's work, spending time in meetings at night can be exhausting. We are lucky if our cover job brings us in direct contact with targets of interest. Many books published on intelligence activities, fiction and nonfiction, fail to mention the stress and strain on case officers maintaining cover jobs to protect their true identity. In reality, spy "tradecraft" is common sense. Humans are human, and all of us share similar emotions, desires, and need for recognition and adventure. We are familiar with using deception as a tool to get what we want. One psychologist likens the process of recruiting an agent to courting a love interest. Consequently, it does not take much to recruit someone who would like to experience his or her adventurous side.

Abort, And Try Again

There are some unique circumstances that case officers often find themselves in. Some situations are hilarious, others deadly serious. For example, on one occasion in foreign country, I had been casing a location on the same day and time for weeks, following the same route. The day before the scheduled package drop, it rained very hard. Nevertheless, the next day the drop conditions seemed the same, so we agreed to implement the operation. That night as I followed my route and approached the drop site, someone on the other side of the street began yelling, but I could not make out what he was saying or to whom he was yelling. It was very dark, and I knew the person could not see who I was, so I ignored him and continued on my predetermined route. Sudden I found myself in the bottom of a large hole, waist deep in water. The city had removed a tree that day and left the hole in the ground uncovered. I aborted the operation. Truthfully explaining why the operation was aborted, and writing a cable to Headquarters describing what happen, was a little embarrassing. A few weeks later, I was obliged to repeat the operation. Happily, this time all went well.

The Doctor's Assistant

Another situation proved unique, and I doubt that many case officers found themselves in this type of situation. An agent complained to me that he was suffering from a bad case of hemorrhoids and asked if I could have an American doctor treat his problem. He told me that in his country, men suffering from hemorrhoids are suspected of engaging in anal sex with other men, and that this would hurt his effectiveness as an agent. In our discussion on how to handle the situation, we agreed that the agent was correct regarding the negative impact on his reputation. A local doctor might be tempted share his medical condition with friends. Because this was a highly valued agent, we concluded that it was worth the risk to bring in a doctor to treat him. We decided to avoid the usual safe house and met late one night in another safe house in the countryside. In order to avoid undo attention from neighbors, I was obliged to hold a flashlight while the doctor lanced the agent's hemorrhoids and closed the exposed veins. I left it up to the doctor to report the success of the surgery to Headquarters.

The Double Agent

An agent that worked with us for almost two years came under suspicion of being a "double agent." The agent was recruited in a third country and turned over to me when he returned to his native country. Shortly thereafter, I turned the agent over to another case officer. During a routine polygraph examination, the agent showed indications of deception on the question of whether he was working for another intelligence service. I was recalled to a third country to attend the polygraph and to translate for the polygraph operator. The agent steadfastly claimed his innocence during my presence. When he realized that the polygraph operator was not going to drop the subject, using excellent English, the agent asked if he could talk to the operator without my presence. This was a shock to both of us. We had no idea what he was going to say, especially if he was going to accuse me of malfeasance or treason. After several minutes, I was asked to return to the room. The polygrapher said that the agent had a confession to make. The agent apologized for his deception and said it was difficult to face me after his duplicity had been exposed. He said that I had been a good friend during the time I handled him, and that he wanted me to forgive his dishonesty. Finally, he confessed to me that he was working for another intelligence service, and that he had been recruited by the other service before CIA recruited him. Further, he swore that he had not revealed his association with the CIA, nor had he identified any of the officers he had worked with. According to the polygraph operator, the agent showed no deception on this point.

The agent identified the foreign intelligence service he worked for, the targets he was given, and the type of information he obtained and reported. Asked why he had agreed to work with CIA, the agent said that it was purely financial. He was being paid by both services. Finally, the agent agreed to work against the foreign intelligence service on our behalf. He agreed to report his tasking by his other intelligence agency, the aliases of his foreign handlers, the individuals he suspected had been recruited by the foreign intelligence service, and to identify all the indoor and out-door meeting sites and safe houses used by the foreign intelligence services. Doubling-back agents often netted a wealth of information on how other foreign intelligence services did business.

Caught Between Aliases

Operating under alias can be problematic. Improper backstopping can prove disastrous to an operation and to the safety of a case officer if the backstopping agency, company, or person forgets to follow procedures when contacted by someone investigating his background. On occasion, I have been in an awkward position because the backstopping person has gone on vacation or lunch without briefing his or her replacement. This is always a most worrisome problem for case officers working undercover in foreign countries. If arrested while working under nonofficial cover by a foreign government security service, one rarely has diplomatic immunity.

Once, I met an ambassador from an important country that agreed to discuss his country's position on a delicate international situation. We met at a foreign-policy forum and luncheon. This was a good cover for our meeting. While chatting with the ambassador before the event, I happened to look over his shoulder and saw another diplomat smiling and waving to me. This diplomat knew me by a different name, and I had no idea that he would be at this forum. Acting quickly, I excused myself from the ambassador and intercepted the diplomat before he could reach us. I pulled him aside and told him that I had been looking for him and wanted to arrange a lunch with him. I promised to telephone him the next day at his office. The diplomat was pleased and walked off to talk to someone else. This was not the end of the story. While sitting with my first ambassador friend, I just happened to notice an empty seat at a table next to ours. The name card was readable from where I was sitting. I almost fell out of my chair when I realized that person was a graduate school alumnus. I had not seen him in some time, and I knew he would react with pleasure to seeing me and want to introduce me to his friends.

I was in a quandary as to how to handle this situation, but I had to move fast. I had several choices. None of them were good. I could feign illness and leave the conference the moment I saw him enter the room, which meant losing an opportunity to continue my debriefing of the ambassador. I could approach my friend and explain to him that I was a last-minute arrival and took the place of a fictitious person that did not show. Under no circumstances could I reveal my CIA affiliation. The problem solved itself. My friend did not show at the luncheon. This type of situation explains why a case officer will not sit with his or her back to the entrance of a bar or restaurant. If a case officer is engaged in meeting, he or she can acknowledge or intercept friendly visitors while at the same time hiding the face of the person he is meeting with.

The Fleeting Walk-In

Once a visitor walked into our embassy and asked to talk to someone about a problem. The receptionist asked the man what he wanted to talk about so that he could contact the appropriate office. The man said that he was looking for political and financial support to send all black people in his country back to Africa. The receptionist, maintaining his professionalism, telephoned me and explained the purpose of the man's visit. He told the visitor that someone would see him as soon as possible. When I exited the elevator, I saw a tall white European man standing in the lobby. I approached him, identified myself as the officer on duty, and asked him how I could help him. He shook my hand and said, "I think I have my answer. Thank you," and departed. It was very difficult for the receptionist to maintain his composure, but he lost it after the man left, and so did I.

Me, Retired.

The Double Walk-In

On another occasion, two men came to our office and asked to talk to someone in the CIA. Only one of the men spoke. He told the receptionist that he was a local national but that his friend was from another country and wanted to defect to the United States of America. The receptionist contacted the duty officer, who happened to be me, and relayed the man's request. The two men were ushered into a conference room to wait for my arrival. In cases like these, there are certain procedures that we use for such eventualities. During our meeting, the local interpreter said that his friend did not speak English. I asked the interpreter how they met. He said that he had met the defector a couple of hours before on a street corner near the train station. The defector had approached him and asked if he spoke his native language. By chance, he spoke the defector's language.

This was a very awkward situation since we did not have anyone in the office that spoke the defector's unusual language. Consequently, his interpreter friend, who was a local national, was aware of everything we said to the person about his desire to defect, and why. Through the interpreter, the defector attempted to describe the kind of information he wanted to share with the US government in exchange for resettlement in the United States. I stopped him from sharing his information in order to protect our defector procedures should the information prove useful. I made the decision to refer the defector to a special refugee center for protection and promised to contact him later in the day. I gave both people strict instructions not to discuss their contact with anyone. They agreed. Unfortunately, the defector was adamant that the interpreter remain with him during his discussions with US government officials. Since the defector was from a country that was adversarial to US interests, we flew in an officer who spoke the defector's native language to debrief him. In the meantime, I was able to convince the defector that sharing his intentions and sensitive information with his interpreter was unfair, as it put his interpreter friend in danger if the wrong people learned that he had helped the man defect. The results were positive; the man agreed to meet with an officer that spoke his language without his interpreter friend.

Cover And Its Implications

Cover is used by many people in some fashion or another, but more formally by intelligence services and certain elements of law enforcement. The use of cover implies the use of deception regarding one's identity, organization, or motives. Usually, there are some aspects of cover that require a measure of reality. For example, cover can be used to provide a plausible explanation for one's motives or actions. A false driver's license cannot say that you are six feet tall when you are only five feet tall, or list that you are male when you are obviously female. On the other hand, details about family, education, travel, and occupation can be used to explain who you are, where you are from, and why you are present at a certain location. If caught in the wrong place with an agent, one might confess to the so-called "real" reason for being there: having an affair, or any other reason to avoid confessing that you are engaging in espionage.

Reflections On Race And Spying

On occasion, I have been asked if my race was ever a negative factor in conducting spy operations. Actually, I found it useful to play the "race card" when it served my purpose. Once, an East European diplomat became suspicious of my line of questions and asked me I worked for the CIA. I told him that he should know that the "CIA doesn't hire black people." The idea fit his country's view of America as a place where most blacks lived in total servitude, and he opened up and provided me with intimate details on his background, training, and function at his embassy. We established a friendly relationship, and I introduced him to one of my colleagues, who eventually elicited important intelligence information from this diplomat.

At a reception in a foreign capital city, a diplomat commented to one of my colleagues that he had visited New York City recently and was astonished to see so many American blacks in responsible positions on television and in business. My colleague decided to play a game with this foreign diplomat. He called me over and introduced me to him. He told the diplomat that I was his boss. The diplomat seemed dumbfounded but managed to keep his composure. We chatted for a few minutes and I excused myself. A few months later, the diplomat walked into an American embassy and requested political asylum in the United States. He said that he was upset that that his government had lied to him about social conditions in America. He also said that he had sensitive information to share.

At first glance, many foreign diplomats often assumed that I was an official from an African country. When they learned that I was American, I became a drawing card. They assumed that I must be important or well-connected politically to be in the US Foreign Service. One perceptive diplomat suspected that I worked for CIA and that I was probably the "CIA station chief" because I was "different" and drove a big American car.

Luck sometimes played a big role in our operations. Once, I met a diplomat at a party hosted by a European ambassador. A diplomat from a third country observed that I was American and approached me, seemingly eager to speak to me. He asked if we could have lunch in the coming weeks. Seeing that this diplomat was from an important nation, I accepted the invitation, and we decided on a date, on the spot. At the lunch, the diplomat confessed that he had not been paid in three months and that he had some information to share about the new government in his country. Surprised, he handed me several official documents labeled "Secret," then asked me for a loan. He promised more documents in exchange for money to feed his family, and said he would like to discuss a formal arrangement. Ironically, he never questioned whether or not I was an intelligence officer. Nonetheless, the information proved useful, and we were able to establish a long-term working arrangement.

On the other hand, there were racist ideas within the agency that often surfaced. A few senior white colleagues, who claimed to have a unique understanding of certain areas of the world, argued that black Americans were not suitable for working in certain countries because they were vulnerable to recruitment by a foreign power or because some foreigners, especially Asians and some Europeans, did not respect American blacks and saw them as "rehabilitated slaves." How they came by this information is a mystery. On one occasion, headquarters (HQ) rejected a request from a chief of station (COS) in Asia that my TDY assignment be cancelled because, being black, he did not think I would be effective for a certain operation. On arrival, despite his misgivings, the COS greeted me cordially and explained his reasoning. In spite of his opinions, he agreed to allow the operation to go forward with all the support I needed. I looked forward to the challenge. The operation was more successful than expected. Moreover, it turned out that an aide working in the foreign minister's office in this country was an alumnus, and he arranged for me to meet several of the country's high officials socially that our COS had been unable to meet. Just before my departure, the COS dropped by my hotel room to apologized to me and to admit that he learned a valuable lesson. In addition, he wrote a very flattering cable to HQ lauding my accomplishments.

There was one other case where a COS was anxious to debunk racist ideas floating around the Agency. I was tasked to meet a white foreign diplomat from a country generally characterized as racist toward foreign minorities. In addition, this diplomat was cool to every American diplomat that had previously approached him. At a reception, I introduced myself to the diplomat and after a long conversation, he accepted my invitation to have lunch together. The diplomat shared information with me that confirmed our suspicions about his political views. In some circumstances, foreigners viewed meeting an American minority official as a unique experience. It was easier for me to establish and maintain contact with foreigners that liked Americans but were concerned about being seen with a white American diplomat, the assumption being that the majority of white American diplomats were CIA officers. Amazingly, it took the CIA many years to accept this reality, and it was not until the late sixties that the agency made a concerted effort to recruit case officers from minority groups that could work effectively in certain foreign environments. I suspect the inroads the Soviet Union and China were making to recruit third world nationals were an important factor in this change.

Several older retired case officers admit that they could not identify more than one or two African-American case officers working undercover overseas before the seventies. In addition, promotions for minorities to higher positions in CIA were slow due to this mentality. Speaking from experience, some minority officers were assigned to high positions at HQ such as division chiefs, chiefs of stations overseas, and other positions but were not promoted to the appropriate grade level normally associated with these high level positions. Instead, financial bonuses and certificates acknowledging Exceptional Performance or service were given to employees and noted in their personnel files. Fortunately, by the time I retired, this mentality had changed dramatically.

Overall, spying is a unique profession, and understanding human nature and being able to assess our situational environment accurately are essential elements in being a successful case officer. History has shown that intelligence collection is an integral part of a government's responsibility to protect its citizens and itself. A country that ignores the signs that another country might want to conquer it or take its resources will soon find itself in slavery and poverty. HUMINT is designed to confirm or deny the truth about an adversary's intentions where technology has its limitations.

Determining what is in the mind of a foreign leader usually requires some form of personal contact. There is no excuse for self-deception or naiveté with regard to foreign relations when a nation's people, values, and culture are potentially threatened by adversaries.

Chapter Eighteen

Conclusion—How I Got Over

My greatest personal achievement was learning to decouple my self-image from my negative childhood experiences.

Odell Lee

I have tried to imagine what my life would be like if I had linked my self-worth to my negative childhood experiences. It was not easy bearing up under the forceful hand of my mother and the fiery darts of my last stepfather. My Uncle Johnnie helped me to maintain my sanity by encouraging me to look forward to the day when I would put it all behind me. However, my conflict with Shorty had become more violent, and I was sure that the next fight would be more than just a standoff. I feared that one of us would get hurt. Despite Mother's frequent outbursts and her brutal use of her ironing cord to punish her children, I believe she cared deeply about each of us. Looking back, it was Mother's advice to me that proved to be the single most important factor in helping me see my own strength and courage. She urged me to trust the integrity of my inner voice and muster the courage to follow my dreams. Mother was a fighter all her life and dared to go against the tide. Unfortunately, too often she took her honesty to an extreme and refused to step back or seek an honorable compromise when faced with logical opposition to her point of view. I never heard Mother blame others for her shortcomings nor claim that she was pushed into making certain choices. Nevertheless, she confessed to me that there was also a downside to being her own person: in her twilight years, she found herself alone.

My stepfather was not all bad, either. Despite Shorty's antagonistic attitude toward me, I will always admire his survival instincts and his commitment to support our family. He taught me a good deal about life on the street, including how to watch my back, how to assess potential risks, and how to respond calmly to the unexpected. I am sure that this influence was a factor in my courageous decision to join the CIA. In addition, Shorty was always honest with me, but in a brutal way. He did not pretend to like me, even when I was his "bagman." He had no qualms about calling on me for help when the family was in jeopardy. I learned to adjust to his changing reactions to me, which were often difficult to predict. Uncle Johnnie helped me to temper my anger at Shorty for the better part of my youth. He stressed that I could handle my difficulties if I learned patience and perseverance. This strategy worked for a while but began to fray as Shorty's attitude became increasingly hostile toward me. Mr. and Mrs. Hooks were always willing to entertain me when I had a few minutes to get away from my parents. I felt a sense of well-being around them. My memories of their compassion and gentleness will always remain dear to me, and I still wonder how my life would have been different had the Hooks agreed to adopt me.

As I adjusted to navy life, I discovered that my caregiving responsibilities had inculcated in me a spirit of compassion for others. I saw that people needed friendship and respect no matter what their lot in life. I learned that I was not alone, and it was heartening to know my shipmates' basic psychological needs were no different from my own. My friendships with Boyson, Mike, Jim, Bill, and others proved the commonality of our life circumstances.

Meeting my biological father filled a deep void in my life. Dad and I spent many nights talking about our life experiences. Ironically, neither of us saw great merit in discussing what might have been if he had been with me during the whole of my childhood, although the thought was never far from my mind. On the one hand, I was disappointed that Dad had not taken me by the hand and told me what to do with my life. I can thank him for not trying to direct my steps or make me his clone. Dad knew that being reunited with him would not solve my problems, and that being together might even surface a few new ones. I can recall the night he asked me, "What are you going to do when you get out of the navy?" I realized for the first time that I was an adult, and that Dad expected me to think for myself and determine my own way.

My brothers and sisters on Mother's side of our family trusted me to take care of them, and I loved them for it. I was their second father. On my dad's side of the family, my brothers and sisters accepted me as their big brother and let me be the icon of unity for the family. I felt loved by all of my siblings, except one: my brother Willie. I learned a valuable lesson from him, as well: on occasion, it is necessary to fight for freedom and personal dignity. I am glad that I did not let my negative experiences with Mother, Shorty, Willie, and others turn me against the world, and against myself.

Friends have played a significant role in helping me to overcome my childhood disappointments and adolescent indiscretions. Who knew that letting people into my life, despite the potential dangers of betrayal, would prove my psychological salvation? I was blessed with certain personality traits that make it easy to win the affections of friends and colleagues. Whatever the source of this gift, people seemed to notice my compassion for others.

Friendship And Good Character

Some years ago, I addressed a group of high school seniors that were preparing to go off to college. Every year my church invited a speaker to offer his or her thoughts to the graduating high school seniors about life in the real world. In my talk, I recalled my recent experiences while teaching a course at a local community college. I counseled young men and women who had high academic potential, but had lost their way because of misplaced loyalty to rebellious friends, blind associations with social movements, or just simply faulty thinking about things important in life. Speaking to the students about my childhood relationships, I commented on how fortunate I had been to make friends that offered sound advice on how to manage my life. I admitted that not all the advice offered fit my developing personal outlook, but I was willing to listen, and I tried to discern the best road to travel. For example, a friend talked me into joining the US Navy, thus helping me to escape my psychologically and physically abusive dysfunctional family; friends helped me adjust to the US Navy's well-constructed value system; and after returning home from the navy, a friend helped me find my first real job. I acknowledged that a friend goaded me into going to college and helped me to achieve a measure of academic success. In addition, a friend helped me to revisit my faith in God, which allowed me to develop a spiritual mindset that has guided me to this day. Finally, a friend recommended me for a job in the US Central Intelligence Agency, where I had a successful career as a case officer. The straight talk seemed to resonate with the seniors and their parents, and I ended my talk with the following comments:

"No matter what road you take in life, choosing your friends will have a lot to do with your personal happiness and professional success. Whether in school, on the job, or at church, people will always judge you by the company you keep. Believe me; it is true, though it may seem very unfair. Is it not logical for people to assume that birds of a feather flock together? Indeed, our understanding of nature shows this idea to be generally true: people tend to keep company with those who think like them and desire the same things as they do. So how can it be too harsh when others judge you as being of the same character as those you run with? Don't we all pre-judge others, from time to time?

"In my life, I have been privileged to make friends with people of many different nationalities, ethnic groups, and value systems. In these relation-ships, I have tried to choose people of good character and personal integrity as my friends. Let me tell you what I mean by good character and per-sonal integrity. By good character, I mean compassionate people who have respect for others, intelligent people who have the mental toughness to do the right thing and are not ashamed of what others may think and finally, people who understand that there is more to life than what we possess or being a member of the so called "in crowd." By personal integrity, I mean people with honest hearts—people who respect themselves, and are willing to do what is right because it is the right thing to do. I firmly believe that no other human trait can make up for the lack of personal integrity. It is the most essential trait of honorable men and women. People of good char-acter and personal integrity will always respect you in good and bad times.

They will help you reinforce your strengths as you grow and mature in your personal, professional, and spiritual life. I encourage you to choose friends that will help you to develop a large measure of personal integrity and good character. I know you will make some mistakes—we all do; but keeping your spiritual focus will lessen the power of those who seek to mislead you or bring you down." I pointed out to the students that I had derived some positive lessons from my turbulent childhood which helped me to develop an important insight into the good and bad aspects of human nature. This helped me to keep a cool head in the face of antagonistic and ambiguous situations—an essential requirement for intelligence work.

The Things That Kept Me Focused

In my first adult "one-on-one" conversation with my mother, she told me that I had a tendency toward personal integrity and independent thinking even before I knew what the words meant. She reminded me that in high school I did not try to fake it when schoolmates asked me about why I did not play sports or participate in extracurricular activities. Instead of laughing at me, most understood and sympathized with me. I learned a profound measure of openness from my seventh-friend Orville. He shared with me his distress about moving to another school because his parents were getting a divorce. I felt a deep compassion for him, and at my young age, I was moved to put my arms around his shoulders as he cried in a corner of the boys' restroom at school.

Creating a dream world to escape my dysfunctional family situation did not fully mask my deep frustrations. My unhealthy attitude toward my mother and stepfather improved when I shared my feelings with Uncle Johnnie. He helped me to understand the good I was doing for the little ones, and to appreciate that my caregiving responsibilities were not in vain. He persuaded me to accept my responsibilities and persevere until I had a viable plan for leaving home. Finally, Uncle Johnnie encouraged me to be honest with my mother about wanting to leave home. To my surprise, she understood and agreed to let me go.

Besides Uncle Johnnie, my post office friend Joe was the first person to offer me practical advice on how to think for myself. He taught me the importance of intellectual openness, and showed me that no new idea should be feared. Instead, ideas must be examined, taken to task, and that

233

they must prove their practical worth. If an idea did not work for me, I should file it away and move on. Joe refused to let me content myself with vague notions and lofty principles. He helped me to examine my core beliefs and to live by them. Finally, he goaded me into going to college where, with his help, I discovered an academic prowess that I never knew I had.

My friend John taught me that I did not need to have all the answers to life's questions. Indeed, I learned that the good life is more than the sum of our creature comforts and accolades. John introduced me to the spiritual side of human nature that he said could not be fully nourished by wealth, fame, or longevity. For the first time in my life, I understood the essential relationship between spirituality, ethics, and morality, and I could fully articulate what I was for and against, and why. I learned what it meant to live by faith, and not by sight, and to accept that there are things about the universe that we cannot know. I concluded that to demand a logical or scientific explanation for everything that happens in nature is a manifestation of human arrogance and delusions of grandeur. We could never live long enough to know everything even if it was possible to know all there is to know.

Greg showed me that instead of being embarrassed by misfortunes and disappointments in life, I might learn to overcome them by sharing them with a friend. He personified my Uncle Johnnie, although less than half Uncle Johnnie's age. Greg's willingness to stand up with me against racism and sexual innuendos was a testimony to his integrity and loyalty.

Self-Definition, Common Sense, And Change

I have come to believe that most of us know exactly what we want in life and what it takes to make us happy. We also know that, too often, what we want or desire in life may not be what is best or possible for us. Understanding these concepts is very important for a case officer who must be prepared to meet and greet people all over the world. Refusing to acknowledge our deep personal desires can stir within us a kind of frustration that gnaws at our sanity, and denying what we know we want can cause us to accept bad compromises for the real thing. I have a friend that wanted to commit adultery or try some unusual sexual experience because he believed everyone else was doing it. He knew that what he wanted to do could cost him dearly, so he embarked on a phony soul-searching trek to "find himself," hoping to reach some sort of moral compromise as a cover for what he wanted to do. Eventually, he imploded and lost everything.

My experiences at Patton State Hospital had a negative impact on my idea of wholesome social relationships. I got involved in relationships and activities that were confusing and wrong for me. Yet I knew in my heart of hearts that I wanted to escape from that situation. Afraid of losing my friends and my social standing, I was seized with fear. Mother forced me to face the reality of my situation, and she convinced me that I was strong enough to do what I knew I needed do, something my father had alluded to.

As a result, I tried to examine what I wanted from life in an objective manner. I asked myself, "What kind of person do I want to be?" I knew that I had to be honest if I was going to make any meaningful changes in my life. Finally, I asked if I was being honest with myself concerning what I wanted to do with my life. My answer was, "yes, and no." I wanted to be honest, even when I was being dishonest. I can recall many times when honesty did not pay, but I wanted it to pay; and it bothered me when I had to hide the truth. I tried to acknowledge the positive and the negative aspects of my character, to admit guilt when I knew that I was wrong, and I pardoned myself when it made sense.

Many of my issues boiled down to a preoccupation with past hurts, fear of change, being unloved, and the ever present regrets over missed opportunities. I wanted to make up for what I thought I missed or lacked, despite the personal cost. I realized that every issue affecting my life centered on my relationship with people and my social environment. It was not until I resurrected my interest in spiritual matters that I made practical progress with these issues. With regard to my parents, I resolved to accentuate the positive: I asked myself, what if I made life as difficult for them as they made it for me? Was my struggle with Shorty and Willie so one-sided? Was I always the innocent victim? Was I blameless? These were painful and necessary questions, but they had to be answered. When people made faulty assumptions about me or my character, or penalized me because I am a black man, I was disappointed, yes, but not destroyed. It was their loss not wanting to know me. I know how to be a faithful friend, and I know that only God can define our true worth. Therefore, if I am maligned or ignored for being me, my conscience is clear. I began to incorporate these ideas and thoughts into a new set of personal values.

Taking a stand on what I truly believed required a good measure of personal integrity. I confess that developing and sustaining personal integrity demands that we acknowledge reality, whether we like what we see or not. Only then can we resolve the age-old contradiction between moving forward in life and holding on to the dead past. Without integrity there was no way that I could make positive changes in my personal and world outlook. In this regard, I had to accept that my guilt and pain did not always come from the hurt inflicted by others, but possibly from the guilt I felt because of what I had done. I had to rethink my ideas about the value of criticism.

None of us enjoys being criticized, judged, measured, analyzed, assessed, evaluated, or stereotyped. Yet we do it to others all the time. On the other hand, self-criticism can be equally harmful. There are several kinds of criticism: positive and negative, constructive and destructive, just and unjust, objective and subjective. Nevertheless, what is important is the purpose of criticism. Some people criticize themselves constantly for some perceived wrong they have done, often without justification. Indeed, when we criticize someone, including ourselves, what are we trying to achieve? What are we criticizing the person for? What behavior or attitude are we against? Will the criticism put the person back on track? For criticism to be effective, both parties must understand the purpose of the criticism. How else can it produce the desired results? Healthy criticism is to make us a better person, not to tear us down. Therefore, it is important to know why we are criticizing someone, and ourselves.

Finally, we can make criticism a bad thing when we criticize things that a person can do nothing about. For example, since we cannot change the past. I learned avoid such self-critical comments like, "Why did I do that?" "Why did I allow him/her to take advantage of me?" "Why did I not scream for help?" "Why did I not tell the truth?" "Will I ever forgive myself for not standing up to him/her?" I am talking about reflections on events and circumstances that cannot be changed. Misguided and faulty criticism of ourselves and others can cause us to distrust people and often prevent reconciliation.

Growing up, I had to deal with a host of feelings that I did not like. Despite my best efforts, I harbored negative feelings about people, places, and relationships without understanding why. Eventually I realized that many of my negative feelings and prejudices were holding me back from developing potentially positive relationships with people. I could have been good friends with certain colleagues and shipmates if only I had gotten to know them better.

Another issue I had to face while working toward self-definition was learning self-discipline. The lack of self-discipline is a phenomenon that afflicts us all. It becomes a very important factor when trying to manage the heart and mind. The unfocused, unstable, and undisciplined mind can never develop the fortitude required to change what must be changed. I had to develop a compelling reason for wanting to change things in my life and to stick with it. To change, we must be committed to the values that we adopt. I am convinced that the reason I had so many abortive affairs with women is that none of us entered the relationship with an honest heart.

The Greatest Challenge Of All

"He has showed you, O man, what is good. And what does the Lord require of you? To act justly and to love mercy and to walk humbly with your God."
Micah 6:8

The greatest challenge we face in life is to remember who we are and what is required of us, even in the midst of psychological chaos.

Odell Lee

I am certain that I would not have managed my world successfully if I had refused to let others into my life. To do so required a radical departure from my childhood fears and disappointments. Consequently, former habits had to be broken and new attitudes established. Past wrongs done to me, or by me, had to be forgiven, and whenever possible, forgotten. This was not easy, but it was required. In other words, I was forced to let go of old resentments that I had carried into adulthood. In the end, I learned no one is all good or all bad, and that I must give people space to prove which is the dominate aspect of their character. This outlook proved immensely helpful to my success as an intelligence officer. Effective officers cannot fear close interaction with others if he is to elicit information or recruit agents in the short, as well as in the long-term.

As a teenager, I folded into myself and spent most of my spare time in a dream world. I used to get depressed thinking about the bad things that had happened to me, and wondered whether or not there was anything I could have done to change the situation. With each thought, my nurturing of the old hurts and painful experiences prevented me from looking to the future. It was like ink being poured slowly into a glass: life became darker and darker with each recollection. I credit Mother who forced me to stand up for myself even though the circumstances for doing so were not pretty, and friends that helped me to see my potential for achieving more than I thought possible. I loved my mother despite her inappropriate use of tough love. On the other hand, I did not know the meaning of parental love until I met my dad. He stirred in me something deep, true, and wholesome. I loved him because I could see that he loved me. My wife Nora was the first woman that I fell in love with. She captured my heart and soul. I knew enough to tell her so, and proposed marriage on our third date. I am convinced that openness to friendship, accepting good advice when offered, and accepting the peculiarity of my parents, siblings, friends and colleagues, allowed me to develop and sustain my emotional and psychological balance. In short, I learned how to walk the walk, and to walk the talk.

Appendix

Books About The Central Intelligence Agency

Ashley, Clarence. *CIA Spymaster*. Gretna: Pelican Publishers, 2004.

Bear, Robert. *Blow the House Down*. New York: Crown Publishers, 2006.

Cherkasin, Victor, and Gregory Feifer. *Spy Handler: Memoirs of a KGB Officer*. Johnson City: Basic Books, 2005.

Divomlikoff, Lavr. *The Traitor*. Translated from French by J. F. Bernard. New York: Popular Library, 1973.

Dulles, Allen. *The Craft of Intelligence*. Guilford, Conn: The Lyons Press, 2006.

Hitz, Fred. *The Great Game: The Myths and Reality of Espionage*. New York: Knopf, 2004.

Hitz, Fred. *Why S Why Spy? Espionage in an age of uncertainty*. New York: Thomas Dunne, 2008.

Ludlum, Robert. *The Tristan Betrayal*. New York: St. Martin's Press, 2004.

Mitnick, Kevin. <u>*The Art of Deception.*</u>, New York: Wiley Publications, 2002.

Olson, James. *Fair Play: The Moral Dilemmas of Spying*. Dulles, Virginia: Potomac Books, Inc., 2006.

Paseman, Floyd. *A Spy's Journey: A CIA Memoir*. Minneapolis: Zenith Press, 2004.

Popov, Dusko. *Spy Counterspy*. NewYork: Grosset & Dunlap, 1974.

Shackley, Ted, and Robert Finely. *Spymaster: My Life in the CIA*. Dulles, Virginia: Potomac Press, 2005.

Wise, David. *The Spy that Got Away*. New York: Random House, 1988.

Articles Published In The Ucla Daily Bruin Newspaper

Lee, Odell. "Courtesy." *UCLA Daily Bruin*, April 12, 1968.

Lee, Odell. "Black Newspaper Defended." *UCLA Daily* Bruin, March 3, 1969.

Lee, Odell. "TJ Club–SDS Not So Close." *UCLA Daily Bruin*, January 28, 1969.

Narda Zacchino. "Jefferson Club backs SDS, Planks, not Methods: Interview with TJ Club President, Odell Lee." *UCLA Daily Bruin*, January 22, 1969.

Students for Democratic Society. "SDS Commends Thomas Jefferson Club." *UCLA Daily Bruin*, January 24, 1969.

Miscellaneous Items

Lee, Odell. "A Black Man's View of Campus Strife." *California Townhall Journal*, Fall, 1969.

Adams, Russell. *Great Negroes: Past and Present*. Afro-Am Publishing Company, 1969.

Aquila, Richard. *That_Old-Time Rock & Roll*. Chirmer Publications, 1989.

Bennett, Jr., Lerone. *Before the Mayflower: A History of Black America*. Johnson Publishers, 1966.

Bronoski, Jacob, and Bruce Mazlish. *Western Intellectual Tradition: Leonard to Hegel*.

Clark, Colin. *The "Virgin" Encyclopedia of R&B and Soul*. London: Virgin Publishing, 1998.

Connolly, Francis. *Man and His Measure*. Harcourt, Brace & World, Inc., 1964.

Cornforth, Maurice. *The Theory of Knowledge*. Little World Paperbacks, 1955.

Fromm, Eric. *The Art of Loving*. Harper Perennial Modern Classics, 1956.

Holy Bible, New International Version (NIV). Zondervan Press, 1985.

Lee, Odell, "Reflections on Communist Ideology." The Dialectical Studies Institute, Falls Church, VA, 1991.

Lee, Odell. "The Church and Social Progress." *The Gospel Advocate Magazine*, January, *1990*.

Stephens, Charles J. *Louis E. Stephens: His Life in Letters.* Jay Publishers, 1999.

Zedong, Mao. *Five Essays on Philosophy*. Peoples' Liberation Press, 1968.

18686351R00150

Made in the USA
Middletown, DE
17 March 2015